# Economic Restructuring, Technology Transfer and Human Resource Development

# Economic Restructuring, Technology Transfer and Human Resource Development

B.R. Virmani
Kala Rao

Response Books
A division of Sage Publications
New Delhi/Thousand Oaks/London

338.95
V 8le

First published in 1997 by

**Response Books**
A division of Sage Publications India Pvt Ltd
32 M-Block Market, Greater Kailash-I
New Delhi 110 048

**Sage Publications Inc**
2455 Teller Road
Thousand Oaks, California 91320

**Sage Publications Ltd**
6 Bonhill Street
London EC2A 4PU

Published by Tejeshwar Singh for Response Books, and typeset and printed at Replika Press Pvt Ltd, Delhi 110 033.

**Library of Congress Cataloging-in-Publication Data**
Virmani, B.R.
    Economic restructuring, technology transfer, and human resource development/B.R. Virmani, Kala Rao.
        p.   cm.
    Includes bibliographical references and index.
    1. Asia—Economic policy—Case studies. 2. Technology transfer—Economic aspects—Asia—Case studies. 3. Industrial organization—Asia—Case studies. 4. Human capital—Government policy—Asia—Case studies. I. Rao, Kala, 1963–    II. Title.
    HC412.V57    338.95—dc20    1996          96-35427

**ISBN:**   0-8039-9346-3 (US-hb)
          81-7036-585-6 (India-hb)

**Sage Production Editors:** Rakhshanda Jalil and Evelyn George

*To the memory of*
### Ashish
*and*
### Seshasai
*who had everything in them, but the longevity, to make a difference in this field*

# CONTENTS

of Reforms in the 1990s • Foreign Direct Investment •
Infrastructure • Science and Technology Policies in
India • Suggested Measures for India • Conclusions

## part three—Organization Case Studies

## part four—Lessons and Directions for the Future

# PREFACE

The past decade has witnessed phenomenal changes the world over, especially with the collapse of the communist system, and the breakup of the erstwhile USSR. Economic barriers between various nations are being steadily dismantled. There is an increasing free flow of goods, services and manpower. At the same time, regional economic blocs are also being formed. There is an increasing pressure on industries to meet the demands of a competitive environment.

Technology has played a crucial role in enhancing this competitiveness. With the emergence of transnational and multinational corporations, technology is no longer confined to a particular country. Some countries, however, cannot afford to develop their own technologies. They, therefore, seek technology from those transnational corporations (TNCs) and multinational corporations (MNCs) which have the resources. However, for any transfer of technology to take place, some conditionalities are always attached which have to be mutually beneficial. Also, there is the important issue of the capacity of newly developed countries to not only attract new technologies but also to absorb, assimilate and further develop them. Closely linked to these issues are the economic policies of individual countries, and the business environment and infrastructure they need to provide for both internal and external investments in technology development and upgradation. Human resources also play a crucial role in not only the transfer but also the assimilation and further development of technology.

Some countries, especially those in the Asian region, have, in the last 20 years, successfully developed their economies and achieved some of the highest growth rates in the world. In fact, their growth rates have been higher than those of some of the developed countries or even that of Japan. On the other hand, there are some countries, such as India, Bangladesh, Pakistan and Nepal who are at the threshold of development and are still searching for appropriate models of growth.

This issue was discussed in a seminar organized by the Asia Pacific Centre for Technology Transfer (APCTT) in collaboration with the United Nations Economic Social Council for Asia and the Pacific (UNESCAP) in Seoul, Korea, where one of us (B.R. Virmani) was invited as a resource person. It was felt that a comparative study of some of these rapidly developing countries could provide useful lessons and models which the relatively less developed countries could emulate. It was in this context that we undertook a comparative study of Malaysia, Singapore, Thailand and India which forms the basis of this book.

The book is based on extensive interviews conducted by us in India and during various visits to Malaysia, Singapore, Thailand as well as some interviews done in Korea. We have also reviewed and incorporated some of the literature available on the subject, especially that produced by the Asian Productivity Organization. Questionnaires were also sent to various organizations. Suggestions from numerous individuals connected with policy formulation and implementation on economic development, technology transfer and HRD were also reviewed and considered. We held detailed discussions with over 400 officials at various levels in each of the countries and the organizations studied. In certain cases, information and data were also culled from the records in the organizations. In the course of interaction with many officials, their perceptions on various related issues were also discussed. Our interviewing strategy was such that it encouraged the interviewees to respond freely. Owing to the paucity of time and resources, we were compelled to limit the study, in the main, to only certain aspects in the four countries.

The initial focus of our study was the analysis of technology transfer, assimilation and related human resource development aspects. However, during the course of the study, it was found that any technology transfer, assimilation and upgradation process is very much linked to economic policies, process of industrialization, investment policies and infrastructure availability. Hence, subsequently, the scope of this study was enlarged to encompass aspects of economic development, investment climate, and structural adjustment programmes including financial reforms and incentives which contributed to technology transfer and development. This book concentrates mainly on the macro-level approaches and gives less emphasis to the micro-level policies of an organization. This is mainly because the organizations studied, especially those in Singapore and Thailand, were not willing to share complete data because of the sensitive nature of some of their projects. However, some of the managers in these organizations were interviewed to elicit their personal views. At the macro level, however, we were able to conduct extensive interviews across a cross-section of administrators, managers and even workers. All these in-depth interviews provided us with reasonable information and projections at the micro level also.

This book is organized into four parts. Part I outlines the concept and definition of technology transfer, human resources and economic development. It also describes in detail the policy issues connected with economic restructuring, globalization, regionalization and their relevance to technology transfer. This part elaborates some of the issues connected with technology policy and enhancement of human resources. It also discusses the issue of investment climate to receive new technology.

Parts II and III describe the experiences of four countries, viz. Malaysia, Singapore, Thailand and India. The economic restructuring aspects of these four countries have been dealt with in detail in Part II, including the evaluation of the process of economic reform and infrastructure development. Part III comprises micro-level case studies of a few organizations, especially those in India and Malaysia, and discusses how they went about the process of technology transfer and human resource development. The lessons one can draw from their experiences are also included in this Part.

Part IV presents the conclusions and provides some useful lessons one can draw from these macro-level and micro-level experiences. Part IV also gives some suggestions and the directions which can help countries at the macro level as well as at the organizational level in improving the processes of technology transfer, human resource development and economic restructuring.

**B.R. Virmani**
**Kala Rao**

# Acknowledgements

Many individuals and institutions have contributed to the completion of this study. Mr D. Sravan Kumar and Ms Tara Rajagopalan helped in collecting secondary data. The National Institute of Public Administration (INTAN) played a major role in facilitating data collection in Malaysia. Our special thanks are due to Dr Mohd. Ghazali Bin Md. Noor, formerly of Institut Tadbiran Awam Negara (INTAN) Malaysia (National Institute of Public Administration), presently Special Assistant to the Deputy Prime Minister of Malaysia, Mr Chan Yuen Hung, Mr Chew Kar Eng and Mr Shukri Ibrahim, all belonging to the faculty of INTAN. We are grateful to the Director of INTAN, Dr Halim Bin Shafie for facilitating the study.

Professor Nawaz Sharif, formerly Director of the Asia Pacific Centre for Technology Centre and later Professor at the Asian Institute of Technology, Bangkok, was the main source of inspiration who prompted us to do the study. Dr Chira Hongladarom, Director of the Human Resource Institute, Thammasat University, Bangkok, gave some useful ideas and suggestions. Ms Juniper Chua of the Singapore Institute of Standards and Industrial Research and Mr Chi Pang Chee of the Economic Development Board were helpful in facilitating the study in Singapore. Mr Paul Chandran of the National Productivity Board, Singapore was helpful in giving information about past and recent trends on the different aspects of technology transfer in Singapore. Thanks are also due to the various organizations and the officials who responded to the questionnaires and spared their valuable time for discussions.

The Friedrich Ebert Foundation, New Delhi, has played a major role in this project by funding the study. Our grateful thanks to Dr Heinz Bongartz, Representative in India of the Friedrich Ebert Foundation, Bonn, Germany and Mr Kabir Seth who lent administrative support on behalf of the Friedrich Ebert Foundation.

A project of this nature could not have been undertaken but for the support from all the colleagues at the Administrative Staff College of India (ASCI), Hyderabad. We are grateful for their suggestions and comments at various stages of the project. Special mention should be made here of Dr B. Bowonder, Dr Sunil Unny Guptan and Mr B. Muralidharan. We are also grateful to Mr T.L. Sankar, Principal, ASCI for providing all the necessary support from time to time. We acknowledge with gratitude Mr A.V. Satish for his help in analyzing the data, Mr H.K. Srinivas for collecting secondary data and helping to give shape to the revised manuscript, and Mrs Edna John, Mr A. Parthasarathy Swamy and Mr K. Shekhar for their secretarial assistance. Our thanks are also due to Mr C. Martin and Mr D. Jaya Kumar of the Production Unit of ASCI for facilitating the preparation of the final manuscript.

**B.R. Virmani**
**Kala Rao**

# part one

# INTRODUCTION

# 1

# THE CONCEPTUAL FRAMEWORK

## ECONOMIC DEVELOPMENT AND TECHNOLOGY TRANSFER

The economic development of a country is dependent on two important factors. One is its industrial development, and the other is its economic, social and political environment. A conducive environment not only helps in the growth and development of industry, it also encourages internal and external investments. During the past decade, there have been major global economic changes which have led to economic restructuring in many countries. With the signing of the GATT agreement and formation of the World Trade Organization, trade barriers all over the world are being either reduced or eliminated. At the same time, more and more regional trade blocs are also being formed. All this has created tremendous competition among nations, and each and every country has been compelled to gear itself to meet new challenges.

Technology plays a crucial role in this process of restructuring. There is urgent need for continuous innovation, especially in the high-technology-based industries. The policies followed in each country determine the extent to which the need to introduce sophisticated technology is being fulfilled. Use of new technology can increase the product range for tapping new markets and meeting competition as well as provide better customer service, while saving time in developing new products and process technologies.

Technology can mean different things to different people. The definition of technology can vary from the very general to serving a very specific function. One generic definition of technology is that it is 'the relationship between man and nature'.[1] In more specific terms, technology can be defined as 'the combination of types of knowledge indispensable to carrying out the necessary operations for transforming the factors of production into products, the use of that knowledge or the provision of services'.[2] One can also use the term 'technology' to refer to new and better ways of achieving economic ends that contribute to economic development and growth.[3] Similarly, technology transfer has been given many meanings. Essentially, however, the major motive of transfer is the technology gap that exists between the supplier of technology and its recipient.

Technology transfer involves four main stages—negotiating, setting-up, starting-up, and sustaining growth. The negotiations for technology transfer involve the initial interaction among the buyers and suppliers, the country officials wherever applicable, the joint venture partners, etc. The setting-up involves detailed design, modifications and adaptations, while the start-up stage will involve proactive training, infrastructure development and redeployment. The sustained operations of a transfer will be reflected in the uninterrupted use of technology as well as in its successful adaptation and upgradation.

Any appropriate transfer of technology should include not only shifting of technology from one place to another but also its assimilation, adaptation and transmission of complete knowledge pertaining to its various stages. It is through such transmission that the recipients can make efforts to adopt the technology to work on a permanent basis. The recipient organization can not only understand but also upgrade the technology, where ever required, to suit local conditions. This implies that any technology transfer will entail the appropriate blending of technology between the recipient and the host countries/organizations, and the making of suitable adjustments to the existing skill levels as well as norms, culture, values and environment. Unfortunately, in many cases such absorption or blending does not take place. In such instances, the process is neither a transfer nor a transmission, absorption nor assimilation, but merely a 'rental' or 'transplant' of technology.[4]

The extent of absorption and assimilation of technology by the recipient organization/country is a true measure of the actual transfer of technology for manufacturing/production purposes without developing the appropriate capabilities of the recipients. The recipient organization should have developed its capabilities to utilize the technology on its own.[5] Absorption could mean the process of learning about the imported technical knowledge and its consolidation and adaptation into local systems where required. Proper assimilation of technology is necessary for recipient countries to enhance and derive maximum benefits from a technology alliance.

The level of sophistication of technology is determined by the component of labour involved in the usage of technology. Low technology may require the application of scientific devices for different aspects of production without displacing labour. Intermediate technology refers to the production of finished goods and intermediary products. High technology refers to the use of highly complex processes and machinery using capital goods, such as in the manufacture of steel, communication equipment, space and nuclear installations, etc. Factors such as production facilities, availability of resources, technical know-how, etc. determine the appropriateness of the technology being introduced.[6]

Technological capability and its transfer involve intangible assets such as design and engineering plans, models, patents (for process and product) and tangible assets such as capital goods, machinery and pilot plants. Human assets include skills and know-how. Technology is constantly generated, absorbed, applied, utilized, adapted, exchanged, bought and sold, and upgraded. The institutionalization of technological generation and innovation, its market orientation, intellectual property rights, etc. have subtly altered the methods of diffusion of technology as also its acquisition for commercial production. Since the funds for investment in R&D and technology imports are limited, a suitable and efficient mix of technology needs to be put together, both at the macro and micro levels. A dispassionate assessment of opportunity costs as well as benefits of each investment decision should be made.

## TECHNOLOGY TRANSFER THROUGH ALLIANCES

Multinational corporations play a major role as transferors of technology. They also help in forming alliances with recipient organizations since they are provided with the latest technology and know-how. The need for entering into alliances among one or more organizations is to basically meet the emerging challenges and bridge the technological gaps in some aspects, such as R&D, manufacturing, marketing and at times for general purposes. The type of alliances entered into would directly reflect the objectives to be achieved. Some of the important. types of alliances are given below.

♦ *R&D Alliances*   These alliances comprise licensing agreements, cross-licensing, technology exchange, visitation and research participation, personnel exchange, joint development and technology acquisition investment.

♦ *Manufacturing Alliances*  These alliances include original equipment manufacture, second sourcing, fabrication agreement, assembly and testing agreements.

♦ *Marketing and Service Alliances*   Procurement agreements, selling agents, servicing agents are some examples of this type of alliances.

♦ *General Purpose Tie-ups*   These cover standards coordination and joint ventures.

The types of alliances would eventually depend upon the need and strengths of the parties to effectively negotiate with each other. In some countries, the government has actively helped the parties by way of sourcing of technology, offering of special incentives and deciding the pattern of alliances. For example, India at one time only encouraged licensing type of agreements. Gradually, with liberalization, joint ventures began to be preferred and now, free import of technology is increasingly being encouraged.

The price of technology is normally determined by market forces, especially by the negotiating capability of the parties. In the process of negotiations for technology transfer one has to keep in mind the indirect cost of technology which normally arises from the conditions or restrictive practices imposed by the parent company on the recipient. These restrictions normally include:[7]

❑ Territorial market restraints

❑ Linking technology transfer to the purchase of goods or services

❑ Restrictions on the recipient of technology from entering into agreements involving competing or complementary technology

❑ Restrictions on R&D

❑ Restrictions on adaptation or innovation of technology

All these restrictions can have an adverse effect on the recipient. For instance, export capacity gets restricted, import costs climb higher, and expansion of the technological capacity is restricted. At times, the loss from such restrictive practices is considerable and should be considered as part of the total cost of technology transfer. Such restrictions can also have repercussions on the balance of payments and the overall economic development of the country.

The technology transfer process can also take place through various agencies, such as business firms, governmental or non-profit organizations or even universities. Some international organizations, such as the World Bank, Asian Developmental Bank, US Agency for International Development (USAID) and Japan International Co-operative Agency (JICA) have also played a predominant role in technology transfer. However, multinational enterprises directly or indirectly continue to be one of the major sources of technology transfer including technology-specific training. However, it must be pointed out that in the case of multinational enterprises, technology transfer is only incidental as their major objective remains seeking markets, suppliers and profits. In this process of seeking markets and meeting competition they also transfer technology. In the case of proprietary technology, the firms are, at times, reluctant to transfer technology unless there are commensurate returns.

Other indirect agents of technology transfer have been trained personnel leaving one organization to join another who in the process carry knowledge about new technology, including sources of new technology, and disseminate it in the new organization. Some organizations send their professionals for training to their collaborators or partners who act as carriers of technical know-how. They, in turn, pass on their knowledge and skills to others in the parent organization. This kind of indirect transfer is possible only if there is a systematic documentation of the knowledge gained through training experience, R&D, etc. within the organization.

The entry of multinational corporations can influence the industrial structure, conduct and performance of local enterprises. Blomstrom and Persson (1983) suggest three ways in which spill-overs can occur. First, the presence of multinational corporations can change the extent of competition in a particular industry because foreign firms can have better chances of overcoming entry barriers. Increased competition can force local firms to adopt more efficient techniques. Second, the training of labour and management and entrepreneurial initiatives can eventually become available to the industry or to the economy in general. Third, the presence of multinational corporations can stimulate local firms to speed up their adoption of new technologies via demonstration effects. In addition, multinational corporations can also have a spill-over effect on the economy of the recipient country by the creation of vertical linkages through outsourcing wherein a technology may also be transferred to the supplier.

## KINDS OF TECHNOLOGY TRANSFER

There can be a variety of technology transfer mechanisms depending upon the type of technology. The extent of transfer is also dependent upon the capability of the recipient to receive the technology.

One of the major mechanisms is direct investment by multinational enterprises which includes training for the skills needed to implement new technology. This could be a fully owned subsidiary or a joint venture with a local firm. In some cases, training is also provided by multinational enterprises for local suppliers. Another method of technology transfer could be through the purchase of license by paying a certain fee or royalty including the training of professionals. Another mechanism of technology transfer has been reproduction through reverse engineering. This process entails first the breaking up of a product or process and then rebuilding it with one's own knowledge and resources. However, the process of reverse engineering does require considerable design capability as well as some investment capability. It has, at times, created controversies of proprietary rights apart from the disputes arising out of the improvements made in the product or process. Turnkey projects and investment is another mechanism which facilitates technology transfer, though in this case the transfer may be limited operational capability without development of any innovative capabilities.

The process of technology transfer by foreign direct investors normally consist of:

❑ Recruitment and training of local workers, including those at the managerial level and professionals, in the requisite skills

❑ Training of workers to shoulder higher responsibilities mainly to replace expatriates and

❑ Through turnover of trained and experienced managerial and technical personnel in so far as they employ their skills in starting new domestic enterprises or modernization of existing enterprises

The major variable in the case of technology transfer by direct investors would, to a large extent, be dependent upon the total amount of investment, that is more the investment, the greater is the technology transfer potential because of larger training base and consequent larger turnover of employees.

## TECHNOLOGY, HUMAN RESOURCES AND ECONOMIC DEVELOPMENT

One of the crucial factors in technology transfer is the capability and extent of human beings to receive, assimilate and absorb the new technology. The capacity to receive technology is dependent upon one's general education and training. 'No developing country can make use of technology flows unless it has an appropriate receiving system composed of scientific and technical infrastructure in the public, private, educational and corporate sectors. It is of no value to develop a technical training system or R&D institutes when companies are not interested in using it.'[8] General knowledge through education and technology-specific know-how required for new production techniques are preconditions for technology transfer and absorption. The existing values and culture of a society should also be kept in mind when considering technology transfer, since resistance to change is a major inhibiting factor in the absorption of technology. The problem of resistance to change can be reduced to some extent by appropriate blending of technology as well as managerial practices.

Another related factor is the state of economic growth and development of the country. This would indicate the country's readiness for change and its capacity to absorb new technology. If any of these factors are missing, then effective technology transfer cannot take place. There is a close linkage between technology development and economic growth. The capacity of a country to receive new technology is again dependent upon the internal and external investment pattern in industry, related government policies, availability of appropriate human resource skills, and a conducive environment for rapid industrial and technological development.

Many of the developing countries before they embarked upon their economic reform process were predominantly agrarian economies. Another common characteristic was that at the initial stage of development they gave special emphasis to the policy of import substitution. Poverty was another major social problem faced by these countries. Alleviation of poverty and improving the standard of living remained a primary objective in the early years. The workforce in these countries too was not endowed with skills or managerial expertise. In order to move towards manufacturing and industrialization, major re-adjustments in certain policies were carried out. Singapore, for example, with its total dependence on other countries for raw material, expertise, technology as well as markets, had to take the initiative in building up an infrastructure and an extremely conducive climate for investment. To effectively utilize the latest technology, efforts to upgrade human skills were extensively undertaken by the government of Singapore.

Technology-based industries, also known as 'sunrise' industries, are growing rapidly, especially in the highly industrialized and developed countries. These industries are highly competitive and often research-intensive. They also need a high level of human skills which are not easily available in developing countries and need to be honed, as was done in the case of Singapore.

The recent global trends towards internationalization of production and, more importantly, the role of Asia's newly industrialized countries in manufactured exports has influenced the restructuring process in several countries, including Malaysia, Thailand, Singapore and India. Due to the dominance of multinational companies in world trade, export-led industrialization has become an increasingly difficult task unless it is attempted with their partnership. Economic adjustments have become necessary and these are manifesting themselves through the changing dynamics of comparative advantage among various countries, according to their different stages of industrialization. The importance of technology, finance and market channels has been increasingly demonstrated by the activities of foreign companies, especially the multinational corporations. It is important, therefore, to ensure that effective transfer of technology takes place including the spin-off and linkage effects of foreign investment.

For the purpose of this book, technology has been considered in relation to the level of economic development of a country. The definition of technology transfer has been confined to the narrow sense and includes some aspects of technology absorption and assimilation and development of human resources in relation to technology transfer, upgradation and absorption.

The experience of some of the recently developed countries in technology transfer can be helpful in formulating appropriate policies in newly developing countries who are in process of initiating rapid economic change. This book aims to analyze various issues connected with technology transfer, human resource development and economic restructuring processes in some of the fast developing countries of the Southeast Asian Region, such as Malaysia, Thailand and Singapore, with a view to draw certain lessons, wherever appropriate. These lessons can be emulated by emerging South Asian countries such as India, Pakistan and Bangladesh. It may be argued that these countries are not comparable since Singapore is a city-state and even Malaysia and Thailand are much smaller countries in comparison to India which has a much larger population and distinct socio-economic features. Keeping this in mind, no attempt has been made to make a point-by-point comparison of each stage of development.

The focus of this book is to show how these countries went about restructuring their economies, developing their technologies and human resources, and achieved comparatively much faster rates of growth in their economies. Despite differences in terms of size, resources, etc., there are certain areas, such as fiscal policies, factors of investment climate, technology usage and skill development of manpower, where the strategies and policies adopted by these countries can be successfully emulated by the under-developed and newly-developing countries, and their mistakes avoided. This book has focused attention on these issues, and towards that end, has suggested some lessons that can be drawn and adopted.

# References

1. CHOPRA, O.P., 'Technology Transfer to India: Perceptions of British Firms', paper presented at the Seminar on International Programme on Innovation and Technology Transfer, at ASCI, Hyderabad, April 22–24, 1992.
2. Comision del Acuredo de Cartegene, *Decision* 84
3. STEWART, CHARLES T., *Technology Transfer and Human Factors,* Lexington Books, D.C. Heath and Company, Lexington, Massachusetts, Toronto, 1992.
4. CAPRILES, ROBERTO SAKAS, *Integrated Technology Transfer,* London Publications, 1979.

5. Konz, Leo Edwin, 'The International Transfer of Commercial Technology: The Role of the Multinational Corporation', New York, Arno Press, 1980.

6. UNCTAD, *Guidelines*, Supra note 6, p. 5, and 'Science and Technology in India: A Review of the Role and Impact of S&T on the Development of the Country', *Spectrumindia*, 1991.

7. 'Intra-Regional Investment and Technology Transfer in Asia', a symposium report, Asian Productivity Organization, Tokyo, 1994.

8. *Fund for Multinational Management Education*, Public Policy and Technology Transfer, 4 volumes, sponsored by FMME, Council of the Americas, US Council of the International Chamber of Commerce, and the George Washington University, March 1978.

**2**

# THE SIGNIFICANCE OF APPROPRIATE NATIONAL POLICIES

## IMPORTANCE OF TECHNOLOGY IN DEVELOPMENT

In the present context, technology is the key to the growth and development of any nation. Because of their innovative practices and inventions, some countries have been able to develop technology at a much faster pace resulting in better living standards for their people. However, there are a vast number of less developed countries who, for historical reasons, have not been able to keep pace with the technological developments of the more developed nations. Also, with changes in incomes pattern, close communications among the nations of the world and their people, it has become a wasteful exercise for each country to develop its own technology from scratch every time. In the present environment, nations are, therefore, much more interdependent on each other. While some countries have developed their expertise and technology in certain areas, others have evolved different kinds of expertise and resources. Therefore, it becomes imperative that technology is shared for achieving better living standards among all nations for mutual gain. Transfer of technology from one country to another is also desirable from the point of view of bilateral trade and national gain for the transferors of technology. Technology transfer also means that any developer of technology within a country transfers the new technology for production and commercial purposes. The development of technology will have practically no meaning if it has no productive use. Transfer of technology, therefore, raises the following issues:

❑ Is the technology appropriately transferable for large-scale production?

❑ How does the technology transfer take place?

❑ How can a large number of people be trained to make use of the technology?

❑ What will be the gains for the developers of the technology?

❑ Should the technology be transferred wholesale or in parts or should the transferors themselves enhance their R&D efforts?

❑ What will be the cost of transfer of technology and benefits to the transferee?

To find an answer to these issues, each country or firm has to develop its own policies of technology transfer.

Sometimes, there can be an 'information paradox' in the transfer of technology. The buyers of technology may not have access to full information on what they are buying. The seller of technology may also not like to give full information about the technology until the buyers have signed the purchase contract. In such a situation the buyers of technology must develop their own sources of technology information, or end up acquiring inappropriate technology. For example, at the national level, one can develop a policy that by transfer of some basic know-how, the rest of the development will be indigenously planned through one's own efforts. Another alternative could be through wholesale import of total technology which could ultimately help boost exports generated through the new technology. Similarly, at the micro level, the individual firms also need to develop broad policies and guidelines for themselves on these issues. The importance of technology for socio-economic development is recognized by most countries and is reflected in their technology policy formulations. It is important to integrate a nation's technology policy with its industrial policy and also to articulate the objectives and direction of envisaged growth. Policy objectives should give attention to various aspects, such as creation of technology, indigenous capacity, energy, consolidation of existing structures, labour-intensive measures, relation to science, R&D for the development of a dynamic production structure.[1]

The issue here is not only of technology transfer but also the availability of resources, including human resources, with the recipients. Major resources can be categorized in the following areas:

- ❑ Capital required for the purchase/import of technology
- ❑ Availability of raw material required for the use of the technology
- ❑ Infrastructure facilities
- ❑ Availability of skilled human resources for the use of technology

In any technology transfer process, experience suggests that it is necessary that every recipient has all the resources required for technology absorption. Initially, some goods and services could be imported and later re-exported with value addition, which could generate sufficient capital to obtain more resources. The steel industry in Japan is a classic example of this nature, where they import iron ore as raw material, convert it into steel through technological processes and then export the manufactured steel which is able to command a high market value. In the initial years, Japan had to purchase the conversion technology from other countries, which they refined and improved through their own R&D efforts. This is a good example of technology absorption, assimilation and development.

Any proper technology transfer and development ultimately leads to production of quality goods and services at a cheaper price. It also results in growth and development of the economy, resulting in increased purchasing power and thus better living standards for the people. However, the benefits of technology development are also linked to economic policies, investment climate, import-export strategies, etc. The money generated through the export of goods produced by the technology helps in purchasing different goods and services. Singapore is a good example where they import technological know-how, convert it to high-tech goods, export them and with the surpluses generated, buy essential commodities, of the best quality and at the cheapest price, required for its people. In Singapore one can get the best wheat at the cheapest prices even though it is not a producer of wheat itself.

A country must identify the areas in which it should transfer and develop technology. This will again depend on the stage of their growth, availability of skills, economies of scale in terms of export and their R&D capabilities. For example, Korean firms have achieved an impressive degree of development through technology absorption and innovation in industries such as plywood, textiles and shipbuilding. Singapore has largely concentrated on electronics and oil refining, while Japan is concentrating on technology-intensive industries such as electronics, automobiles and steel. In the initial years, Japan's efforts were in the textile field, they gradually vacated the textile field to other countries and branched off into the electronics industry.

The take-off stage of economic development in most South and Southeast Asian countries has given rise to new business opportunities and newer markets due to expanding production bases. These changes have been brought about by changes in technology. The action and counter-action between markets and technology has resulted in combined upward improvements as well as economic development. The shift of emphasis from a strong government role to vigorous private sector participation is also another common feature. The need for competitiveness and quick entry into markets has been reflected in increased dependence on foreign investment. Thus, technology transfer becomes an important yardstick of foreign investment.

The newly industrializing economies are largely dependent on the large-scale transfer of technology from developed countries. The availability of market or cheap labour is not always the major incentive for foreign investors as is evident from the examples of Singapore or Malaysia. The other factors which can attract foreign investment and technology transfer are the availability of proper infrastructure, government policies that encourage foreign investment, and the capacity of the recipient country to absorb the technology. The experience of many host countries is such that complaints by foreign investors gradually declined as the country gained experience with foreign investments and as their capacity to absorb foreign technology developed. The experience of some of the Southeast Asian countries is such that investors will still be motivated to transfer higher level of technologies for the host country as the capability to export increases. The experience of Singapore and Malaysia suggests that the host country could actively improve its capacity to absorb sophisticated technology by investing in education and training and by supporting the development of scientific and industrial engineering.

## IMPACT OF TECHNOLOGY TRANSFER

Any technology transfer can have a positive as well as negative impacts on recipient countries, both at the macro and micro levels. On the positive side, the countries are compelled to reconsider their policies to give meaningful direction to industrial investment, especially in sophisticated technologies. This can result in opening up of new markets, availability of quality goods at cheaper prices, and paving the way for innovation of new products and better service to consumers due to increased competition. The other indirect benefit of technology transfer is upgradation of educational and training institutions to meet the increased skill requirements. Therefore, the human resource development aspects also receive an impetus. In the ultimate analysis, the economy is given a boost and there is a corresponding overall increase in employment and living standards of the people at large.

There is an on-going debate about the effects of technology transfer by developed and newly industrializing countries on the recipient countries. It is argued that technology transfer by MNCs of developing countries is more appropriate than the technology transferred by those of developed countries. In one of the studies conducted by the Asian Productivity Organization, it was found that MNCs of developing countries tended to use less capital-intensive technology than their developed country counterparts (Chen, 1990). The lower capital intensity of the developing countries technology was related to such factors as their lower dependence on the parent firm's technology, greater autonomy in the choice of technology and smaller scale of production. The MNCs of developing countries also tend to use a higher proportion of second-hand machinery, and equipment made from local material and components. Thus, the developing countries' MNCs create more spill-over and linkage effects. However, the MNCs of developing countries tend to undertake less R&D activities in recipient countries than their counterparts in developed countries.[2] While there is an overall positive impact, there can be certain negative factors which can adversely affect the economy in the short-term. Table 2.1 lists the positive and negative effects of technology transfer.

**TABLE 2.1:** Impact of Technology Transfer

| Sl. No. | Positive | Negative |
|---|---|---|
| 1. | Policies to give direction to industrial investment in high technology/sophisticated technology. | Disincentive to local entrepreneurs (imports are cheaper). |
| 2. | Increase in demand and opening up of new markets. | Reduced incentive for indigenous R&D. |
| 3. | Availability of quality and cheaper products. | Redeployment problems due to new technology and new skill requirements- resulting in redundancies in some sectors and shortages in others. |
| 4. | Increased competition leading to new product improvements and innovation as well as better service to consumers. | Emergence of new competition in domestic markets. |
| 5. | Long-term employment generation due to spurt in industrial investment and growth. | Problems due to restructuring of organizations because of technological changes. |
| 6. | Increase in demand for sophisticated skills, need for establishment of education and training institutions. | Human resource related issues:<br>— Obsolescence<br>— Wage disparity<br>— Employee alienation and resistance to change |
| 7. | Ultimate boost to the economy, more employment, better living standard and more export earning. | |

For instance, change in policies to bring in sophisticated technology can affect local enterprises as imports of the already available products may become cheaper. The recipient country has to take into account such factors to minimize this adverse impact. The local industry may also regard import of technology to be more lucrative in comparison to investments in indigenous R&D. This can, at times, result in repeated purchases of similar technology without proper assimilation or absorption. Technological change can also result in the need for restructuring of organizations leading to problems of redeployment and other human resource-related issues. Any sophisticated technology will require a highly skilled workforce which may not be readily available. At the same time, it can make the old workforce redundant, especially those who are not trainable. This can create a problem of surplus labour in certain areas, and shortages in some other areas, thus creating industrial relations problems, as well as resistance to change.

New technology can also result in industry-wide disparities in terms of wages and skill requirements where the entry of MNCs can widen the competitive edge between the existing local industries and the new entrants. Another adverse effect, especially in the short term, can be that local enterprises who are not very competitive and do not have the means or resources to upgrade their technology may get adversely affected or may even be forced to wind up.

## HUMAN RESOURCE DEVELOPMENT AND TECHNOLOGY TRANSFER

The extent of technology transfer is dependent upon the absorbing capacity of the human resources in the recipient country/organization. This absorptive capacity, in turn, is dependent upon the availability of a workforce with the general educational background and technology-specific training. At times, even if there is abundance of an educated workforce trained in specific skills, it may still lack the skills and abilities to digest, absorb and diffuse modern technology.[3] Normally, MNCs do not take the responsibility of general education. Therefore, this becomes the primary responsibility of the host country. The training is restricted to operating and maintaining the technology brought in for production purposes.

Human resource development is the key to any technology transfer and upgradation. The Japanese or the Korean success in technology transfer, absorption and development can be largely attributed to their human resource skill development efforts. In Korea and Japan there are built-in incentives for personnel, especially skilled personnel, to upgrade their knowledge and skill by passing certain tests and examinations which are linked to salary increases or rewards. There are some issues involved here. The first issue is: How does one upgrade the skill of the people to understand and use the new technology? The second is related to imparting constant, conducive education and training towards R&D efforts in the recipient country to upgrade their technology. The willingness on the part of the transferors of technology to not only appropriately train the manpower for operational aspects of the technology but also in the analysis and development assumes critical significance. This raises the issue of proprietary rights over technology and to what extent should the transferees be allowed to acquire and upgrade the technology. Human beings who are accustomed to a certain technology and way of life often resist change. Thus, one is faced with the problem of overcoming such resistance to develop a climate which is conducive to change.

Any technology transfer and upgradation will initially have an impact on the employment situation. This is because any change will lead to redundancy or the requirement of different kinds of skills, resulting in surpluses in certain areas and shortages in others. This calls for retraining and redeployment, which is again linked to the policies regarding training and development of skills.

## TRAINABILITY AND CHANGES IN SKILL DEVELOPMENT

With changes in technology, the skill and knowledge components of the human resource have to be constantly upgraded, otherwise the assimilation or absorption process is weakened. The Technology Atlas (United Nations Economic Social Commission for Asia and the Pacific–UNESCAP) defines the various stages of sophistication of increasing human abilities starting from operating, setting up, repairing and reproducing to adapting, improving and innovating abilities.[4] All these call for strengthening skill levels not only at the advanced stages but right from the elementary educational level so that the workforce can increase their trainability later on when they join an organization. With rapid upgradation and changes in technology, the trainability component assumes much greater importance than training the persons for a particular skill, the requirement of which may only be temporary. Trainability implies that with the change in technology, the person could be retrained to handle new technology. The assumption is that he or she has the basic knowledge and capability to absorb new technology and new ideas. This obviously requires a mix of basic and technical education with on-the-job training at the organizational level. The trainability traits include:

- ❑ Reasoning skills
- ❑ Development of cognitive ability
- ❑ Development of a scientific attitude
- ❑ Mastery over appropriate language

❑ Development of communication skills
❑ Development of interpersonal skills
❑ Development of self discipline and responsibility

Singapore and South Korea have gone ahead in a much more systematic way in developing their human resources. For example, to increase the trainability of manpower in Singapore, programmes in basic mathematics and English have been developed to improve the analytical abilities and skills to help people better adapt at operating computers. All such programmes are state supported. Similarly, for quick development of resources to catch up with fast-changing technologies, some special programmes, known as 'Fast Forward', have been developed which are meant not only for younger people but for those over 40 years of age.

In South Korea, a system of built-in incentives for employees have been developed for clearing different grades of examinations as and when they upgrade their skills, and employees are given enhancements in salaries. When an employee reaches the Master Craftsman level, South Korean law prescribes that he will draw a salary equivalent to that of a Professor. Such incentives provide necessary motivation to the people to constantly strive to upgrade their skills. In addition, there are social pressures to develop oneself and correspondingly increase one's standard of living by earning higher salaries. This, to a great extent, has resulted in the reversal of 'brain drain', which was a problem earlier. South Korean workers who had gone abroad are coming back as they can now enjoy the same standard of living in their own country. In contrast, in countries such as India, Pakistan or Bangladesh, even highly trained technical personnel have an increasing urge to go abroad as there are no incentives to stay back in their own countries. The pace of industrial development and need for skilled professionals are still low in these countries since they are unable to find appropriate jobs at home. This, obviously, calls for a review of national policies.

The mode of technology transfer is largely dependent on the level of formal education and training available in the recipient countries. There is a tendency in the developing countries to concentrate on professions such as teaching, law and social sciences, while the requirement may be for agronomy, maintenance, technical, marketing and production skills. The transferors of technical know-how have, therefore, an obligation to guide the recipient countries to reshape their education and training policies and establish the essential infrastructure required for successful acquisition of organizational and technical skills.

There are various ways to enhance human resource skills to absorb technology. Different countries have been able to achieve this by successfully adopting distinctive approaches. The Middle Eastern countries, since they have the capacity to pay, rely on the skills and experience of foreign workers to operate their most sophisticated technology. Singapore, on the other hand, adopted a strategy of developing skill-intensive activities within the country. It, therefore, encourages foreign partnerships to help build the operating, repairing and management skills geared to domestic and regional production. The South Korean experience has been to similarly build local operating, maintenance and management skills through foreign subsidiaries and joint ventures. Brazil has also depended upon development of local skills with foreign direct investment partnerships, while Mexican engineering and development skills were built up through joint ventures.

While technology transfer does help in skill upgradation and appropriate development of human resources, it can, at the same time, create certain human relations related problems which need to be given due attention to minimize their adverse impact. Any sudden transfer of sophisticated technology can bring about worker alienation as it may lead to more specialization in respective skills or areas, resulting in a feeling of collective powerlessness arising due to organizational or fiscal changes. Prolonged dehumanization at work due to technology can also lead to the breakdown of functional patterns and give rise to problems of discipline. This may necessitate an appropriate HRD approach at the micro level with an in-built system of career development, job enrichment, employee participation, etc. to improve the quality of work life.

Similarly, executives may offer resistance to change owing to technological change. Induction of computers, for example, can minimize the importance of middle management. Similar resistance could also be there due to the human obsolescence of middle-aged managers faced with increasing demands to learn new skills and techniques. It has been observed that the capability of an individual to learn new technology often declines after a certain age. High technology can also create problems of wage disparity, and lead to the development of high-tech wage islands. In addition, there could be a problem of wage disparities between multinational and domestic sectors resulting, at times, in labour unrest. To reduce all these problems there is a need, both at macro and micro levels, to adopt better HRD approaches. This calls for heavy investments to provide intensive training and retraining facilities for the middle management and for enhancing the skills of operations.

There is also an equally pressing need to develop a more effective interface between R&D and other related functions within an organization. Organizations need to create new HRD systems and specialized cadres that would replace the traditional power and authority culture by a culture adaptable to and supportive of the technological change. Similarly, customers, dealers and suppliers need to be trained to accept the new products and services as a result of new technologies. The HRD efforts from government quarters should be similarly related to education and increasing the trainability of the workforce. This can culminate in personnel at various levels imbibing technological culture, especially in the spheres of policy making, designing administrative procedures and laying down criteria and controls. Therefore, development of personnel at the policy level is as crucial as development of skills at the implementation level.

# Research and Development

R&D plays a crucial role in any technology transfer, absorption, assimilation and upgradation. R&D is also in the forefront in developing leadership in the competitive market, and in the long run pays a return on investment.

R&D can be of two types:

- ❑ Basic R&D where the emphasis is on development of technology or processes for production increases and design of new products
- ❑ R&D for development of capabilities to absorb, assimilate and upgrade technology brought in from other countries

In many advanced countries, R&D as a percentage of GDP is characterized by their technological competition and its role in the global economy in terms of its commercialization and transfer to other countries on commercial basis. Japan's investment in R&D is around 2.98 per cent of its GNP while South Korea spent 1.83 per cent and Taiwan 1.41 per cent in 1990. In Japan, the governmental support to spending on R&D has been specially in the area of computer technology (See Table 2.2).

**TABLE 2.2**: R&D Spending in 1990

| Country | US $ Million | As % of GDP |
|---------|-------------:|------------:|
| Japan | 85,640 | 2.98 |
| South Korea | 3,210 | 1.83 |
| India | 2,500 | 0.88 |
| Taiwan | 2,075 | 1.41 |
| Singapore | 180 | 0.88 |
| Indonesia | 155 | 0.18 |
| Malaysia | 35 | 0.10 |
| Thailand | 105 | 0.21 |
| Pakistan | 320 | 0.98 |

*Source:* World Economic Forum, 1994.

South Korea's national system of innovation has been characterized by closely related economic, industrial and R&D import promotion policies. Industrial R&D in South Korea is supported by government policies and incentives such as subsidization of development costs and prototype manufacturing, favourable tax incentive system, investment and loan financing, promotion of venture capital, etc. Singapore has 26 research centres, while Hyundai in Korea has 17 research centres only for their automobile engines. In India, government agencies and public sector companies accounted for 87 per cent of the Rs 42 billion spent on R&D in 1990–91. Of the 87 per cent, 56 per cent was on defence research, space research and atomic energy alone. The Council for Scientific and Industrial Research (CSIR) runs 41 laboratories in India. The 1,000 or so private sector companies in India with R&D facilities spend only an average of 0.7 per cent of their revenue on R&D and even this is not on original applications research.

Some of the trends observed in technology transfer in developing countries indicate that R&D has not been playing a leading role. It, is normally the operations/production personnel who are involved in the choice of technology, training, operations, etc. The role of research comes in later, mainly in trouble-shooting, with the result that assimilation and absorption of technology is poor. Whenever there is a change or upgradation of technology, the machinery and the technology have to repurchased. The ideal course would be if the technology is first transferred to R&D which, in turn, should take the responsibility for training of personnel. This can, then, possibly pave the way for proper assimilation and upgradation of technology in the future. However, at times, the licensors of technology are reluctant to involve R&D professionals as they like to maintain strict secrecy about their know-how and future business. There are, at times, new R&D efforts within the country but even these do not get passed on to entrepreneurs for manufacturing purposes. Sometimes, the firms prefer to import technology from foreign companies having a better brand image. This helps them in marketing their products better in a competitive environment.

## PROBLEMS IN EXPLOITING INDIGENOUS TECHNOLOGY

The innovations and new technologies developed in the laboratories are often not effectively utilized by the industry owing to various reasons. The lack of proven manufacturing process development, such as non-availability of pilot plants, and improper documentation makes the transfer of technology from the laboratory to the industry extremely difficult. There is also a bias in favour of investments in foreign technology specially in countries such as India, Pakistan, etc. The reasons could be any of the following:

- ❑ Misgivings about manufacturability
- ❑ Lack of faith regarding quality and maintainability
- ❑ Doubts about the gestation period
- ❑ Delays in dealing, especially with government laboratories
- ❑ Doubts regarding the ability to market products without a foreign tag/name
- ❑ Preference to turnkey projects from abroad due to lack of proper technical base within the organization/country

Technology transfer to developing countries poses a different set of problems, such as non-availability of foreign exchange, high cost of transfer, problems in adaptation to local conditions, poor level of skills available, inadequate socio-economic infrastructure, new material quality, etc. The developing countries are often at a disadvantage while negotiating the purchase of technology due to inadequate knowledge regarding the price, type/generation of technology, etc. It is imperative that these countries take into account the following before importing the technology:

- ❑ Obsolescence of technology
- ❑ Adequate information for import substitution

❑ Adequate supply of raw material and components

❑ Continued supply of technology information

❑ Freedom to export products

❑ Training

❑ Guidance for R&D

The need for investment at the organization level must take into account the following:

❑ Stay competitive in the present areas of business

❑ Enter into new areas of business and develop new products

❑ Maintain a pool of talent for problem-solving

❑ Exploit outside discoveries

❑ Anticipate outside threats to the present market from new inventions and discoveries

❑ Avoid an adverse patent or know-how situation which may erode the present business or throw the company out of a new area of business

❑ Give the firm an image of progressiveness

## TECHNOLOGY TRANSFER AND ECONOMIC DEVELOPMENT

There are various issues related to economic development and restructuring that help or hinder the process of technology transfer, absorption, assimilation and innovation. Some of these issues are discussed below.

### Government Policies

Government policies regarding investment and technology transfer will eventually have a bearing on the nature and kind of technology to be transferred, including the policies on foreign investment, the type of technology to be acquired and so on. For example, till 1991 India followed a national policy that imposed restrictions on foreign investment. Equity participation by foreign partners was either discouraged or restricted to a limit of 40 per cent, and that too in certain specified industries. This affected the flow of technology into the country; prior to 1991 substantial technology transfer was only in the 'packaged' form.

When there is a restriction on equity participation to less than 50 per cent, MNCs may be reluctant to transfer the latest technology. Similarly, restrictions on participation in technology transfer imply that technology suppliers are at times reluctant to transfer technology in the 'unbundled form', especially when the transfer is through technical assistance and licensing. In such a situation, the transfer is more a case of a technology transplant rather than technology transfer, since the latter implies a certain level of absorption and assimilation.

Another national policy issue is the approach to imports and exports. Some countries believe in import substitution. In such case the policies are mainly confined to curbing the import content and developing an indigenous capability to save scarce foreign exchange. For example, the policy in India has been directed at developing import substitution capability. Such a policy has its own limitations as it entails heavy capital investment to build indigenous industries and the required infrastructure. On the other hand, in countries such as Singapore and Malaysia, the national policies give a thrust to exports rather than import substitution. These countries import raw material or semi-finished goods which they re-export after value addition. This enables them to earn sufficient foreign exchange to take care of their own import needs.

National policies on industrial development that clearly define the priority sectors can also give an impetus to the accelerated development of these sectors. For example, Japan identified electronics as its priority sector, especially the computer-related fields, for government investment. This gave the electronics industry in Japan a tremendous boost, with the result that the country emerged as a global leader. Malaysia has also shifted its focus from the agro-based sector to the electrical and electronic sectors and is now emerging as one of the major exporters in this field.

The continuity of economic development and industrial policies also play a significant role in attracting investments, both foreign and domestic. Trends indicate that there have been much higher investments in countries where there has been greater political stability or at least an assurance about the consistency and continuity of policies even with changes in the government. Another important variable of investment is the existence of a sound financial system, backed by good fiscal and monetary policies and mature capital markets. The availability of capital for investment is also dependent upon the policies on interest rates.

## Investment Incentives

Technology transfer is also affected by the national policies on investment incentives, both internal and external, since most Less Developed Countries (LDCs) have a shortage of investment funds. Therefore, they try to encourage foreign direct investment by offering incentives through reduction of tax liabilities or lower import tariffs. The level of sophistication of technology could also depend upon the extent of investment or equity participation of foreign investors. The higher the stakes of investors, the higher the chances of their bringing in higher technology to the developing countries. 'Similarly, the government policy of tariff exemption for certain machinery may bias investment towards capital-intensive products and processes. This may involve substantial technology transfer but also at times result in the transfer of inappropriate technology.'[5]

Trade policies and market protectionism can also affect the level of technology transfer. In case there is a protected domestic market, there could be inducement for foreign investment. This can, however, also act as a disincentive for bringing in the latest technology because of the absence of market competition. The functioning of the bureaucracy within the country can also have a bearing on investment. Investors naturally prefer countries where rules, regulations and procedures for clearance of investment proposals are faster and the clearance agencies are fewer in number. Simplified customs and excise clearance procedures also play a major role in encouraging and facilitating industrial activity.

## Intellectual Property Rights and Patent Rights

Many multinational enterprises would like to protect their property rights including risks of nationalization, procedures for compensation, repatriation of profits and royalty payments. Signing of bilateral and multilateral trade and investment guarantee agreements have had a positive influence on technology transfer and foreign direct investment. Absence of any such protection will restrict the extent of technology transfer to licensing type of agreements. At times there are ceilings put on royalty payments and if such ceilings are low, it can encourage the transferor to earn additional income by other means which could mean even resorting to unfair practices or putting other conditionalities such as supply of raw material, spares, etc.

## Infrastructure

Some of the infrastructure facilities and services that affect investment and technology transfer are the existence of an effective transport system, a sound legal framework, utilities, financial services and material testing laboratories. At times the government policies and standards regarding infrastructure can affect the extent of technology transfer. 'Much of the technology that flows across national boundaries is not effectively transferred on two counts: control over it is not passed from one set of institutional actors to another and the capacity to take further steps in elaborating technological modifications or improvements is likewise not vested in new hands, in particular indigenous third world ones.'[6]

There is always some distinction between the skills required for technology transfer and the skills needed for production processes. While the former have to be created and developed by the firms transferring the technology, the latter have to be taken care of by the country's educational system. One of the reasons for some of the South Asian countries, such as Hong Kong, Singapore and Malaysia attracting heavy foreign investments is the effort put in by their governments in the development of conducive infrastructure facilities, including development of ports, transportation, warehousing, industrial estates, power, etc. The government of Singapore has also taken the initiative of establishing technical institutions not only for education but for continuous skill development and upgradation.

## Cultural Diversities in Technology Transfer

There are differing schools of thought regarding the evolution and transfer of management concepts from one country to another. One school of thought believes that along with the technology transfer, managerial concepts could also be transferred since they are universally applicable, while the other view is that most management concepts are culture specific and cannot be transferred. There is a third view that advocates the transfer of concepts with appropriate blending with local practices and values. This view holds that otherwise the policies and practices do not get properly implemented, resulting in a hiatus between what is intended and what actually happens (Virmani and Guptan, 1992). Transferring managerial technology from one country to another is far more complex than transferring physical technology because the former are less codified and more intertwined with the social context.[7]

Therefore, in any technology transfer including managerial technology, the cultural diversities should be kept in mind. Regarding transfer of managerial know-how, there are normally two or three stages which are followed. The first involves the physical transfer of managerial know-how from the parent company to the recipient company. The second is the process of indigenization of personnel as well as managerial culture. The third stage is the integration and assimilation with the social background of the recipient country and diffusion of know-how to other firms. In the transfer process, it has also become important to blend some of the new approaches to management, such as just-in-time (JIT), produced to order, total quality management (TQM), multi-skilled workers, etc.

The success in transferring organizational innovation will largely depend upon the harmonization of human relationships, the style of doing work and the creation of a conducive work environment.[8] The Japanese were the first to demonstrate that changes in management techniques are equally if not more important than process technology in raising efficiency and productivity. A crucial question that still remains is whether superior management techniques practised in the parent company are culture specific. While the earlier belief was that many such techniques were indeed culture specific, recent experiences tend to suggest that some of the Japanese management techniques such as JIT, TQM, etc. can be transferred with appropriate modifications and blending.

The focus of this book is the coverage of the technology transfer and various macro- and micro-level issues which affect not only technology transfer but also its assimilation, absorption and upgradation. Some of the issues studied in detail are represented in Table 2.3. The subsequent chapters discuss all these issues with reference to the four countries, namely Thailand, Malaysia, Singapore and India including the case studies of a few organizations in these countries at the micro level.

**TABLE 2.3:** Key Policies Concerning Technology

| *Sl. No.* | *Macro* | *Micro* |
|---|---|---|
| 1. | National Development Policies<br>— Economic policies<br>  (Import/export policies)<br>— Development incentives<br>  • Infrastructure<br>  • Investment climate<br>  • Industrial policies<br>  • Others | Organization Policies<br>— Technology<br>  • Industry research centres<br>  • Core competencies<br>  • Diversification/expansion<br>  • Assimilation, absorption and<br>    upgradation<br>  • Blending of external and<br>    indigenous technology |
| 2. | Science and Technology Policies<br>— R&D policies<br>— Strategies<br>— National research laboratories<br>— Technology policies<br>  • Priorities<br>  • Types of alliances<br>  • Government's role | Human Resource Development<br>— Manpower planning<br>— Skill classification<br>— Skill upgradation training<br>— On-the-job training |
| 3. | Human Resource Policies<br>— Education policies<br>— Technical/vocational training<br>— Skill development and<br>  upgradation | Labour<br>— Grievance handling system<br>— Redundancy and redeployment<br>  policies |
| 4. | Industry-University Collaboration<br>— Industry-sponsored projects<br>— Research parks | Organization Capability Building<br>— Information flow and<br>  documentation system<br>— Choice of technology<br>— Alliances<br>— Negotiation capability<br>— Organizational restructuring for<br>  change<br>— Optimum utilization of incentives,<br>  e.g. R&D, training, etc. |
| 5. | Labour Policies<br>— Exit policy (redundancy and<br>  redeployment)<br>— Job reservations<br>— Legislation regulating employer/<br>  employee relations | |
| 6. | Financial Sector Reforms<br>— Banking policies<br>— Exchange regulations | |

# References

1. Kanthi, M.S., *A Compendium of Technology Plans and Policies in Selected Developing Countries,* UN Industrial Development Organization, June, 1986.
2. 'Intra-Regional Investment and Technology Transfer in Asia', a symposium report, Asian Productivity Organization, Tokyo, 1994.
3. Myint Hla, in Spencer, Daniel L. and Alexander Woroniak (eds.), *The Transfer of Technology to Developing Countries,* New York, Praeger, p.156, 1967.
4. *Technology Atlas,* Asian and Pacific Centre for Transfer of Technology, UNESCAP, Bangalore, India, September, 1988.
5. Stewart Jr., Charles T. and Yasumitsu Nihei, *Technology Transfer and Human Factors,* Lexington Books, Lexington, 1987.
6. Goulet Denis, in Sagafi-nejad, Richard W. Moxon and Howard V. Perlmutter (eds.), *Controlling International Technology Transfer: Issues, Perspectives and Policy Implications,* New York, Pergamon Press, p. 321, 1981.
7. 'Inter-regional Investment and Technology Transfer in the Asia', a symposim report, Asia Productivity Organization, Tokyo, 1994.
8. *Ibid.*

*part two*

# **C**OUNTRY CASE STUDIES

In recent years, some countries especially those in the Southeast Asian Region, have shown rapid economic growth. For this reason, countries such as Malaysia, Singapore, Thailand and Hong Kong have been called the 'Asian tigers'. On the other hand, economic progress in the countries of South Asia, such as India, Pakistan or Bangladesh, has been slow. This has been attributed by some to unavoidable environmental constraints, such as the pressures of population, political system, geographical diversity, etc. However, it has also been argued that these countries could have progressed much faster but for their faulty industrial and economic policies, more so when a country such as India has an abundance of internal resources—both natural as well as human. It is also interesting to note that some of the emerging Asian countries, such as Thailand and Singapore, have higher growth rates even though they do not have sufficient internal resources or trained manpower. Many attribute the fast-growing economies of some Southeast Asian countries to their conscious development policies, timely structural reforms, creation of a conducive climate for technological advancement and emphasis on human resource development.

While recognizing essential differences among the various countries, there are certain commonalities in terms of the socio-economic and political features which lead to faster development in countries such as Singapore, Malaysia and Thailand. Singapore at one time had no resources or trained manpower, yet they have been able to attain one of the highest growth rates and efficiency levels in the world. Malaysia had an abundance of natural resources such as petroleum, tin and rubber but suffered from a shortage of skilled and qualified manpower. Yet, it emerged as one of the largest exporters of manufactured electrical and electronic goods. In Thailand, despite political instability and a shortage of skilled labour, economic development continues at a reasonably fast rate. India, on the other hand, has an abundance of natural resources, reasonable political stability and good number of educated manpower. Yet the economic progress in the country has been slow. Compared to the first three decades after Independence, India's economy fared much better in the 1980s and more so in the 1990s. During the latter period, certain major decisions pertaining to structural reforms were undertaken, especially in the areas of technology and human resource development. This clearly indicates that a conscious following of certain policies can lead to economic growth.

Keeping the above in view, we made a comparative study of the structural reform processes, economic and industrial policies and other factors that have facilitated industrial growth, economic development, technology transfer and human resource development in four select countries—Malaysia, Singapore, Thailand and India.

We felt that such a study could enable some of the developing countries to draw certain useful lessons in planning their development.

# 3

# MALAYSIA

Malaysia was a British colony which gained independence in 1957
Till then the country's economy was dependent on agricultural produce
such as cocoa, rubber, palm oil and minerals such as tin.

The first policy initiatives towards industrialization were made
from 1958 onwards with the first phase of planning focusing on
economic self-reliance through import substitution and domestic
market orientation. Initially, the small and medium private sector
was encouraged to set up industries for the domestic market as well
as support import substitution. In addition to financial incentives,
certain other incentives were given to private enterprises such as tax
holidays, creation of industrial estates, etc. The major investments
were in agro-based industries, drawing upon the abundance of the
country's natural resources, such as rubber, cocoa and palm. The
economy was regulated and controlled. There was a heavy influx of
labour from India and neighbouring countries who came to work on
the plantations.

However, the growth rate remained sluggish and progress in
industrialization was less than expected. There was a lack of qualified
technical manpower and financial resources for the manufacturing
industry. The economy became inward-looking and exports were

confined to agro-based products. There were inequities in income distribution with a majority of the population living below the poverty line. Thus, a need was felt to re-orient the planning objectives and bring about structural re-adjustments in the economy. The Investment Incentives Act, 1968, brought in major structural changes such as encouraging export-oriented production rather than catering to only the small domestic market. Figure 3.1 traces the evolution of economic reforms in Malaysia.

| | | | |
|---|---|---|---|
| PHASE I | Pioneer Industries Ordinance Act, 1958 | → | Import substitution, promotion of private sector, tax holidays, industrial estates, etc. |
| | | → | Domestic market orientation |
| PHASE II | Investment Incentives Act, 1968 | → | Export orientation |
| | | → | New economic policy |
| | Industrial Coordination Act, 1975 | → | Free trade zones |
| PHASE III | Launching of Fourth Malaysian Plan, 1981-85 | → | Export-led growth |
| | | → | Heavy industries programme (import substitution) |
| | | → | Industrial master plan (1986–1995) |
| | Promotion of Investments Act, 1986 (Foreign Investment) | → | Action plan for industrial technology development |
| PHASE IV | Vision 2020 1992 onwards | → | Projected growth of GDP |
| | | → | Structural reforms in bureaucracy |

**FIG. 3.1:** Evolution of Economic Reforms and Policy Initiatives

The new economic policy moved the economy from being exclusively agro-based to a manufacturing giant. Inadequate financial resources for investment and lack of an industrial base necessitated value-added export-led growth. This was done through easing of import restrictions, especially in exportable value-added items. The small size of the domestic market also facilitated easy exports.

The second phase saw the introduction of the New Economic Policy (NEP). This was intended to attract foreign investors with restricted equity participation and conditions for employment of local manpower. This led to the import of foreign technology into free trade zones. Export orientation gave an impetus to foreign investors for setting up industries in these free trade zones. The 1970s saw the entry of large investors in export-led products, while the development

**TABLE 3.1:**  Major Economic Indicators

|  |  | 1992 | 1993 | 1994 | 1995* | 1996* |
|---|---|---|---|---|---|---|
| Gross domestic product | % change | 7.8 | 8.3 | 8.5 | 8.5 | 8.0 |
| Agriculture | % change | 4.3 | 3.9 | 0.5 | 2.3 | 3.0 |
| Industry | % change | 8.9 | 10.0 | 11.4 | 10.8 | 8.5 |
| Services | % change | 8.1 | 8.3 | 8.4 | 8.3 | 9.2 |
| Gross domestic investment | % of GDP | 33.5 | 35.0 | 37.2 | 37.6 | 36.0 |
| Gross domestic saving | % of GDP | 35.5 | 35.9 | 35.6 | 36.7 | 35.1 |
| Inflation rate of CPI | % of change | 4.7 | 3.6 | 3.8 | 4.2 | 4.4 |
| Money supply growth | % change | 19.1 | 23.5 | 22.0 | 18.0 | 15.0 |
| Merchandise exports | US $ billion | 39.6 | 45.9 | 57.0 | 68.9 | 82.6 |
|  | % change | 18.1 | 15.9 | 24.2 | 20.8 | 20.0 |
| Merchandise imports | US $ billion | 36.2 | 42.5 | 57.8 | 65.6 | 78.1 |
|  | % change | 9.8 | 17.3 | 36.0 | 13.5 | 19.0 |
| Current accounts | US $ billion | −1.6 | −2.1 | −6.4 | −4.9 | −3.6 |
|  | % of GDP | −2.8 | −3.3 | −9.0 | −6.1 | −4.0 |
| External debt outstanding | US $ billion | 20.0 | 23.3 | 25.0 | 27.0 | 28.0 |
| Debt-service ratio | % of exports | 6.6 | 7.9 | 4.7 | 5.0 | 6.0 |

*Estimates.

*Source:*  *Asian Development Outlook 1995 and 1996,* Asian Development Bank, Oxford University Press, 1995.

**TABLE 3.2:**  Growth Rate of Per Capita GDP

| 1989 | 1990 | 1991 | 1992 | 1993 | 1994 | 1995 | 1996 |
|---|---|---|---|---|---|---|---|
| 6.6 | 7.2 | 6.2 | 5.3 | 6.1 | 5.7 | 6.4 | 5.9 |

Per Capita GNP US $ = 31.60 in 1993.

*Source:*  *Asian Development Outlook 1995 and 1996,* Asian Development Bank, Oxford University Press, 1995.

of infrastructural facilities and bases remained the major responsibility of the government.

The Fourth Plan (1981–85) reverted to promotion of import substitution with heavy industries, such as petrochemicals, fertilizers, automobiles and electronics, receiving a high level of protection. The growth so far had not been complemented by an expansion of the indigenous technological capability. The focus on technology development and internal capability building remained with the identified industrial sectors within the domestic industry. The Investment Act, 1986, on the other hand, was intended to attract direct foreign investment in industries other than the identified sectors and for hundred per cent exports. The critical role of technology and upgradation of human resource skills were highlighted in the action plan for industrial and technological development. In the initial years after independence, there was hardly any science and technology base in the country. A policy of encouraging internal capability building through import of appropriate technology was developed by entering into various agreements with foreign agencies.

Through the NEP the government consciously tried to create a conducive environment to attract foreign investment by fewer government controls and regulations. Some of the major factors that attracted investment in the manufacturing sector were:

❑ Simpler licensing policies

❑ Free monetary exchange regulations

❑ Encouraging joint ventures philosophy

❑ Opening up the economy with a free market philosophy

❑ Financial incentives.

With this favourable climate for investment, Malaysia attracted the second highest amount of direct foreign investment in the world valued at US $2.90 billion in 1990. The World Competitiveness Report accorded Malaysia the highest marks for 'a highly conducive business environment, attitude to work, technology, government and international influence'. In terms of ratings of investment risks in selected economies (1991) by the International Country Risk Guide, London, the Malaysian economy's rating comes almost close to developed countries such as USA, Japan and Singapore. In fact, it is rated slightly higher than the Republic of Korea.[1]

The net impact of the various policies resulted in a faster rate of growth of the economy with the Gross National Product (GNP) growing from US $3,881 in 1970 to US $64,450 in 1993 and the per capita steeply rising from US $360 to US $3,160 during the same period. There was hardly any manufacturing base in Malaysia before 1970 but with conscious encouragement given to this sector, there was a sharp increase in the percentage share of manufacturing in the GDP from 13.4 per cent in 1970 to 45.4 per cent in 1994. Electrical and electronic machinery within the manufacturing sector has shown a remarkable increase in production capacity from Malaysian Ringitt (RM) 52 in 1970 to RM 55,230 in 1993. Chemical and petrochemical sectors also indicate a rising trend in production capacity from RM 196 in 1970 to RM 5,882 in 1993. There has, however, been sharp decline in agriculture and mining sectors as shown in Tables 3.3 and Table 3.4.

**TABLE 3.3:** Percentage Changes in Overall Sectoral Share of GDP

|             | 1980 | 1994 |
|-------------|------|------|
| Agriculture | 22.9 | 14.8 |
| Industry    | 35.8 | 45.4 |
| Services    | 41.3 | 9.8  |

*Source: Asian Development Outlook, 1995 and 1996,* Asian Development Bank, Oxford University Press, 1995.

**TABLE 3.4:** Sectoral Distribution of GDP

|                              | 1970 | 1980 | 1990 | 1991 | 1992 | 1993 |
|------------------------------|------|------|------|------|------|------|
| GDP* RM (millions)           | 12,308 | 44,511 | 79,430 | 86,302 | 93,624 | 101,084 |
| Percentage Share of GDP      |      |      |      |      |      |      |
| Agriculture                  | 30.8 | 22.9 | 18.6 | 17.2 | 16.0 | 15.0 |
| Mining and quarrying         | 6.3  | 10.1 | 9.7  | 9.2  | 8.7  | 8.0  |
| Manufacturing                | 13.4 | 19.6 | 26.9 | 28.2 | 29.3 | 30.9 |
| Construction                 | 3.9  | 4.6  | 3.6  | 3.8  | 4.0  | 4.1  |
| Electricity gas and water    | 1.9  | 1.4  | 1.9  | 2.0  | 2.1  | 2.2  |
| Transport, storage and communication | 4.7 | 5.7 | 6.9 | 7.0 | 7.1 | 7.2 |
| Wholesale and retail, hotels | 13.3 | 12.1 | 11.1 | 11.7 | 12.0 | 12.1 |
| Finance, etc.                | 8.4  | 8.3  | 9.8  | 10.1 | 10.4 | 10.7 |
| Government services          | 11.1 | 10.3 | 10.8 | 10.4 | 10.1 | 9.8  |
| Other services               | 2.5  | 2.3  | 2.1  | 2.1  | 2.1  | 2.1  |

*RM = Malaysian Ringitt in millions.

*Source: The Malaysian Economy in Figures,* January 1993, Economic Planning Unit, PM's Dept., Kuala Lumpur, Malaysia.

*Note:* One US $ = 2.50 Malaysian Ringitt in April 1993 and equal to 2.61 MR in February 1996.

# CHALLENGES OF VISION 2020

The Prime Minister of Malaysia, Dr Mahathir Bin Mohammad, in his address to the Malaysian Business Council in 1991, gave an outline of the mission for Malaysia which is popularly known as Vision

**TABLE 3.5:** Major Exports

(Figures in RM millions)

| Exports | 1970 | 1980 | 1990 | 1991 | 1992 | 1993 |
|---|---|---|---|---|---|---|
| Total RM millions | 5,163 | 28,172 | 79,646 | 94,497 | 110,372 | 123,365 |
| Manufacturing products | 614 | 6,319 | 46,833 | 61,427 | 77,386 | 90,541 |
| Textiles | 32 | 806 | 3,983 | 4,805 | 5,803 | 6,791 |
| Chemical and petroleum | 196 | 278 | 3,174 | 3,539 | 4,642 | 5,882 |
| Electrical and electronic machinery | 52 | 3,016 | 26,504 | 35,602 | 46,432 | 55,230 |
| Iron and steel, and metal | 34 | 249 | 1,625 | 1,883 | 2,398 | 2,987 |

*Source: The Malaysian Economy in Figures,* EPU, January 1993, PM's Dept., Kuala Lumpur, Malaysia.

*Note:* One US $ = 2.50 Malaysian Ringitt in April 1993 and equal to 2.61 MR in February 1996.

2020. According to Dr Mohammad, 'By the year 2020, Malaysia can be a united nation, with a confident Malaysian society, infused by strong moral and ethical values, living in a society that is democratic, liberal and tolerant, caring economically just and equitable, progressive and prosperous, and in full possession of an economy that is competitive, dynamic, robust and resilient.'[2]

To achieve these objectives, the Prime Minister, highlighted nine strategic challenges which the country had to work out if it wished to achieve Vision 2020:

❑ The challenge of establishing a united Malaysian nation with a sense of common and shared destiny

❑ The challenge of creating a psychologically liberated, secure and developed Malaysian society, with faith and confidence in itself

❑ The challenge of fostering and developing a mature democratic society, practising a form of mature, consensual, community-oriented Malaysian democracy

❑ The challenge of establishing a fully moral and ethical society whose citizens are strong in religious and spiritual values

❑ The challenge of establishing a mature, liberal and tolerant society

❑ The challenge of establishing a scientific and progressive society that is innovative and forward-looking

❑ The challenge of establishing a fully caring society and a caring culture

❑ The challenge of establishing an economically just society in which there is fair and equitable distribution of wealth

❑ The challenge of establishing a prosperous society with an economy that is fully competitive, dynamic, robust and resilient

The Prime Minister's mission and the related challenges have become a topic of much public debate. All the sectors of the economy, the industry and government departments have been involved in identifying their respective roles in meeting these challenges as well as developing strategies to meet the goals.

## Areas of Reforms

In Vision 2020, it is envisaged that by the year 2020 Malaysia will be a fully developed society. In economic terms, it is envisaged that GDP would be eight times more by the year 2020 than it was in 1990. In other words, GDP should double every 10 years. This would require a growth rate of around 7 per cent annually over the next 30 years. The mission also envisages balanced growth in all sectors of the economy and equitable development of all ethnic groups from different regions.

The economic objective is to secure a competitive economy which is self-sustaining, having 'a modern and mature agricultural sector, and an efficient productive and equally mature service sector'. The economy has to be technologically proficient, innovative and moving in the direction of higher levels of technology. The economy will be characterized by a low inflation rate and subject to the discipline of market forces. The government role will be proactive 'to ensure healthy fiscal and monetary management and smooth functioning of Malaysian economy. While the process of deregulation will continue, the government will play a role in ensuring laws and regulations which are productive of the societal objectives'.

The local entrepreneur will be encouraged, especially in the small and medium sectors, to meet the goals of development and necessary encouragement will be given to R&D. It is also clearly indicated in the mission that though Malaysia will be an economically developed and industrialized society, it will preserve its social, ethical and spiritual values.

## Science and Technology Policy

With the intention of encouraging faster growth in the area of science and technology, the government launched the Action Plan for Industrial Technological Development (APITD). The objective of APITD was to strengthen scientific and technological capability through indigenous technological development and acquisition of selective technology from abroad, and at the same time develop requisite human resources and infrastructure.

The Fifth Plan endeavoured to bring in greater coordination between internal R&D and technological development in identified priority areas in the public sector. A budgetary allocation of US $ 414 million was provided for R&D which was 0.8 per cent of the GNP. Fifty per cent of the budget was provided for agriculture, 34 per cent for industries and 17 per cent for other sectors. Private sector participation in R&D expenditure continued to be low as they relied more on foreign sources of technology rather than in-house R&D. Even domestic adaptations and modifications of externally-sourced technology in the form of new and imported products and processes were not substantial. However, in some areas such as telecommunications, there were extensive product diversifications and innovations which catered not only to the requirements of the domestic market but also to the exports. Similarly, there were innovations in the plantation sector. The country also established a Technology Park to promote private sector participation in technological development.

## Policies on Technology and Investment

The import of technology continues to play a significant role in the country's industrial development. Contractual agreements for technology imports increased from 58 in 1975 to 198 in 1989, a substantial percentage of which were in the nature of technical assistance (see Table 3.6). Though there was openness in the economy to import technology, guidelines were developed to ensure that technology transfers were planned to enhance domestic technological capabilities and that there were mutual benefits for the receivers and suppliers of technology. In addition, steps were taken to strengthen the technical capabilities of the institutions involved in the evaluation, selection, processing and enforcement of technology transfer agreements. In spite of technology transfers from abroad, the innovations have resulted in only incremental

**TABLE 3.6:** Technology Imports by Type of Agreement, 1985–90

| Type of Agreement | Number of Imports | | | | | |
|---|---|---|---|---|---|---|
| | 1985 | 1986 | 1987 | 1988 | 1989 | 1990 |
| 1. Joint venture | 9 | 19 | 11 | 11 | 15 | 16 |
| 2. Technical assistance | 46 | 47 | 50 | 64 | 64 | 75 |
| 3. Know-how | 5 | 3 | 3 | 3 | 13 | 11 |
| 4. Licenses and patents | 14 | 27 | 22 | 37 | 35 | 15 |
| 5. Management | 6 | 10 | 5 | 7 | 12 | 5 |
| 6. Services | 1 | 1 | 1 | 2 | 12 | 5 |
| 7. Trademark | 5 | 6 | 8 | 7 | 18 | 19 |
| 8. Turn-key and engineering | 0 | 1 | 0 | 1 | 1 | 1 |
| 9. Supply and purchase | 1 | 0 | 1 | 0 | 6 | 2 |
| 10. Sales, marketing/ distribution | 7 | 7 | 7 | 10 | 6 | 5 |
| 11. Others | 2 | 2 | 2 | 8 | 16 | 4 |
| **Total** | **96** | **123** | **110** | **150** | **198** | **156** |

*Source: Malaysia, Sixth Malaysian Plan, 1991–95,* National Printing Dept., Kuala Lumpur, 1991.

*Note:* There were less technology transfer agreements in 1990, though the number of approved manufacturing licences was substantial. This is because many of these projects were expected to lift off only during the Sixth Plan and the relevant technology transfer agreements were expected to be submitted for approval much later.

improvements or marginal adaptations to meet local needs rather than the design and development of new products and processes. Thus, in Malaysia, the indigenous capability and ability for technological development has continued to be weak. This calls for strengthening domestic consultancy, design and engineering capabilities.

Government policies have been the major facilitating factor for technology transfer and foreign investment. The manufacturing sector has been given a major thrust with special incentives for export-oriented industries. The Industrial Coordination Act of 1975 requires a licence for industries with shareholder's funds of US $2.5 million and above or engaging 75 or more full-time employees. The Act also provided that industries exporting 80 per cent or more of their products do not require approval. Industries were allowed to diversify for export purposes without prior approval.

The government also developed certain guidelines for protection of foreign investment in Malaysia. The equity participation is allowed on market criteria, i.e. the total export or domestic market share, apart from other factors such as the level of technology, spin-off effects, size of the investment, location, value-added benefits and utilization of local raw materials and components. Certain assurances on equity were given, such as companies were not required to restructure their equity even after expansion or diversification provided they met the original conditions of approval. Malaysia also concluded investment guarantee agreements with a number of countries which provided protection against nationalization and expropriation, prompt and adequate compensation in the event of nationalization or expropriation, free transfer of capital, profits or other fees and settlement of investment disputes under the Convention of the Settlement Disputes.

**TABLE 3.7:** Technology Imports by Industry Group, 1985–90

| Industry Group | Number of Imports | | | | | |
|---|---|---|---|---|---|---|
| | 1985 | 1986 | 1987 | 1988 | 1989 | 1990 |
| 1. Food | 10 | 8 | 8 | 16 | 21 | 14 |
| 2. Textiles and wearing apparel | 1 | 7 | 2 | 6 | 4 | 8 |
| 3. Leather and leather goods | 0 | 0 | 0 | 1 | 0 | 1 |
| 4. Wood and wood products including furniture | 0 | 4 | 1 | 0 | 0 | 6 |
| 5. Paper and paper products including printing and publishing | 3 | 4 | 1 | 3 | 0 | 4 |
| 6. Chemical and chemical products including pharmaceuticals | 16 | 15 | 18 | 29 | 27 | 24 |
| 7. Petroleum and coal | 0 | 0 | 0 | 6 | 2 | 0 |
| 8. Rubber and rubber products | 4 | 13 | 8 | 22 | 18 | 8 |
| 9. Plastic and plastic products | 0 | 4 | 0 | 2 | 6 | 5 |
| 10. Non-metallic mineral products | 7 | 7 | 12 | 4 | 10 | 7 |
| 11. Basic metals | 1 | 1 | 2 | 0 | 6 | 4 |
| 12. Fabricated metal products | 9 | 22 | 21 | 17 | 7 | 4 |
| 13. Manufacture of machinery | 0 | 0 | 0 | 0 | 7 | 6 |
| 14. Electrical and electronic products | 20 | 12 | 29 | 37 | 40 | 41 |
| 15. Transport equipment | 20 | 15 | 4 | 1 | 15 | 18 |
| 16. Hotels and tourism | 4 | 4 | 1 | 2 | 6 | 3 |
| 17. Agriculture | 0 | 0 | 1 | 1 | 7 | 0 |
| 18. Miscellaneous | 1 | 7 | 2 | 3 | 22 | 3 |
| **Total** | **96** | **123** | **110** | **150** | **198** | **156** |

*Source:* *Malaysia, Sixth Malaysian Plan, 1991–95*, National Printing Dept., Kuala Lumpur, 1991.

The Promotion of Investment Act, 1986, provided for special incentives for the manufacturing sector in terms of relief from taxes. A company with a 'pioneer' status was granted partial exemption from payment of income tax and could pay tax only on 30 per cent of its statutory income. This is still applicable for five years from the date of production. Strategic projects of national importance having high technology and heavy capital investment can be given 100 per cent exemption.

Similar reliefs were also given in the shape of investment tax allowance and re-investment allowance. There were special incentives for exports, such as the Export Credit Refinancing Scheme, abatement incentives for export, double deduction for promotion of exports as in overseas advertising, export market research, exhibitions, etc. Incentives were provided for R&D which include double deductions for cash contributions made to approved research institutions. A tax exemption for a period of five years was granted to companies established to undertake R&D.

Special incentives have been given for skill upgradation of human resources. Double deduction has been allowed for expenses incurred on approved training of employees, especially to small and medium industries which employed 50 or less workers. A special Human Resource Development Fund (HRDF) has been created where companies are required to contribute at the rate of 1 per cent of the wages of employees. Large and medium enterprises can draw assistance from the HRDF for training for specified and approved courses. An industrial building allowance has been granted to companies for buildings used for industrial training. The incentive consists of an initial allowance of 10 per cent and an annual allowance of 2 per cent.

Incentives are provided for Industrial Adjustment Allowance (IAA) by a particular industry to undertake restructuring exercises. This could be by way of reorganization, reconstruction or amalgamation with the intention of strengthening the basis for industrial self-sufficiency, improving industrial technology, increasing productivity and efficient management of manpower, and is made available to companies in the form of IAA loans at concessional rates from the IAA fund. It applies to specific industries in the sectors of wood, textiles, machinery and engineering. There are other incentives for small-scale companies, agricultural sector, tourism industry, etc. Certain exemptions were provided from import duties on the manufacture of goods for export. Exemption from import duty was also allowed on raw material, components and machinery used for manufacture of goods for the domestic market, if these were not manufactured locally. Taxation laws, rules and regulations were also simplified. Similarly, rules and regulations regarding employment of expatriate personnel were simplified.

## Transfer of Technology

In order to facilitate the process of technology transfer, the government streamlined the policies and procedures for approval of transfer of technology agreements. The authority for approval and policy making for transfer of technology rests with the Ministry of International Trade and Industry (MITI). The MITI tries to ensure that any technology transfer agreement: (*a*) does not impose unfair restrictions or handicaps on the local party; (*b*) is not prejudicial to the national interest; and (*c*) is one where the payment of fees is commensurate with the level of technology to be transferred. The projects with an investment of RM 2.5 million or with 75 or more employees only need to seek approval. There are no controls or restrictions on technology transfer for industries with investment below RM 2.5 million or employing less than 75 people.

Normally, technology transfer agreements fall into the following categories: joint ventures, technical assistance and know-how, licence agreements, patents and trademarks, turn-key contracts, management agreements, etc. Gradually, turn-key services, management and sales, marketing and distribution type of agreements have been phased out while technical assistance, know-how, trademark, licensing and patents, and joint ventures have been increasing. This indicates that gradually internal expertise has been developed in services, management and marketing areas.

The Ministry evaluates the agreements on the basis of the following criteria:

❑ Access to improvements

❑ Remuneration for technology

❑ Methods of payment

❑ Duration and renewal (normally five years)

❑ Training

❑ Patent and trademarks

❑ Confidentiality and secrecy

❑ Guarantee/warranty

❑ Withholding tax

❑ Sales territory

❑ Governing laws and Arbitration

The withholding tax levied on payments made to suppliers of technology is also eligible for double deductions on application. The royalty payments are normally to be paid on net sales. While approving agreements, MITI has evolved a formula based on a point system for evaluating the amount of royalty payments. The points are allocated on the basis of the following factors:

❑ Level of technology—low, medium or high

❑ Equity participation

❑ Patents/trademarks

❑ Source of raw materials

❑ R&D

❑ Market for products—domestic or export

❑ Number of training programmes

❑ Category of industry—priority or others

The royalty normally varies between 2 and 5 per cent depending upon the rating.

Applications are initially processed by the officer at the MITI in accordance with the guidelines laid down. The processing officer

**TABLE 3.8:**  R&D Budget
(in US $ million)

|  | *Fifth Malaysian Plan (1986–90)* | *Sixth Malaysian Plan (1991–95)* |
|---|---|---|
| Direct R&D | 413.8 | 600.00 |
| S&T Infrastructure | 126.7 | 560.30 |

*Source:* Malaysian Sixth Five Year Plan.

*Note:* One US $ = 2.50 Malaysian Ringitt in April 1993 and equal to 2.61 MR in February 1996.

then makes a presentation to the Technical Committee which ultimately gives the approval. The Committee comprises representatives from the Ministry of Science and Technology, Ministry of Environment, Standards and Research Institute and the Treasury. The proposals are cleared within two to three weeks of submission provided all the necessary details are furnished. Malaysia provides adequate protection to the manufacturers under the Patents Act, Trademarks Act and Copyright Act. Technical R&D capabilities have been weak and reliance has been mainly on foreign technology. R&D is encouraged for internal capability building. The nodal agency for all technology transfer approvals is the MITI while the Ministries of Science and Technology and Environment are basically funding agencies for R&D and for granting approval of projects from the environment angle.

Some initiatives have been taken by the Ministry of Science and Technology to assess the status of existing technology in the country in selected industries and also to identify the emerging technology trends. Correspondingly, studies have been undertaken to identify the available skills and skill requirements for the future. These studies have been quite extensive, not only in identifying gaps in technology or skills but also in suggesting action plans to fill these gaps. The starting point was strengthening the school curriculum with greater focus on science and technology. A special skill development fund has been created to continuously upgrade the skills of the existing workforce.

So far, R&D has not been given much importance as the focus has been on transferring 'readymade' technology. The R&D expenditure in 1990 was a mere 0.8 per cent of the GDP. However, it is estimated that this will increase to 1 per cent by AD 2000, 2 per cent by 2010 and 2.3 per cent by 2020. Though the government has been encouraging R&D projects and their commercialization, the progress in this respect has been rather slow. Malaysian scientists and technologists only managed to commercialize 35 out of the 292 new products, knowledge and technology developed during 1990–92. It is estimated that 83 more new products and technologies have the potential for commercial use.[3]

The Action Plan of the government has recommended self-financing targets for research institutions to the extent of 30 per cent by 1995. It is expected that new approaches will induce technology ventures and entrepreneurship for commercializing and diffusing new technology. The infrastructure for initial downstream activities such as upscaling, prototyping, financing and marketing will need to be developed. Due to high-risk uncertainty and the long gestation period of the commercialization process, the government is considering establishing special funds within the existing financial institutions or in new venture capital corporations which will advance funds to enterprising firms, consortia or individual entrepreneurs on concessional terms.

Simultaneous reforms have also been carried out in the areas of banking, finance and exchange control. The banking system and financial institutions provided the necessary financial support for industrial activity. Special funds were created to assist and stimulate growth in the priority sector. The government has also been encouraging venture capital financing for development of technology-based small and medium industries involved in R&D commercialization and product development.

Strategic industries enjoy protection for 8 to 10 years before allowing competition to enter the areas to ensure competitiveness and efficiency of these sectors, e.g. roads, automobiles, power, etc. Electricity generation was initially started by the government and later privatized. This has greatly enhanced the efficiency of the power sector. Government policies regarding some of the infrastructural industries are based on the philosophy of Build-Own-Transfer (BOT); Build-Own-Operate-Transfer (BOOT) or Build-Own-Operate (BOO).

## Partnership between Government and Private Sector

To achieve the goals of an industrial economy, Malaysia realized the need for a closer partnership between public and private sectors. This led to the development of the 'Malaysia Incorporated Policy' which envisaged a closer partnership between the two sectors. The private sector is expected to be the commercial and economic arm while the public sector will be the service arm to support its private sector partner. The Malaysia Incorporated Policy includes redefining the role of the public sector, bringing in an attitudinal change among civil servants in their dealings with the public, development of institutional mechanisms for public-private sector collaboration, and review of the systems, structure and performance of the civil service. In line with the Malaysia Incorporated Policy the government went in for a 'privatization policy' and a corresponding reduction in the size of the public sector to reduce the public sector budget deficit.

The policy resulted in saving of the operating expenditure to the extent of 10 per cent of the total public expenditure up to 1993.

As a part of the partnership between the private sector and the government, the Malaysian government embarked upon bringing an attitudinal change among the civil servants. As a first step, the effort was to introduce the concept of total quality management in the civil service. This necessitated a systematic approach of preparing the civil servants for their changing roles and acceptance of the greater role of the private sector. Some of the steps taken in this direction were consensus building among civil servants for administrative improvement programmes, documentation and information dissemination, specialized training for skill and knowledge development to implement the new programmes, and development of follow-up strategies to ensure the implementation of new programmes.

## Infrastructure

In accordance with the guidelines outlined in Vision 2020, the government has already taken the initiative of developing a conducive climate for industrialization as well as development of an appropriate infrastructure. The clearance procedures for investment have been simplified. Each state/region was asked to prepare their industrial development plans keeping in view the available infrastructure for their special needs. Special attention has been given to development of power, transportation, ports, industrial estates as well as changes in customs clearances, etc.

## Human Resource Development

With the rapid growth of the Malaysian economy, there has been an increase in demand for appropriately qualified human resources. Initially, the emphasis was on agricultural labour. However, realizing that the growing industrial sector based on high technology required technically skilled manpower, the government has set up technical institutes. It has also been taking various measures to increase the number of engineers, technicians and other skilled personnel.

During the 1980s, there was rapid expansion of technical and vocational schools, polytechnics and industrial training institutions. In addition, the government also set up an institute for training instructors and established a National Vocational Training Council under the Ministry of Human Resources. The Council coordinates the planning and development of vocational training activities and programmes. It also assesses the existing and future skill shortages, evaluates vocational training programmes and establishes National Trade Standards.

## Development of Youth

The Ministry of Education has taken up the major responsibility of increasing the trainability of youth by laying emphasis on subject areas such as language, science, mathematics in their vocational and technical institutes. The Ministry of Youth and Sports has been assigned the special responsibility of preparing the youth for the job market. It has established seven technical and vocational institutes to conduct special employment-oriented long duration training programmes. The programme duration ranges from six months to two years. There are special entrepreneurship development programmes for young people after completion of high school. The objectives of these courses is to prepare them to set up their own small enterprises such as restaurants, automobile workshops, etc. There are also special sandwich courses under the apprenticeship scheme where they are given training partly in the industry and partly at the institute. There are special schemes in collaboration with the Ministry of Agriculture on entrepreneural development for rural youth to take up agro-based activities.

## Development of Women

Women constitute about 50 per cent of the total population in Malaysia. The government recognized the role women could play as early as 1983 when the Women's Affairs Division (HAWA) was established initially under the Prime Minister's department. The objective of HAWA was to promote participation of women in national development and to ensure that the National Development Plans take into consideration integration of women through the provision of equal opportunities and access to facilities and resources. With the articulation of Vision 2020, HAWA has also been assigned the responsibility of ensuring women's contribution to economic development. At present, 44 per cent of Malaysian women are employed. The targets are to increase this number to 52 per cent in the next five years. It is interesting to note that in Malaysia more girls are going in for higher education to universities than boys, though a majority of them have opted for the arts stream. However, their representation in politics is marginal. Also, there is discrimination in salaries paid to female employees in the private sector (70 per cent of the salary paid to males). Incidentally, the ILO convention on gender equality has not yet been signed by Malaysia.

## Training

There are 10 major industrial training institutes set up by the Training Division of the Manpower Department. Some of the programmes conducted by these institutes are:

♦ *National Apprenticeship Scheme (NAS)* The training programme under NAS is to further upgrade the skill of industrial workers sponsored by their employers. The duration of the NAS is three years which includes 18 months training at the Institute and another 18 months practical training in the industry. The apprentices are required to pass an intermediate level of examination set by the National Vocational Training Council after which they are awarded the Certificate of National Apprenticeship.

♦ *Trade Skill Certification Course* This fully sponsored government course is meant for fresh school-leavers. It is of two years' duration with 66 weeks of institutional training and 22 weeks of on-the-job training. After passing an examination, they are awarded Skill Proficiency Certificate.

♦ *On-site Training Scheme for Construction Workers* There are separate three months' specialized courses for construction workers with the objective of developing skilled and semi-skilled workers for construction.

♦ *The Week-end Course in Industrial Skills* This part-time course is conducted on Saturdays and Sundays entailing a total of eight hours of training per week. The course is open to anyone who wishes to acquire basic industrial skills.

♦ *Instructor and Advance Skill Training* The Centre for Instructor and Advanced Skill Training (CIAST) under the Manpower Department provides training for instructors from training institutions as well as supervisors and skilled workers from industrial sectors. The courses are module-based to encourage participation from employees from the industrial sector.

Despite the above measures to increase availability of skilled/qualified persons, shortages still exist and are likely to increase further. Malaysia has reached almost a full employment level as shown in Table 3.9.

**TABLE 3.9:**   Employment Trends

|  |  | 1970 | 1980 | 1990 | 1991 | 1992 |
|---|---|---|---|---|---|---|
| Employment | (thousands) | 3,396 | 4,835 | 6,621 | 6,849 | 7,060 |
| Growth rate | (%) |  | 2.6 | 4.3 | 3.4 | 3.1 |
| Agriculture | (% of total) | 50.5 | 37.2 | 27.8 | 26.8 | 25.2 |
| Mining | (% of total) | 2.6 | 1.3 | 0.6 | 0.6 | 0.6 |
| Manufacturing | (% of total) | 11.4 | 15.5 | 19.5 | 20.0 | 21.0 |
| Construction | (% of total) | 4.0 | 5.6 | 6.4 | 6.7 | 6.8 |
| Services | (% of total) | 31.5 | 40.4 | 45.7 | 45.9 | 46.1 |

|  | 1971–80 | 1981–90 | 1971–90 |
|---|---|---|---|
| Growth Rate | 3.6 | 3.2 | 3.4 |

*Source:  Malaysian Economy in Figures,* 1993. Economic Planning Unit, Malaysia.

The labour force in Malaysia had more than doubled from 1970 to 1992 with the growth rate being 4.3 per cent during 1980–90. The overall growth rate of employment has been above 3 per cent. Agriculture and fishing, which accounted for 50 per cent of the total employment in 1979, had reduced to almost 25 per cent in 1992. On the other hand, employment in the manufacturing and services sectors increased from 11.4 and 31.5 per cent in 1970 to 21 and 46.3 per cent in 1992, respectively.

The capacity of the local institutions to meet existing demands has not kept pace with local requirements and, as estimated by the government, is likely to further worsen. This situation has necessitated individual organizations to take up their own in-house training programmes for initial training as well as skilled upgradation training. In addition, the private sector needs to take a lead in establishing training centres or institutes.

The unemployment rate in Malaysia fell to 2.9 per cent of the labour force in 1994. This was mainly because of the employment growth in manufacturing, construction and services. The employment in government services is increasing at about 0.5 per cent per year.

In contrast, the employment in the agriculture sector has continued to reduce. The major demand has been in the manufacturing sector and thus labour shortages are now apparent in both skilled and unskilled occupations.[4] The government is taking new steps to tackle the problem of shortfall of skilled manpower required mainly by the manufacturing industries.

## Skills Upgradation Programme

With the rapid growth of the economy and the corresponding increase in demand for skilled labour, there has been a growth of various training institutions in the country. It is estimated that there are 125 organizations conducting a whole variety of training programmes. According to a study by the National Productivity Council (NPC), 77.4 per cent of the organizations are in the private sector. However, the study also indicated that 75 per cent of the training institutions use external resources.[5] Many of them, therefore, function more as coordinators rather than regular training instructors. The training offered by government institutions is open to both private and government sectors.

With a view to develop the skills of the workforce and involve the private sector in the process, the government introduced the Human Resource Development Fund (HRDF) by the Act of 1992, whereby organizations employing 50 or more employees were required to contribute 1 per cent of the total emoluments to the HRDF. The major objectives of this fund are:

❑ Retraining of workers to equip them with the latest and specialized skills

❑ Skill upgradation to facilitate technology transfer and development

❑ To inculcate training as a culture in the industry.

The fund is managed by a Human Resource Development Council comprising 14 members from the private sector, the government and other bodies. There are various training schemes approved under the HRDF wherein the contributing organizations can claim reimbursements ranging from 50 to 80 per cent of the training expenses incurred (provided they are sponsored for the courses approved by the HRD council, including overseas training). The fund was initially confined to mainly the large enterprises in the manufacturing sector.

However, in 1994 it has been extended to the service sector and also, to a limited extent, to small- and medium-scale industries. The main beneficiaries of this fund have so far belonged to the high-tech sectors such as electronics and electrical industries while the traditional industries have not yet come forth actively to avail these benefits.

However the government has now started giving incentives to larger companies to train workers belonging to small and medium sectors, especially their out-sourcing channels. Certain groups of industries are also being encouraged to start their own training institutes. Industries such as textiles, plastic, timber, electronics, etc. are taking a lead in establishing skill training centres to meet their specific skill requirements. Some of the larger industrial houses and MNCs such as Texas Instruments and oil companies such as Shell and Petronas have their own well-equipped training centres.

To partly meet the acute labour shortage in the country, Malaysia has been importing foreign labour in both the skilled and unskilled categories. The labour shortage has also led to a sharp increase in wages in relation to increases in productivity. In 1994, the wages increased by 10 per cent while productivity increased by only 2 per cent. This had an adverse effect on inflation which also rose to 3.7 per cent in 1993–94 in comparison to the earlier 1.7 per cent. The manufacturing sector, which has been identified as the lead sector in Vision 2020, has shown a marked dependence on foreign labour. The government plans to gradually reduce the dependence on foreign labour by concentrated efforts on training, especially of the rural workforce, and also by bringing in automation and more sophisticated technology.

## Industrial Relations

The government has tried to provide a conducive industrial relations climate to encourage foreign investment and facilitate industrial growth. It has instituted a legislation to regulate the dispute resolution machinery and functioning of trade unions. The effort has been directed at resolving disputes and at the same time preventing the exploitation of workers, without adversely affecting the smooth functioning of the industry. Employees belonging to the managerial, executive and security cadres have been excluded from registering themselves as trade unions. Matters relating to promotion, transfer, dismissal, re-instatement and allocation of duties has also been excluded from the collective bargaining machinery. Strikes cannot be organized on any of these matters and are permitted only after first obtaining the consent by a secret ballot of at least two-thirds of the total members. Strikes or lockouts are also prohibited in case there are any pending disputes in courts. Special protection is given to newly set up industries during the initial years of their establishment against any unreasonable demands from trade unions. All their demands have to be within the framework of the terms of employment stipulated under the Employment Act of 1955.

The efforts of the government have been directed at not replicating the British model of industrial relations based on adversarial relationships and collective bargaining practices. Trade unions are being involved in developing industrial relations policies, though at present only around 12 per cent of the workforce is unionized in Malaysia. For non-unionized establishments a grievance machinery has been provided. In case the employee is still aggrieved, he can lodge a complaint with the Ministry of Human Resources which can further investigate the matter. Though there are no minimum wage laws applicable in the manufacturing sector the government has tried to ensure that the workers are not exploited by laying down certain terms and conditions of employment, including working hours, overtime, leave, etc. under the Employment Act of 1955. Similarly, there are legislations regarding provident fund, social security, medical benefits, regulation of foreign workers, etc.

## Civil Service Reforms

As a part of its TQM philosophy, Malaysia has been making efforts to change the attitude and work culture of its civil services and make them more customer-driven. Each government department is asked to prepare a charter specifying the service standards to be rendered to the public. This, in turn, is further elaborated in the sectional and individual charters. Such a 'client charter' is normally a written undertaking to deliver goods and services prescribing to a specific quality in line with the requirements of the public (customer). If the public is aggrieved, they are free to report the matter to a especially constituted complaint cell which is expected to initiate action on such complaints.

Human resource management in the civil services has been given a fresh impetus to meet the emerging challenges of Vision 2020. The thrust has been on decentralization, deregulation and right-sizing of the government sector. Specific steps include improvement in the recruitment and selection of staff, induction training for new entrants, training for productivity and quality improvement, improvement in the performance appraisal system and enforcement of proper discipline. A new remuneration system was introduced after a thorough restructuring of the public sector, whereby over 9,000 posts were abolished and 19 new service classifications were introduced to facilitate the recently-introduced system of remuneration administration. Certain specialized sectors were identified which suffer from a chronic shortage of personnel. These sectors were provided special incentive payments to attract and retain workers. Special training programmes have been developed at INTAN for all cadres of employees, from the lowest to the highest level.

To encourage innovation in the civil services, certain special incentives and awards have been introduced by the Malaysian Administrative Modernization and Management Planning Unit (MAMMPU) with the Prime Minister's department acting as the nodal agency to implement such schemes. The major criteria for these rewards is reduced operational costs, time saving, increased work output and enhanced customer satisfaction. Some of the innovations have been in relation to improvements in manpower, systems and procedures, organizational structure, management style, work environment, technology and capital equipment.

## MICRO-LEVEL ORGANIZATIONAL CASE STUDIES IN MALAYSIA

In this section two organizations have been taken up for an illustrative micro-level study. The first is Texas Instruments Ltd, a US-based multinational electronic industry. The second is the government-owned Petroleum and Petrochemical industry (PETRONAS).

### Texas Instruments Ltd

Texas Instruments Ltd is a wholly-owned subsidiary of Texas Instruments Incorporated a US-based company with 100 per cent foreign members on its Board of Directors. It has a 100 per cent export unit located in one of the free trade zones in Malaysia. The company operates with four major divisions, the semi-conductor division being the largest employing 2,000 workers, and the remaining 1,100 employees are with the other three divisions. There are 250 personnel at the managerial level. 10 per cent of the 3,000 workers (in 1995) are technicians and the balance belong to operations and administrative levels. Another remarkable feature of the operation is that there are no operator supervisors in the entire plant.

About 75 to 80 per cent of the plant and equipment is designed and supplied by the US parent company, and the rest by local suppliers. The semi-conductor division is the largest producer of integrated circuits in the world, with a production level of over four million pieces a day. About 50 per cent of the finished products are shipped back to the USA, another 30 per cent to Japan and the rest to the Pacific region. The technology process is highly automated. Though the company has no R&D set up in Malaysia, the latest developments and innovations in technology are brought in from the parent company. The company had obtained ISO 9000 Certification in the early stages. One of the major incentives for setting up the plant in Malaysia was the conducive human resource environment. Barring the three top managerial posts (manned by expatriates), the entire manpower is recruited locally. In a majority of cases, the recruitment is drawn from school freshers who are made to undergo an intensive six-month induction training in the company before being hired for the job. Diploma holders are recruited after the induction training as technicians, while managerial-level personnel mostly possess professional qualifications.

The company believes in intensive training. The key personnel are sent to the parent companies or the plants run by the suppliers for training in new processes or for upgradation, who, in turn, train the workers within the company. The organization has a full-fledged training department with 15 full-time trainers and 90 part-time specialist trainers. It is estimated that every workman undergoes, on an average, 37 hours of training per year, while managers/engineers undergo more than 40 hours of training per annum. Because of the high technology, there is very little multi-skilling at the workman level though at the managerial level there is systematic job rotation. The company believes in developing a long-term relationship with suppliers and vendors and, wherever required, gives training to the suppliers' representatives. The company is highly regarded for its employee relations and has won a number of awards. Traditionally, Texas

Instruments does not have a trade union. However, their remuneration package and perks are above the industry average in Malaysia. In addition to salaries, the company provides various perquisites and benefits, such as free medical treatment for staff and dependants, vacation leave, two months' salary as bonus, life and accident insurance, meal and transport subsidy, housing and other loans, etc.

The company has a good internal grievance procedure and believes in an open-door policy regarding the settlement of grievances. Even the Managing Director is available to all employees for grievance handling. There is a formal weekly dialogue session. The company also conducts yearly attitude surveys and, wherever required, takes corrective action. It is interesting to note that there is no punch card system for the employees. For the administration staff a flexi-time is applicable, though the staff is expected to spend certain fixed hours at work each day. However, the company does believe in discipline and there have been cases where the employees have been asked to leave when they have not conformed to the standards. Owing to the concern of the company for human resources, the employee turnover is as low as 2 per cent. The company has to date not retrenched any employee though there have been instances of redeployment after appropriate training. With regular transfer of technology and upgradation from the parent company, the company has successfully expanded its production from 33 million pieces to over 100 million pieces over the past one-and-a-half decade without increasing the workforce.

According to the company's top management team, the major factors that affected the adoption of certain technology development strategies were R&D budgets, developability, internal R&D strategy and the technology development efforts of the competitors. Their developmental priority was aimed at improving manufacturing effectiveness, expanding the product line and adhering to the policy governing intellectual property. They also felt that the government policies on research, financial affairs and technology parks have had little or no impact on the company's development strategy. This was possibly due to the fact that there was no R&D set-up in Texas Instruments in Malaysia. The technology development planning and R&D was centralized at the Texas Headquarters in USA.

The executives of Texas Instruments felt that there was negligible influence of the government on the development of technology strategies since they had ample freedom to operate within the broad policy guidelines. However, they did mention some positive factors, such as the government's technology-oriented procurement policies, investment tax credits, the political situation, labour and export policies, monetary policies, and R&D tax credits. They also felt that the research policy at the agency level, the science and technology policy, results from government research facilities, direct R&D funding by the government and R&D related loans had no influence on the firm's technology development strategy.

The company has found the human resource policies of the government quite satisfactory and conducive to their own human resource development, especially the training of technical manpower and the level of funding in technical areas. Similarly, the training of scientific and management manpower imparted by the government as well by private/autonomous bodies have also had a somewhat positive effect. Government dissemination of scientific and technical know-how has, however, exercised no influence on the options for development or on interest groups such as entrepreneurs, unorganized labour and managerial unions. Another factor that has played a positive role is the government's education policy for private educational institutions. The policies on the linkages between institutions and industry and on redeployment, retraining and redundancies have also been found to be helpful.

By and large, the human resources policy of the company has been based on the parent company's practices. Though for government companies there are restrictions regarding recruitment of local personnel (who are referred to as *bhumiputras* or sons of the soil), no such restrictions are applicable to private companies such as Texas Instruments. As has already been mentioned, the company gives considerable importance to employee training. Around 1.5 per cent of the net sales amount is spent on training with a budget of RM two million with 15 full-time trainers and 90 part-time trainers. As much as 80 per cent of the training is equipment-specific while 10 per cent is technical training, with the balance devoted to managerial and behavioural training.

The company has undergone technological changes in the recent past on the basis of technology imported from the parent company. This has been mostly related to automation and new technology in information processing. The main reasons for introducing new technology were factors related to production, expansion, reduction in employees' workload, labour and capital cost reduction, safety, quality improvement and market competitiveness. However, there were no redundancies as a result of the technological changes since the company ensured that their expansion projects absorbed and redeployed the surplus employees.

## Petronas (Petroleum Nasional Berhard)

The history of hydrocarbon exploitation in Malaysia began in 1909 when the Anglo-Saxon Petroleum Company (a forerunner of Shell) was granted the sole right to explore petroleum in Sarawak. Later, more companies began exploring for oil. The oil crisis in 1973 compelled Malaysia to realize the importance of managing their own petroleum industries. This led to the formation of the National Oil Company, Petronas, to develop petroleum resources within the country.

The Petroleum Nasional Berhard (Petronas) was incorporated in 1974 and was vested with the entire ownership of oil and natural gas resources in the country. Today Petronas is a fully government owned integrated oil company engaged in all spheres of petroleum operations, right from oil exploration, refining, production, marketing, natural gas processing and distribution to manufacturing of allied products including fertilizers. It employs around 12,000 employees, 40 per cent of whom are at the managerial levels and 60 per cent in workmen and first-line supervisory categories.

Initially, the first major refinery project was the result of a joint venture agreement among Petronas, Shell and Mitsubishi in 1978. A technical consultant was engaged for the basic engineering design from Shell International. The RM 7.2 billion investment in the gas project was raised from both international and domestic sources, 50 per cent of which was raised in the Eurodollar market. The Japanese part of the contract included a 20-year shipment contract to the Tokyo Electric Power and Tokyo Gas Company. The project became operational in 1983. In 1996 there were four refineries in Malaysia with a capacity of 265,000 barrels per day (bpd). Shell has two refineries accounting for a capacity of 135,000 bpd, while Esso has a refinery with a capacity of 42,000 bpd (1995). The Petronas refinery produces 30,000 bpd, with another Petronas refinery under construction.

Though the investment pattern in Petronas is basically self-financing or of the joint-venture type, the technical know-how and design has been brought in from outside. Petronas, by and large, believes in the principle of importing proven technology. In almost all the major technical fields, Petronas has collaborations with foreign licensors since the company depends mainly upon foreign technology for production. Though the company has a separate R&D set-up, its main contribution is to maintain quality of its products and undertake research in areas such as corrosion and crude oil. Over the years, Petronas has been able to develop reasonable technical expertise and has now even begun to transfer technology to other developing countries, such as Vietnam and Pakistan.

Along with technological development, Petronas has been giving due importance to human resource development. Initially, it brought in foreign consultants and experts to train its technical personnel. Subsequently it established its own technical and management training centres. At the induction stage, after recruitment, all the workmen have to undergo six months of classroom training at the training institute and another six months of on-the-job training. Manpower planning is done in a systematic manner. All the jobs are transferable both at the managerial and operator levels. The company gives greater weightage to merit rather than seniority for executive-level promotions.

The industrial relations climate in the company has been quite good. The wages and perquisites are comparable or even better than those given by governmental or other oil companies. A three-year wage agreement has been arrived at with the union. About 15 years ago, the company ran into some problems with the trade union, but over the years relations have been cordial.

In most cases of technology transfer, consultants have been hired to help in selecting technical collaborations. All projects are essentially technical know-how arrangements without equity participation, and targetted to meet domestic market requirements before exporting. In general, the licensing fee and royalty is paid on lump-sum instalments. The company's technology development strategy is evolved through a semi-formal discussion within the different divisions of the organization. The company has been paying considerable importance to quality and have already obtained 150,000 specifications.

The focus of the company's strategy has been on improving its manufacturing effectiveness and adhering to the intellectual property policy. The non-government market incentives, R&D budgets and technology development efforts of the competitors are considered important elements in the technology development strategy.

The gestation time span before the technology strategy becomes operational is generally two to three years. With regard to the government policy, R&D tax credits, the National Science and Technology Policy and investment tax credits are some of the factors that can play an important role. Conducive government policies for training can also prove to be extremely helpful. The manning norms by and large are based on licensors' recommendations. There have been technology changes in 1995 for automation in production. The reasons for introducing new technology have so far been to expand production and meet competitive market requirements. There have been no redundancies arising out of upgradation of technologies as all the employees have been redeployed as a result of expansion.

## CONCLUSIONS

From the above two case studies in Malaysia, it is apparent that the government has followed a liberal technology transfer policy with limited controls. The major factors attracting foreign investment and transfer of technology relate to financial incentives, a conducive industrial relations climate, and cheaper labour costs as compared to other developed countries. The companies also find the superior infrastructural facilities such as power, roads, transport system and custom clearance as added incentives. Through regulatory mechanisms the government has tried to ensure that labour problems do not occur and at the same time employees get a fair deal. The government's efforts in training and retraining have been helpful in providing a skilled workforce. At the same time the companies too have given appropriate training to their own employees. The stable political situation has also contributed to good foreign investments.

Internal R&D continues to be a weak area, though, it has not hampered the country's industrial growth because it has been able to import proven technologies and update them periodically. Internal and external competition has also compelled both companies to upgrade their technology and improve the skills of their employees on a continuing basis. The domestic market being small, the focus has been on export. This has provided the impetus to import and upgrade its technology to keep pace with world standards. This has raised another interesting issue: How necessary is to build internal design, engineering and R&D capabilities when it is cheaper to import proven technology? More so, in the case of MNCs who are mainly exporting their products and are under compulsion to bring in the latest technology for their own survival.

The recent trend towards religious fundamentalism in Malaysia can, however, adversely affect the country's economy in the future. The banking industry has had to make certain changes in its terms and terminology to conform to religious sentiments. The interest rate system is being substituted with a profit-sharing scheme. This shift could retard the progress as the monetary system is not an isolated one and interest rates are common terms of reference in global transactions.

Another trend that could affect the future economy is the increasing emphasis on the role of *bhumiputras* as indicated in their various plans to reduce disparities. There is increasing involvement of *bhumiputras* in technical and managerial jobs. They are given preferential equity participation and are being provided with loans for setting up business ventures. Funds for retraining and skill training programmes for these sons of the soil have also been established. The private sector is now compelled to employ a minimum number of *bhumiputras* in at least a specified proportion of their total employment. An excess of such discriminations can create discontent among the Chinese and other minority communities who form a substantial number of the existing workforce in Malaysia, and may lead to internal strife in the country.

# REFERENCES

1. *International Country Risk Guide,* International Business Commission Ltd., London, 1991.
2. 'Malaysia: The Way Forward (Vision 2020)', working paper presented by the Prime Minister Dr Mahathir Bin Mohammad, Malaysian Business Council, 28 February, 1991.
3. ANSHAR, AZMI M., 'Making Use of Local Incentives', *New Straits Times,* 6 June, 1992.
4. *Asian Development Outlook 1995 and 1996,* Asian Development Bank, Oxford University Press, 1995.
5. NAIDU, GOKUL, The Emphasis on Training in View of the Changing Environment in Malaysia, Paper presented at the Conference on Workers Training held at Singapore on behalf of National Productivity Board, 1991.

# 4

# SINGAPORE

When the British left Singapore, it became a part of Malaysia in 1963. Singapore was considered a marshy land with no natural resources or industries. In 1965, it separated to become an independent country. It has a land area of 641 sq. km and had population of 2,873,800 in 1993. The Republic of Singapore is today a parliamentary democracy. It has four official languages—Malay, Mandarin, Tamil and English. Except for its strategic location, Singapore has no other natural resources. At the time of independence, Singapore had a population mainly consisting of unskilled labour and a low literacy rate. It was in 1965 that the then government of Singapore realized the pressing need for economic growth and development. The people of Singapore, especially the Chinese, were considered, by nature, to be good traders with great acumen for entrepreneurship. While trading remained a major business activity among local entrepreneurs, the government took up the major responsibility of building and developing basic infrastructural facilities, such as the sea port, airport, transport system, industrial estates, a reliable modern communication network, etc.

In 1965 the government also started the process of economic liberalization. Lack of an internal domestic market necessitated export-oriented production. The MNCs were encouraged to invest in Singapore and bring in the latest technology and expertize as well as and internationally competitive products to meet the demands of export.

Initially, local industries were started up as labour intensive units using semi-skilled and unskilled labour, as for example in the textile industry. The focus in the late 1960s was to encourage entrepreneurship and set the ball rolling for industrialization. Gradually, the focus shifted to encouragement of capital-intensive industrialization in the 1970s. In the 1980s greater emphasis was given to knowledge-intensive industrialization with the introduction of increasingly sophisticated technology. The emphasis shifted to the service industries instead of trade and manufacturing activities by the late 1980s. By the 1990s country had reached a saturation point due to its limited size. It was commonly accepted that further development in Singapore was not possible unless there was a shift in focus towards globalization with greater regional thrust. Today industries in Singapore are encouraged to invest or enter into joint ventures with neighbouring countries such as Vietnam, Malaysia, Indonesia, China, Myanmar and India. Presently, there is also a substantive accent on R&D and value-added production processes.

The government has followed a policy of encouraging foreign investment (up to 100 per cent) provided that 50 per cent of the products are exported. In 1990, Singapore ranked fourth in the world in its share of foreign investment. In the World Competitiveness Report of 1995, Singapore was ranked at number two position.[1] In 1996 Singapore was declared a developed country and qualified to join the Organization of Economic Cooperation and Development (OECD). To attract foreign investment, the government offered various incentives such as quick clearance of proposals, tax incentives, modern port facilities which are being continuously enhanced, non-interference by the government, no special protection to any industry, a strong financial market, and a congenial industrial relations climate.

The growth of Singapore's economy has been phenomenal. The Gross Domestic Product (GDP) has increased from S$2,100 million in 1960 to S$89,000 million in 1993. Along the lines of the development plans and priority accorded to different sectors of the economy, Table 4.1 and 4.2 show the trends in the share of these sectors in the GDP.

The GNP has increased to S$55.8 billion in 1993 from S$6.7 billion in 1960. The unemployment rate has dropped to 1.9 per cent as

**TABLE 4.1:** Basic Indicators

| Economic Structure | 1988 | 1989 | 1990 | 1991 | 1992 |
|---|---|---|---|---|---|
| GDP @ mkt. prices S$ bn | 49.5 | 56.8 | 63.4 | 69.5 | 75.0 |
| Real GDP percentage | 11.1 | 9.2 | 8.3 | 6.7 | 5.8 |
| Population (m) | 2.65 | 2.68 | 2.71 | 2.76 | 2.82 |
| Exports c.f. US $ bn | 39.3 | 44.7 | 52.6 | 58.9 | 63.4 |
| Imports c.f. US $ bn | 43.9 | 49.7 | 60.5 | 66.0 | 72.1 |

| Principal Exports 1992 | US $ bn | Principal Imports 1992 | US $ bn |
|---|---|---|---|
| M/C and equipment | 34.9 | M/C and equipment | 34.6 |
| Mineral fuels | 8.3 | Mineral fuels | 9.2 |
| Manufactured goods | 4.4 | Manufactured goods | 9.2 |
| Chemicals | 4.1 | Chemicals | 5.4 |
| Crude net | 1.4 | Crude net | 1.1 |
| Food | 1.8 | Food | 3.0 |

*Source:* The Economist Intelligence Unit, Dartford Trade Bank, Kent UK, 1993.

*Note:* One US $ = Singapore $1.44 1996 (approximate).

**TABLE 4.2:** Major Economic Indicators

| | | 1992 | 1993 | 1994 | 1995* | 1996* |
|---|---|---|---|---|---|---|
| Gross domestic product | % change | 6.0 | 10.1 | 10.1 | 9.0 | 8.5 |
| Agriculture | % change | 1.1 | −2.3 | 0.2 | 0.1 | 0.0 |
| Industry | % change | 5.4 | 9.4 | 13.1 | 9.9 | 8.5 |
| Services | % change | 6.4 | 10.5 | 8.4 | 8.5 | 8.5 |
| Gross domestic investment | % of GDP | 40.4 | 43.8 | 41.5 | 40.6 | 39.9 |
| Gross domestic saving | % of GDP | 47.6 | 47.9 | 48.0 | 45.0 | 45.0 |
| Inflation rate of CPI | % of change | 2.3 | 2.4 | 3.8 | 3.2 | 3.0 |
| Money supply growth | % change | 8.9 | 8.5 | 14.4 | 10.0 | 10.0 |
| Merchandise exports | US $ billion | 62.1 | 72.0 | 89.2 | 107.1 | 123.1 |
| | % change | 8.6 | 15.9 | 24.0 | 20.0 | 15.0 |
| Merchandise imports | US $ billion | 67.9 | 80.0 | 99.2 | 117.1 | 134.7 |
| | % change | 11.3 | 17.9 | 24.0 | 18.0 | 15.0 |
| Current accounts | US $ billion | 3.7 | 2.0 | 6.5 | 7.5 | 8.0 |
| | % of GDP | 7.7 | 3.7 | 9.6 | 9.5 | 8.8 |

*Estimates.

*Source: Asian Development Outlook 1995 and 1996,* Asian Development Bank, 1995.

*Note:* One US $ = Singapore $1.44 in 1996 (approximate).

against 14 per cent in 1960. Another distinctive feature of Singapore is that the domestic saving rate is around 46.9 per cent of its GNP, which is one of the highest in the world.

The government as a policy encourages discipline in every sphere of life in Singapore with an exemplary legal system for punishment in case of any violation. It has always emphasized the need for discipline with a promise for improved quality of life. From the early days of independence, Singapore has followed certain fundamental principles for economic development which have helped in the faster and efficient growth of its economy. These are:

❑ Ensuring a good, corruption-free government

❑ Building an efficient infrastructure

❑ Heavy investment in education and training

❑ Encouragement to free enterprise

❑ Fiscal prudence to build up national reserves

❑ Maintaining a clean environment

The Strategic Economic Plan articulates the Singapore's vision for the twenty-first century:

' ... catching up with the first league of developed nations .... On a moving target basis, by 2020–2030, in four key areas: economic dynamism, national identity, quality of life and the configuration of a global city.'

The strategies being adopted to achieve the Vision stated above are as follows:

❑ Maintaining the fundamentals listed earlier

❑ Reinforcing resilience through international competitiveness and business capability development

❑ Encouraging cluster development by enhancing the base of the existing competencies (of technology)

❑ Bringing in international orientation through regionalization and overseas investment using a 'Singapore Incorporated' approach

❑ Manpower development by constantly upgrading their capabilities to support the industries' need at various stages of growth

❑ An integrated logistical plan model for optimum development of Singapore (housing, industrial estates, etc.)

Tourism is considered one of the major industries in Singapore. The Singapore Tourist Promotion Board (STPB) was established in 1964 to develop and promote tourism and related services. Its services include promotion of exhibitions, conventions, cultural, arts and sports events, cruise development, including the marketing of Singapore itself. The STPB has around 20 offices located in various parts of the world. Singapore received 6.426 million visitors in 1993.

The Singapore Manufacturers' Association, comprising 1,400 members, plays an important role in promoting the interests of the manufacturing sector through its activities and facilities. It also provides business counselling, consultancy and diagnostic services, especially to small- and medium-scale enterprises.

**TABLE 4.3:** Net Investment Commitments in Manufacturing by Industry, 1989–93

| Industry | 1989 | 1990 | 1991 | 1992 | 1993 | 1989 | 1990 | 1991 | 1992 | 1993 |
|---|---|---|---|---|---|---|---|---|---|---|
| | *Million Dollars* | | | | | *Per Cent* | | | | |
| Food and beverages | 34.1 | 43.8 | 39.8 | 76.5 | 92.9 | 1.7 | 1.8 | 1.4 | 2.2 | 2.4 |
| Textiles | 2.0 | 2.8 | 11.2 | 5.2 | — | 0.1 | 0.1 | 0.4 | 0.1 | — |
| Wearing apparel | 0.4 | 0.2 | 5.7 | 10.0 | 0.4 | 0.0 | 0.0 | 0.2 | 0.3 | — |
| Leather and rubber | — | 10.0 | 4.4 | 2.8 | 1.7 | — | 0.4 | 0.1 | 0.1 | — |
| Wood products | 2.1 | 8.6 | 2.8 | 4.6 | — | 0.1 | 0.3 | 0.1 | 0.1 | — |
| Paper products and printing | 93.8 | 76.2 | 109.4 | 89.5 | 87.3 | 4.8 | 3.1 | 3.7 | 2.6 | 2.3 |
| Industrial chemicals | 213.5 | 265.9 | 322.0 | 294.3 | 783.5 | 10.9 | 10.7 | 11.0 | 8.5 | 20.1 |
| Other chemical products | 21.7 | 35.0 | 243.4 | 248.4 | 340.4 | 1.1 | 1.4 | 8.3 | 7.1 | 8.8 |
| Petroleum | 290.0 | 381.0 | 99.5 | 454.2 | 84.6 | 14.8 | 15.3 | 3.4 | 13.0 | 2.2 |
| Plastic products | 37.8 | 8.9 | 87.2 | 110.8 | 48.3 | 1.9 | 0.3 | 3.0 | 78.5 | 81.0 |
| LOCAL | 333.3 | 269.5 | 472.9 | 748.0 | 741.0 | 17.0 | 10.8 | 16.1 | 21.5 | 19.0 |

*Source:* *Singapore 1992, Statistical Highlights,* Department of Statistics, Government of Singapore, March 1992.

*Note:* One US $ = Singapore $1.44 in 1996.

# INFRASTRUCTURE

From the early days of independence Singapore realized that any industrial development process must begin with the development of a strong infrastructure to support its industrial sector. Therefore, it has always given a lot of importance to the development of industrial estates with all the necessary infrastructure facilities, such as wide roads, drainage, water, power, communication network, etc. Keeping this in mind, the government, in collaboration with the industry, has invested heavily in developing such an infrastructure. There is an extensive system of expressways and roads which provide fast and easy access to all seaports and the airport. The airport and sea ports are constantly being modernized and updated. The sea port capacity is being doubled every three to five years.

Another area of concentration has been the development of well-equipped industrial estates. For this purpose, the government has constituted a statutory board, the Jurong Town Corporation (JTC), which is responsible for the development and management of industrial estates in Singapore. It currently manages 24 industrial estates, having around 4,000 companies employing about 70 per cent of Singapore's manufacturing workforce. The JTC tries to ensure that ready built-up modern factories are available for immediate start-up of operations. In addition, fully-serviced industrial land and special industrial areas and offshore islands have been zoned for the development of chemical and petroleum processing industries.

## Sea Port Facilities

To develop its sea ports and make them some of the finest in the world, the government created the Port of Singapore Authority (PSA) in 1964. It is one of the world's busiest trans-shipment ports in terms of shipping tonnage and containers handled, and links around 789 ports worldwide. There are around 700 ships in the port at any

**TABLE 4.4:** Transport

|  | 1991 | 1992 | 1993 |
|---|---|---|---|
| Arrivals of vessels of over 75 GRT |  |  |  |
| ('000) | 70 | 81 | 93 |
| (million GRT) | 537 | 578 | 624 |
| Sea cargo handled (million FT) | 206 | 238 | 274 |
| Container throughput (million TEUs) | 6.4 | 7.6 | 9.0 |

Source: *Singapore in Brief, 1992–93*, Ministry of Trade and Industry, Department of Statistics, Government of Singapore, 1994.

given time Nearly 93,000 vessels called at the port in 1993 with a shipping transage of 624 million gross registered tonnes. The port offers a wide range of ancillary services such as warehousing, shipping, chandeliering, etc.

Singapore is the third largest oil refining and distributing centre in the world, handling over 90 million tonnes of oil annually through its port for import of crude oil and export of refined petroleum products.

## Airport Facilities

In addition to the sea port facilities, Singapore has also concentrated on the development of its airport. The Changi Airport is considered to be the largest in the region and is capable of handling 24 million passenger movements in a year.

**TABLE 4.5:** Cargo

|  | *1991* | *1992* | *1993* |
|---|---|---|---|
| Air cargo handled ('000 tonnes) | 644 | 720 | 840 |
| Aircraft landings ('000s) | 57 | 66 | 71 |

*Source:* *Singapore in Brief, 1992–93,* Ministry of Trade and Industry, Department of Statistics, Government of Singapore, 1994.

The air cargo handled in 1993 was approximately 840,000 tonnes. The Singapore airport has earned a reputation for being the most preferred airport in the world both in terms of passenger traffic and cargo handling.

## Telecommunication Network

Singapore has one of the world's best telecommunication infrastructures and was rated at the top in 1992 by the IMED World Competitiveness Report. Its telecommunication network includes satellite earth stations, digital international gateways, cellular telephones, paging services, skyphone, digital least circuits, photo video texts, etc.

## Singapore Institute of Standards and Industrial Research (SISIR)

SISIR is a self-financing national statutory body established in 1973 to carry out R&D activities as well as to set standards for industrial products, processes and services in accordance with international requirements. In addition to certification, SISIR conducts research, provides consultancy and training, quality assessment and inspection, technical assistance in exports, etc. It also conducts training programmes on total quality management, ISO 9000, etc. There are five specialized divisions within SISIR—Materials Technology Division, Product and Process Technology Division, Technology Transfer Division, Electronic and Computer Applications Division and Standards and Quality Division. SISIR works in close collaboration with the other industry research laboratories and the Singapore University. It is also ideally situated in the Science Park close to the other laboratories. SISIR also works in collaboration with institutions of higher learning, leading R&D establishments and standards authorities the world over.

## Banking and Financial Systems

In any economic development process, the banking and finance sector play a crucial role, not only in encouraging foreign investment but also enhancing the process of internal industrialization through easy availability of funds for investment. These funds can be obtained through a simple and speedy process without bureaucratic delays. Financial incentives to entrepreneurs can also speed up the investment and industrialization process.

Singapore is considered to be one of the model countries in the banking and financial sector. The government created the Monetary Authority of Singapore (MAS) to carry out all the regulatory and monetary functions except the issuing of currency. MAS is also responsible for the development of Singapore as an international financial centre. The country offers a wide range of sophisticated financial facilities to both domestic and foreign investors, lenders, borrowers and traders. Commercial banks in Singapore are licensed under the Banking Act and are categorized as full, restricted and off-shore licensed, depending upon their area of operation.

The creation and growth of the Asian Dollar Market since the late 1960s (the Asian counterpart of the Eurodollar market) has further increased the role of the banking sector. Total liberalization of the exchange control rate in 1978 helped the banks strengthen their participation in the process of investment and industrialization. New instruments such as bonds, fixed and floating rates certificates, etc. have given an impetus to the Asian Dollar Market, placing Singapore as the fourth largest centre after UK, USA and Japan. The banking and financial system in Singapore provides a comprehensive range of incentives to both individuals and companies. Some of the incentives and assistance programmes are described below.

# INCENTIVES AND ASSISTANCE PROGRAMMES

## Development Assistance for Business Enterprises

The government provides numerous investment and export incentives, developmental assistance programmes and financial assistance schemes to promote industrial development. This includes help to new investors as well as, encouragement to existing companies to upgrade their technology and also to introduce new products and services. The main arms of the government to encourage and monitor programmes are the Economic Development Board and the Trade Development Board.

♦ *Economic Development Board (EDB)*  The EDB was set up in 1961 to primarily look into employment generation and promote environment conservation. The EDB also promotes quality improvement and upgradation of technology in the manufacturing sector to prepare it for international competition. Special attention is given to small and medium enterprises. The EDB has a team of qualified professionals in all major technical and commercial disciplines. It maintains links with foreign research centres and plays a substantive role in preparing development plans, both industrial and logistic aspects. One of the unique policy features that attracts investors to Singapore is that no formal approval is required to set up any business/industry. The only formalities required are the registration of the company with the help of lawyers and consultants and obtain environment clearance. The whole process usually does not take more than two weeks. Only in cases where the entrepreneurs/promoters wish to avail of any of the incentives provided by the government or other statutory bodies, do they need to approach the EDB for the necessary recommendation.

Venture capital as a form of equity financing has been encouraged for the development of technology-based companies in Singapore. The EDB promotes the venture capital industry by providing two tax incentives:

❑ Pioneer service status to encourage professional venture capital fund companies with their profits exempted from taxes for five to 10 years

❑ Venture capital incentives to encourage investment in advanced technology projects and allow write-off against income of the full amount of any capital loss

The EDB has also set up its own ventures fund to invest in local projects. The Venture Capital Club provides the venue for meetings of potential investors.

♦ *Trade Development Board (TDB)*   Singapore's trade is three times its GDP and constitutes 2.2 per cent of world imports and 2 per cent of world exports. The role of the TDB is to promote Singapore as a pivotal trading centre for international trading activities, which include third-country trade, entrepot trade, countertrade as well as warehousing and distribution activities. To encourage business collaborations, the TDB has established 28 trade offices overseas. It provides assistance to both domestic and foreign companies and also offers incentive schemes. It also organizes seminars, conferences, trade missions and business delegations. There is no prioritization of sectors which are especially targetted for investment. The major trend is for investments in infrastructure like technology parks, ports and industries such as electronics and aquaculture.

## Tax Incentives

To encourage investment by enterprises in new machinery and equipment for upgrading operations or for higher value addition, the government allows certain investment allowance tax rebates especially to manufacturing, R&D, engineering and other service-related industries including exhibitions, entertainment and leisure. In addition, to encourage exports of Singapore-made goods, double taxation deduction is allowed provided the goods manufactured in Singapore have not less than 25 per cent Singapore content in terms of labour, materials, production overheads, etc.

## Financial Assistance Programmes for Local Enterprises

♦ *Local Enterprise Finance Scheme (LEFS)* The LEFS is aimed to help local companies strengthen their operations and contribute to their growth. It normally covers factory loans, machinery financing and factoring. The loan can be in the form of term loan, hire-purchasing or leasing.

♦ *Special Interest Rate Scheme (SIRS)* This scheme is specially meant for smaller enterprises to upgrade their technology by acquiring more sophisticated machinery and equipment or introduce a more sophisticated manufacturing technique. This can result in significant savings in manpower or in a significant increase in the output per worker. The incentive is in the form of a loan with a low interest rate of 3.5 per cent.

♦ *Local Enterprise Technology Assistance Scheme (LETAS)* This scheme is designed to provide assistance to local enterprises to upgrade their management and operations by engaging external experts or consultants on a short-term basis.

## Computerization

The National Computer Board helps local firms assess their computerization needs under the Requirements Assessment Service (RAS). This low-cost assessment helps to identify a firm's requirement regarding computerization of business functions, cost-benefit analysis and suggested hardware and software. In addition, the Small Enterprise Computerization Programme (SECP) provides assistance in terms of service charges of consultants registered with the National Computer Board for computer-need assessment reimbursement, an education subsidy for seminars, etc. The local enterprise accounting programme also provides assistance to enhance the local firms' accounting and MIS systems through systematic computerization. The government also acquires computer hardware packages in bulk and supplies them to local enterprises at costs which are guaranteed to be lower than market costs.

♦ *Automation Feasibility Study (AFS) Scheme*   With a view to upgrade technology, introduce automation and improve the quality of products, the government introduced the AFS scheme under which companies can benefit from the services of automation consultants for a maximum period of four years. In addition, the EDB provides training grants to assist companies in the training of automation engineers and technicians, both internally as well as overseas. With the intention of improving the product design with greater level of automation, the government also provides financial support for redesigning and effecting significant improvements in the production process. Industry-wide automation programmes are also available under which the government provides grants to cover the approved direct costs of products/process development and/or acquisition of know-how.

♦ *Local Industry Upgrading Programme (LIUP)*   With the opening up of the economy, there are over 600 MNCs operating in Singapore. This has generated a strong demand for parts, components and supporting services in addition to creating opportunities for technology transfer and business collaborations with local enterprises. In the past, of the $16 billion worth of material being sourced by MNCs, only around $3 billion was sourced locally (constituting 18 per cent of the total). LIUP was started in 1986 to develop greater collaboration between local companies and MNCs operating in Singapore. Under this scheme, MNCs are encouraged to help in the joint development of local suppliers. MNCs contribute to transfer of technology and the development of operational and management skills of their local vendors. In return, local suppliers are expected to provide good quality parts and services at competitive prices.

For undertaking this programme, the EDB provides financial assistance in the upgradation and development of projects. The programme includes the provision of experts jointly agreed between the MNCs and the EDB whose role is to select four to five small and medium enterprises for focused assistance in consultation with the EDB. To qualify for this assistance, the local equity should be at least 30 per cent and the fixed asset investment should not exceed Singapore $8 million. Before giving assistance, it is also taken into account that the enterprises have the existing capacity to absorb the technology or skills transfer, in addition to their commitment to quality, reliability, delivery and cost competitiveness.

Special schemes have been designed for business and export development for encouraging local enterprises to expand their operations and pursue opportunities outside the purview of incentives. The schemes cover costs for total business planning, bulk purchasing and joint marketing, studies abroad or visits overseas to explore new technologies or markets or to establish new business contacts, etc. The EDB approves the schemes and monitors the progress of the enterprises.

The other schemes designed to help local companies are the Franchise Development Assistance Scheme which includes assistance to cover costs of franchise development and marketing; the Franchise Development Centre which gets together similar local companies to achieve economies of scale and promotes cooperatives; the Market Development Assistance Scheme which provides assistance for participation in overseas trade fairs, setting up overseas marketing offices, new project tenders overseas, etc. and requires that the local company has at least 30 per cent equity participation of a Singapore citizen; and the Certification Assistance Scheme to help local firms obtain international quality certification (ISO 9000).

# ROLE OF LOCAL ENTERPRISES

In some developing countries there is a widespread belief that opening up the economy to multinational enterprises can stifle the growth of local enterprises which may not have the requisite resources, technology or funds to compete with MNCs. To some extent it is true that there may be an initial adverse impact on the non-competitive and technologically weak local enterprises. However, by adopting a conscious policy of development, local enterprises can, in a short period, learn from the MNCs and give a boost to the national economy. Singapore is a classic example where this has happened.

In most countries, in the initial years of development and planning, local enterprises are given protection by imposing restrictions on the entry of MNCs in some select sectors of the economy. Each country decides its restricted sectors giving due consideration to available local resources, expertise and natural advantages. Singapore consciously attracted foreign investment through MNCs by inviting them to set up industries locally as it lacked natural resources, skills, managerial competence and technology. A country which has been developed with the help of MNCs, Singapore is now increasingly encouraging local enterprises through various incentives and developmental programmes.

Today, local enterprises constitute nearly 90 per cent of the total number of establishments in Singapore. They employ 65 per cent of the working population and contribute to more than 50 per cent of the total value added in Singapore. In terms of value addition, the growth rate has been around 15 per cent per annum. Owing to various incentives offered by the government and National Productivity Board to improve their technology systems, the productivity of local enterprises measured in terms of value added per worker improved by almost 40 per cent from 1987 to 1991. In terms of exports also the growth rate in the manufacturing sector increased by about 40 per cent from 1987 to 1991. To encourage local enterprises, a comprehensive Master Plan for small and medium enterprises was

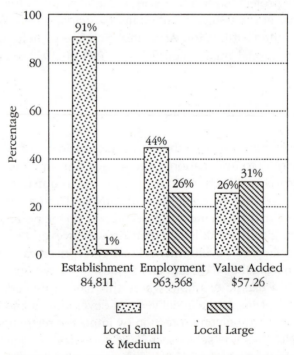

**FIG. 4.1:** Local Enterprises—Manufacturing and Service

*Source: Singapore 1992, Statistical Highlights,* Department of Statistics, Government of Singapore, March 1993.

developed in 1989. The Master Plan contained guidelines for the promotion of technology, business development, human resource management, productivity, fiscal incentives, low interest financing and grants to local companies. All these enabled local enterprises to develop new managerial competencies and better their technologies with the introduction of R&D, and helped them in diversifying their product lines.

The scope of growth being limited in the small territory of Singapore itself, the government has recently been encouraging local enterprises to start overseas operations and projects. The Local Enterprise Finance Scheme (LEFS) provides low interest loans for the purchase of equipment needed for overseas operations. This has given a boost to Singapore companies to start operations outside, and many enterprises have gone to China, Malaysia, Vietnam, Indonesia and India in a big way.

# HUMAN RESOURCE DEVELOPMENT

The government of Singapore has given a major emphasis to skill development and upgradation of human resources to meet the expanding requirements of the industry. It has been the conscious policy of each company to train its human resources in the most modern technologies and systems. At one stage it was felt that the companies were not coming forward with substantive investments in training and skill upgradation of its employees. To meet the expanding requirements of skilled professionals, it was felt that the government itself would have to take the lead. To meet this objective, the government created a Skill Development Fund. It was made mandatory for organizations employing workmen earning S$ 750 or less to contribute 1 per cent levy on workers' earnings per month to the Fund. This limit was raised to S$ 1,000 per month in 1993–94. The assumption here was that employees drawing less than $ 1,000 are either unskilled or semi-skilled and need to upgrade their skills. Training programmes are heavily subsidized, drawing resources from the Skill Development Fund. The National Productivity Board (NPB) of Singapore has been identified as the agency to monitor the Skill Development Fund. Any company which releases an employee for approved skill training can apply to the NPB for reimbursement of the fee which can range from 20 to 70 per cent of the fee charged for the training, including overseas training.

In the area of training, the NPB has entered into a partnership with various large MNCs who have the expertize to conduct specialized training programmes in their own sphere of activities. Some of the major companies who entered into joint ventures with the Board include Motorola, Festo, Philips, IBM, Singapore Airlines, etc. The NPB has also started industry-based training programmes for small and medium organizations including retail outlets, for example, for bakeries, departmental stores, stock markets, medical shops, etc.

The NPB provides strategic assistance to companies with low capital and labour productivity, such as the plastic materials industries. Group pressure from peer companies compels low performers to approach the NPB for conducting training programmes. The Board, in turn, publicizes its successful training programmes to attract companies to attend their programmes. Owing to acute competition, the companies find it necessary to train their workers to keep pace with the industry. For industry-based assistance, the NPB also strives to identify some of the key industries having low capital intensity, low labour productivity and/or total factor productivity. Trade associations are also involved in identifying such industries and special emphasis for training is given in such industries. Wherever required, multi-disciplinary production management and project teams (PROMPT) and production management in small and medium enterprises (PROMIS) are sent to identify their problems and provide the necessary guidance. At times, private consultants are also involved for specialized jobs. The NPB provides all these services on a payment basis, though, at times, these are subsidized. The NPB also gives importance to training based on distance learning, especially in cases where workers cannot be spared from their jobs. Training lessons are taken to the homes or the workplace through television, specialized video programmes, mail, computer-aided instruction programmes (CAI), etc.

With advancements in technology, it was felt that knowledge of computers is essential for all employees. However, a substantial number of workmen lacked the basic numerical ability and knowledge of English to operate computers. Therefore, at the initiative of the government they started Basic Education and Skill Training programmes (BEST) where the main focus was on basic mathematics and the English language. Once the employees have undergone the BEST programme they are put through an advanced programme on numerical ability and then given training on computer operations. In addition, the National Trade Union Congress itself conducts training for the workers. The Singapore Institute of Labour Studies conducts programmes on trade unionism, management skills, industrial relations, etc. at the industry level.

## TRADE UNIONS AND INDUSTRIAL RELATIONS

One of the attractions of doing business in Singapore is the responsible trade union movement in the country. Though the movement did pass through turbulent periods, gradually with the industrialization process and inculcation of a disciplinary spirit, trade unions became more conscious of their responsibility to develop Singapore economically. Interestingly, in Singapore, the movement started in 1946 with the objective of gaining political independence and not protecting workers' interests. In fact, the trade unions came into being even before the political parties were formed. Therefore even today, ideologically, trade unions and political parties are very close, though according to the law trade unions cannot finance political parties and vice versa. There are laws to protect trade union rights, workers' rights, and to regulate employer and employee relations. With high growth rate, prosperity and near full employment, there is reluctance on the part of the younger generation to join trade unions. At present, only around 20 to 22 per cent of the workforce is unionized.

To attract trade union membership, trade unions have started concentrating on non-bargainable activities to enrich workers' lives in recent years. Trade unions are one of the largest promoters of co-operatives specially in the areas of insurance, transportation, consumer cooperatives, health care, etc. They run 8,000 taxis in Singapore and own 47 cooperative supermarkets with the objective of containing inflation and excessive profiteering. The emphasis on these co-operatives has brought in market competitiveness and reduced the inflation rate. Trade unions have also started holiday and recreation clubs not only in Singapore but also in neighbouring countries for the exclusive use of its members. They also run the largest golf course and a club in Singapore for their members. Trade unions have their own radio station which is used to propagate their activities, ideologies and facilities, specially to attract membership from the younger workforce. They are also actively involved in training activities and have even established the Institute for Labour Studies.

To regulate better industrial relations and wage-related issues, a National Wage Council (NWC) was set up in 1972. The NWC is a tripartite body comprising the government, employees and union representatives as well as academicians. The role of the NWC is to advise the government on wage policies and develop wage guidelines in keeping with the economic objectives. Normally, the suggestions of the NWC serve as a basis for wage negotiations between the employers and the unions. Recently, there has been a trend wherein the wage increase has been more than the growth in productivity. The NWC has, therefore, recommended that the built-in wage increase should not exceed productivity growth. However, additional variable rewards linked with productivity have been recommended. There have also been instances in Singapore wherein the emoluments were reduced, such as during the recession period in 1984–85.

Singapore also has a specially constituted Industrial Arbitration Court (IAC) to promote industrial peace through regulation of industrial disputes. Depending upon the nature of the dispute, the IAC consists of one to three persons. In the case of a panel of three members, normally one each is from employer and employee's side. In addition to the arbitration role, the IAC also certifies collective agreements entered between employers and trade unions. The court also provides mediation services to the disputing parties.

# PRODUCTIVITY

To encourage productivity in the country, the government established the National Productivity Board (NPB) in 1972. Initially, help was taken from Japanese experts to develop certain productivity models and the productivity strategy. The NPB started the productivity movement in three phases. The objective of **Phase 1** was to create an awareness about productivity among the people. A number of training programmes were launched with emphasis on positive work attitude, team work, pride in work, customer satisfaction, quality consciousness, the advantage of zero defects, etc.

**Phase 2** concentrated on making companies aware of productivity The idea was to help companies take action at the workplace to increase productivity. The companies were made aware and given training on computation of labour and capital productivity and cost-benefit analysis of quality. A number of training programmes were started on the principles of quality circles, just-in-time and TQM Even some housekeeping programmes were started for workers

**TABLE 4.6:** Key Indicators of Employment and Productivity

| Year | Labour Force | | | Labour Force Participation Rate | | | Unemployment Rate | Self-employed |
| | Total | Employed | Unemployed | Total | Males | Females | | |
| | Thousand | | | Per Cent | | | | Per Cent of Workforce |
|---|---|---|---|---|---|---|---|---|
| 1982 | 1,253.2 | 1,221.2 | 32.0 | 63.4 | 81.5 | 45.2 | 2.6 | 13.0 |
| 1983 | 1,292.8 | 1,251.3 | 41.5 | 63.8 | 81.6 | 45.7 | 3.2 | 13.5 |
| 1984 | 1,304.4 | 1,269.2 | 35.2 | 63.4 | 81.2 | 45.8 | 2.7 | 13.6 |
| 1985 | 1,287.8 | 1,234.6 | 53.2 | 62.2 | 79.9 | 44.9 | 4.1 | 13.6 |
| 1986 | 1,298.5 | 1,214.5 | 84.0 | 62.3 | 79.4 | 45.6 | 6.5 | 13.8 |
| 1987 | 1,329.3 | 1,266.8 | 62.5 | 62.7 | 78.6 | 47.0 | 4.7 | 13.6 |
| 1988 | 1,377.7 | 1,331.6 | 46.2 | 62.9 | 78.5 | 47.8 | 3.3 | 12.9 |
| 1989 | 1,424.7 | 1,394.0 | 30.7 | 63.1 | 78.6 | 48.4 | 2.2 | 13.0 |
| 1990 | 1,516.0 | 1,485.8 | 30.2 | 64.9 | 79.2 | 50.3 | 2.0 | 11.0 |
| 1991 | 1,554.3 | 1,524.3 | 30.0 | 64.8 | 79.8 | 50.5 | 1.9 | 12.3 |
| 1992 | 1,619.6 | 1,576.2 | 43.4 | 65.3 | 79.9 | 51.3 | 2.7 | 12.6 |

*Source: Singapore 1992, Statistical Highlights, Department of Statistics, Government of Singapore, March 1992.*

**TABLE 4.7:** Changes in Productivity by Sector, 1984–93

(in percentage)

| | 1984 | 1985 | 1986 | 1987 | 1988 | 1989 | 1990 | 1991 | 1992 | 1993 |
|---|---|---|---|---|---|---|---|---|---|---|
| TOTAL | 6.9 | 3.1 | 6.3 | 4.8 | 4.5 | 4.8 | 3.9 | 1.5 | 3.3 | 6.4 |
| TOTAL (Excluding construction) | 6.7 | 2.4 | 7.1 | 4.8 | 4.4 | 5.0 | 4.1 | 1.7 | 2.8 | 7.9 |
| Manufacturing | 7.2 | –1.5 | 13.6 | 3.7 | 2.0 | 3.8 | 4.6 | 3.5 | 3.8 | 12.9 |
| Construction | 9.0 | 5.7 | –4.3 | 0.8 | 2.2 | — | 1.2 | 2.6 | 12.3 | –8.1 |
| Commerce | 4.5 | 0.4 | 5.5 | 5.9 | 10.9 | 4.1 | 6.3 | 3.6 | 1.6 | 5.6 |
| Transport and communication | 11.9 | 5.2 | 10.7 | 6.3 | 6.6 | 5.0 | 4.9 | 4.8 | 5.5 | 4.1 |
| Financial and business services | 7.7 | 12.0 | 0.7 | 8.3 | 1.3 | 2.3 | 2.5 | 0.5 | 0.9 | 6.4 |

*Source:* *Singapore 1992, Statistical Highlights,* Department of Statistics, Government of Singapore, March, 1993.

making them aware of how to maintain their workplace properly, including cleanliness in their work habits.

**Phase 3** laid emphasis on making individuals conscious of productivity so that they are able to appreciate the direct benefits of productivity. A number of post-employment training programmes were started, especially for small- and medium-scale enterprises. Consultancy services on productivity and technology aspects are also offered. For the period 1992–99 the emphasis has been shifted to improving the infrastructure to sustain future productivity levels.

## Conclusions

The survey conducted by the Ministry of Trade and Industry in 1995 indicated that there has been a slow-down in the country's economy. The growth rate in 1995 was around 8.5 per cent as compared to over 10 per cent in 1994. There has been an acute shortage of labour leading to a marked increase in salaries. There is pressure to relax the rules regarding the import of labour to ease labour shortages.

The major thrust will continue to be on investment outside Singapore. However, it is acknowledged that Singapore has reached an advanced stage of development with a per capita income of US $ 24,000 per annum in 1995. In January 1996, Singapore was declared a developed country and qualified to join the big league of

**TABLE 4.8:** Key Indicators of Employment and Productivity

| Year | Selected Occupational Groups | | Selected Sectors of Employment | | Median Monthly Income | Average Weekly Hours Worked | Annual Change in Average Monthly Earnings of CPF Contributors | | Labour Productivity Growth |
| | Professional, Technical, and Managerial Workers | Clerical, Sales and Services Workers | Manufacturing | Financial and Business Services | | | Nominal | Real | |
| | Per Cent of Workforce | | | | Singapore Dollar | Hour | Per Cent | | |
|------|------|------|------|------|------|------|------|------|------|
| 1982 | 14.2 | 40.7 | 29.5 | 7.9 | 511 | 45.4 | 15.9 | 11.6 | 1.6 |
| 1983 | 14.9 | 41.5 | 27.8 | 8.1 | 560 | 45.6 | 10.2 | 8.9 | 5.3 |
| 1984 | 16.1 | 41.4 | 27.4 | 8.6 | 613 | 45.6 | 10.7 | 7.9 | 6.9 |
| 1985 | 16.2 | 41.7 | 25.4 | 8.7 | 654 | 44.6 | 7.9 | 7.4 | 3.1 |
| 1986 | 16.9 | 41.1 | 25.2 | 8.7 | 667 | 45.1 | 0.8 | 2.3 | 6.3 |
| 1987 | 17.2 | 41.4 | 26.7 | 8.9 | 687 | 45.5 | 3.2 | 2.6 | 4.8 |
| 1988 | 18.5 | 40.9 | 28.5 | 9.0 | 721 | 45.5 | 8.2 | 6.6 | 4.5 |
| 1989 | 19.6 | 40.5 | 29.0 | 9.2 | 764 | 46.6 | 9.8 | 7.3 | 4.8 |
| 1990 | 24.0 | 26.5 | 28.4 | 10.7 | 818 | 46.5 | 9.3 | 5.7 | 3.5 |
| 1991 | 26.3 | 28.9 | 28.2 | 10.7 | 919 | 46.7 | 9.2 | 5.6 | 1.5 |
| 1992 | 29.5 | 27.9 | 27.5 | 10.9 | 1,002 | 46.6 | 7.5 | 5.1 | 3.1 |

*Source:* *Singapore 1992, Statistical Highlights*, Department of Statistics, Government of Singapore, March 1993.

Organizations of Economic Co-operation and Development (OECD), comprising the rich industrialized nations. Singapore is the first among the developed countries to join the OECD. All this indicates that Singapore's economy has reached a stage of maturity and thus investments, especially in the equipment, slow down in such cases. However, the growth in the manufacturing sector increased to 13 per cent in 1995, compared to 10 per cent in 1993.

Another unique feature of Singapore has been the efficient running of its public enterprises. Singapore Airlines and the Port Authority have often been quoted as being among the most efficiently run and profit-making enterprises in the world. Though public enterprises, they are allowed to function as commercial ventures without any political or bureaucratic interference. Another unique feature has been the phenomenal growth of local industries, in spite of the large number of MNCs freely encouraged to operate in Singapore. This again is due to the special incentives and encouragement given in terms of not only financial incentives but also incentives to upgrade their technology on a regular basis. On the whole, Singapore continues to be a healthy economy because of its positive policies. Despite being a very small country (a city-state, actually), it has made its mark on the world economy.

Since becoming member of the OECD, it has to now compete with the developed countries on an equal footing and has to contribute its share towards the development of the less developed countries. In all likelihood, it will also now face growing competition from the low-cost newly emerging countries such as Malaysia, Vietnam, Thailand, etc. Until now Singapore has relied considerably on foreign capital and ideas but now it has to develop its technological and other capabilities on its own for its future, recognizing the fact that the educational level in Singapore is still lagging behind the industrialized nations. Therefore, in order to sustain its development, Singapore may have to make much more investment in human resource development and further upgradation of their skills to meet future technological challenges.

# REFERENCE

1. 'World Competitiveness Report, 1995', World Economic Forum and International Institute of Management, Geneva, 1995.

# 5

# THAILAND

Thailand is the only Southeast Asian country that was never colonized. Today, it has a constitutional monarchy which has been able to maintain political stability even during periods of crises and transition. Thailand has a population of over 57 million and a fair share of natural resources. Its fertile land and tropical climate make it a flourishing agricultural economy. Its Gross Domestic Product (GDP) grew from 4.2 per cent in the 1960s to 8.3 per cent in the 1970s to 7.5 per cent in the 1980s. Economic growth again accelerated for three consecutive years (1986–88) to around 10 per cent and was around 11 per cent in 1992–95. The economy has undergone significant structural changes due to its planned drive towards industrialization.

Thailand's dramatic growth from an agricultural economy based on rice, rubber, tin and teak to tourism and manufactured goods such as textiles, automobiles and garments, can be attributed to several factors. An important factor was the promotion of private sector investment in the early 1960s with the government concentrating its early economic activity in the provision of infrastructural facilities, such as roads, power generation, irrigation projects, etc. which gave a boost to import substitution-based industrial sector development.

The growth of agricultural exports continued in the early 1970s mainly comprising cassava, sugarcane and pineapple. The early 1980s witnessed an initial setback to the economy mainly because of a sharp increase in oil prices. This necessitated a shift in the investment programme to alternative sources of energy. However, the discovery of natural gas in the Gulf of Thailand eased the situation. Owing to these constraints, the gap in the 1980s on the balance of trade and balance of payments front widened and foreign debt also increased rapidly. The unemployment problems became more acute with increased migration of labour to urban centres. To overcome this problem, there was a shift in emphasis to agro-based labour-intensive industries.

During the fifth plan period in the early 1980s, the focus was on reducing rural poverty and regional imbalances in development. The stress in the late 1980s and early 1990s, was on the involvement of the private sector in the development of infrastructure and commercial agriculture. These policies resulted in a GDP growth of 11.7 per cent per annum between 1988 and 1990. Thus, Thailand emerged as one of the fastest developing economies in the world.

The share of the manufacturing sector in GDP expanded remarkably from 13 per cent to 26 per cent within three decades spanning 1960 to 1990. The initial emphasis of the manufacturing sector on substitution of imported products shifted in the late 1970s to production for export and investment in large-scale industries. Today manufactured exports account for more than 70 per cent of the total exports. The range of export products has also grown vastly, ranging from canned food and fruit to gems, jewellery, toys, computers, integrated circuits (ICs) and electrical and electronic products. The share of agricultural products reduced to 22 per cent in 1990 from 49 per cent in 1980, though the agricultural sector has been the largest employer in terms of the labour force (65 per cent). The agricultural sector was expected to grow at 3.2 per cent per annum in the period 1992–96. The comparative advantage of Thailand lies mainly in its highly competitive industries based on labour-intensive agricultural and agro-industrial products.

The export growth from the 1986–90 period has been expanding at an average annual rate of 26 per cent. There has been a remarkable increase in the export of manufactured goods. Textile exports increased from 31 million baht in 1986 to about 110 million baht in 1991 (one US$ = 26.74 baht in 1996). Similarly, the exports of ICs increased from around 12 million baht in 1986 to about 26 million baht in

**TABLE 5.1:** Major Economic Indicators and Ratios

| Population Mid-1993 | | | | | |
|---|---|---|---|---|---|
| (millions) | 58.1 | | *Income Group:* | *Lower-Middle* | |
| GNP Per Capita 1993 (US$) | 2,110 | | *Indebtedness Level:* | *Less Indebted* | |

| Key Ratios | 1985 | 1990 | 1992 | 1993 | 1994* |
|---|---|---|---|---|---|
| Gross domestic investment/GDP | 28.2 | 41.1 | 39.6 | 40.0 | — |
| Exports of goods and nfs/GDP | 23.2 | 34.0 | 36.3 | 37.0 | 37.0 |
| Gross domestic savings/GDP | 25.5 | 33.6 | 35.4 | 35.9 | — |
| Gross national savings/GDP | 23.9 | 32.4 | 33.9 | 34.3 | — |
| Current account balance/GDP | –4.3 | –8.7 | –5.7 | –5.6 | –5.4 |
| Interest payments/GDP | 2.3 | 1.6 | 1.7 | 1.5 | 1.1 |
| Total debt/GDP | 45.1 | 33.0 | 35.5 | 36.7 | 41.7 |
| Total debt/exports | 171.7 | 90.3 | 92.4 | 94.0 | 107.0 |

| GDP: Production | 1985 | 1990 | 1992 | 1993 | 1994 |
|---|---|---|---|---|---|
| (% of GDP) | | | | | |
| Agriculture | 15.8 | 12.7 | 12.0 | 10.0 | — |
| Industry | 31.8 | 37.0 | 38.5 | 39.2 | — |
| Manufacturing | 21.9 | 27.2 | 28.0 | 28.4 | — |
| Services | 52.3 | 50.2 | 49.5 | 50.8 | — |

| | 1985–90 | 1990–94 | 1992 | 1993 | 1994 |
|---|---|---|---|---|---|
| (Average annual growth) | | | | | |
| Agriculture | 4.3 | 2.5 | 4.2 | –1.7 | 3.0 |
| Industry | 14.9 | 10.7 | 9.6 | 10.8 | 10.1 |
| Manufacturing | 15.6 | 11.6 | 11.3 | 11.5 | 11.5 |
| Services | 10.6 | 7.6 | 6.8 | 10.2 | 7.5 |
| GDP | 10.8 | 8.2 | 7.6 | 9.0 | 8.1 |

| GDP: Expenditure | 1985 | 1990 | 1992 | 1993 | 1994 |
|---|---|---|---|---|---|
| (% of GDP) | | | | | |
| Private consumption | 61.0 | 57.0 | 54.6 | 53.8 | — |
| General govt. consumption | 13.5 | 9.4 | 10.0 | 10.3 | — |
| Gross domestic investment | 28.2 | 41.1 | 39.6 | 40.0 | — |
| Exports of goods and nfs | 23.2 | 34.0 | 36.3 | 37.0 | 37.0 |
| Imports of goods and nfs | 25.9 | 41.5 | 40.5 | 41.1 | 42.6 |

| | 1985–90 | 1990–94 | 1992 | 1993 | 1994 |
|---|---|---|---|---|---|
| (Average annual growth) | | | | | |
| Private consumption | 10.9 | 6.2 | 5.7 | 7.0 | 6.8 |
| General govt. consumption | 2.7 | 6.9 | 6.5 | 7.8 | 6.5 |
| Gross domestic investment | 18.9 | 8.7 | 6.2 | 9.7 | 8.0 |
| Exports of goods and nfs | 20.6 | 14.6 | 12.8 | 19.1 | 11.2 |
| Imports of goods and nfs | 25.3 | 11.3 | 7.5 | 15.9 | 9.1 |
| Gross national product | 11.0 | 8.4 | 8.0 | 8.2 | — |
| Gross national income | 11.2 | 8.0 | 9.4 | 7.2 | — |

*Contd.*

| Prices and Government Finance | 1985 | 1990 | 1992 | 1993 | 1994 |
|---|---|---|---|---|---|
| Domestic prices (% change) | | | | | |
| Consumer prices | 2.4 | 5.9 | 4.1 | 3.6 | — |
| Wholesale prices | 0.0 | 3.5 | 0.2 | −0.4 | — |
| Implicit GDP deflator | 2.1 | 5.6 | 4.5 | 2.4 | 3.0 |
| Government Finance | | | | | |
| (% of GDP) | | | | | |
| Current budget balance | −0.6 | 7.4 | 6.4 | 6.3 | 0.6 |
| Overall surplus/deficit | — | — | — | — | 0.6 |

| Poverty and Social | 1985–90 | 1990–94 |
|---|---|---|
| (Annual growth rates) | | |
| Population | 1.7 | 1.7 |
| Labour force | 2.0 | 1.7 |

| | most recent estimate |
|---|---|
| Poverty level: headcount index (% of population) | 21.8 |
| Life expectancy at birth | 68.8 |
| Infant morality (per 1,000 live births) | 36.4 |
| Child malnutrition (% of children under 5) | 13.0 |
| Access of safe water (% of population) | 72.1 |
| Energy consumption per capita (kg oil equivalent) | 672.6 |
| Illiteracy (% of population age 15+) | 7.0 |
| Gross primary enrollment (% of school-age population) | 97.0 |

| Trade | 1985 | 1990 | 1992 | 1993 | 1994 |
|---|---|---|---|---|---|
| (millions US$) | | | | | |
| Total exports (fob) | 7,120 | 23,053 | 32,466 | 36,391 | 44,419 |
| Tea | 829 | 1,085 | 1,425 | 1,301 | 2,005 |
| Iron | — | 379 | 1,166 | 858 | 738 |
| Manufactures | 2,920 | 13,911 | 21,054 | 25,619 | 30,222 |
| Total imports (cif) | 9,248 | 33,006 | 40,679 | 45,804 | 52,059 |
| Food | 348 | 1,312 | 2,015 | 1,958 | 2,525 |
| Fuel and energy | 2,696 | 5,175 | 5,888 | 6,189 | 6,544 |
| Capital goods | 2,598 | 13,611 | 17,351 | 21,173 | 23,658 |
| Export price index (1987=100) | 73 | 172 | 230 | 234 | 0 |
| Import price index (1987=100) | 72 | 204 | 237 | 240 | 248 |
| Terms of trade (1987=100) | 101 | 84 | 97 | 98 | 0 |
| Openness of economy (trade/GDP %) | 49 | 76 | 77 | 78 | 80 |

| Balance of Payments | 1985 | 1990 | 1992 | 1993 | 1994 |
|---|---|---|---|---|---|
| (millions US $) | | | | | |
| Exports of goods and nfs | 9,100 | 29,230 | 40,661 | 46,511 | 51,676 |
| Imports of goods and nfs | 10,160 | 35,700 | 45,931 | 52,103 | 59,503 |
| Resource balance | −1,060 | −6,471 | −5,271 | −5,592 | −7,827 |
| Net factor income | −643 | −1,024 | −1,461 | −1,648 | −30 |
| Net current transfers | 47 | 26 | 323 | 281 | 333 |

*Contd.*

| Balance of Payments | 1985 | 1990 | 1992 | 1993 | 1994 |
|---|---|---|---|---|---|
| Current account balance | | | | | |
| Before official transfers | −1,656 | −7,469 | −6,409 | −6,959 | −7,524 |
| After official transfers | −1,537 | −7,282 | −6,355 | −6,928 | −7,524 |
| Long-term capital inflow | 1,606 | 3,489 | 4,226 | 4,289 | 2,194 |
| Total other items (net) | 13 | 7,022 | 5,054 | 9,808 | 7,090 |
| Changes in net reserves | −82 | −3,230 | −2,925 | −7,169 | −1,760 |
| Memo | | | | | |
| in (million US $) | | | | | |
| Reserves excluding gold | 2,190 | 13,305 | 20,359 | 24,473 | 29,332 |
| Reserves including gold | 3,003 | 14,258 | 21,183 | 25,439 | 30,280 |
| Conversion rate (local/US $) | 27.2 | 25.6 | 25.4 | 25.3 | 25.1 |

| External Debt | 1985 | 1990 | 1992 | 1993 | 1994 |
|---|---|---|---|---|---|
| Export ratios | | | | | |
| Long-term debt/exports | 129.4 | 63.7 | 58.0 | 53.5 | 59.4 |
| IMF credit/exports | 11.0 | 0.0 | 0.0 | 0.0 | 0.0 |
| Short-term debt/exports | 31.3 | 26.6 | 34.4 | 40.5 | 47.6 |
| Total debt service/exports | 31.9 | 16.9 | 13.9 | 18.7 | 11.3 |
| GDP ratios | | | | | |
| Long-term debt/GDP | 34.0 | 23.3 | 22.3 | 20.9 | 23.2 |
| IMF/credit/GDP | 2.9 | 0.0 | 0.0 | 0.0 | 0.0 |
| Short-term debt/GDP | 8.2 | 9.7 | 13.2 | 15.8 | 18.6 |
| Long-term debt ratios | | | | | |
| Private non-guaranteed/long-term | 25.5 | 36.7 | 46.0 | 44.2 | 48.6 |
| Public and publicly guaranteed | | | | | |
| Private creditors/long-term | 31.3 | 22.6 | 21.2 | 20.0 | 17.8 |
| Official creditors/long-term | 43.2 | 40.7 | 32.8 | 35.8 | 33.6 |

*Estimates.

*Source:* *World Bank Book, Trends in Developing Economies, 1995.*

1991. There was a similar increase in footwear, precious stones, jewellery, etc. At the same time, agro-based products remained almost constant except for a marked increase in the export of prawns from four million baht in 1986 to 26 million baht in 1991.

Of the total population of 32.7 million people, 31.2 million were estimated to have been employed in 1992. The bulk of the labour force continues to remain in the agricultural sector (see Table 5.4). The labour force employed in the manufacturing sector was estimated to be around three million. With the slowdown of labour employment in the agricultural sector, there was a steady increase of unemployed persons during the late 1980s.

**TABLE 5.2:** Exports

| Main Commodities Exported (Bt mn) | 1986 | 1987 | 1988 | 1989 | 1990 | 1991 |
|---|---|---|---|---|---|---|
| Rice | 20,315 | 22,703 | 34,676 | 45,462 | 27,770 | 30,516 |
| Rubber | 15,116 | 20,539 | 27,189 | 26,423 | 23,557 | 24,953 |
| Tapioca products | 19,086 | 20,661 | 21,844 | 23,974 | 23,136 | 24,388 |
| Maize | 9,261 | 3,928 | 3,828 | 4,093 | 4,144 | 3,925 |
| Sugar | 7,261 | 8,573 | 9,664 | 19,244 | 17,694 | 14,782 |
| Tin | 3,097 | 2,344 | 2,229 | 2,497 | 1,880 | 877 |
| Textiles | 31,268 | 48,555 | 58,280 | 74,027 | 84,472 | 109,563 |
| Footwear | 3,185 | 5,915 | 9,624 | 13,524 | 20,213 | 23,800 |
| Integrated circuits | 11,640 | 15,179 | 18,664 | 18,424 | 21,580 | 25,760 |
| Precious stones | 8,150 | 11,550 | 13,958 | 16,419 | 22,045 | 23,433 |
| Jewellery | 5,014 | 8,257 | 9,725 | 11,974 | 12,813 | 12,465 |
| Prawns | 4,391 | 5,749 | 9,698 | 16,057 | 20,454 | 26,681 |
| Canned fish | 8,495 | 9,516 | 14,989 | 15,928 | 15,742 | 18,838 |
| Furniture | 1,866 | 3,387 | 6,635 | 9,672 | 11,511 | 13,626 |
| Total (including others) | 233,383 | 299,853 | 403,570 | 516,315 | 589,813 | 725,777 |

*Source:* Bank of Thailand, *Quarterly Bulletin,* in The Economist Intelligence Unit (EIU), Company Profile, 1992–93, Thailand.

*Note:* One US $ = 26.74 bahts as on February 1996.

**TABLE 5.3:** Imports

| Main Commodities Imported (Bt mn) | 1986 | 1987 | 1988 | 1989 | 1990 | 1991 |
|---|---|---|---|---|---|---|
| Fuel and lubricants | 32,354 | 44,177 | 38,829 | 59,819 | 78,346 | 87,580 |
| Non-electric machinery | 32,299 | 49,653 | 90,850 | 119,917 | 153,629 | 188,003 |
| Base metals | 22,176 | 33,855 | 59,166 | 78,090 | 90,453 | 93,260 |
| Chemicals | 26,106 | 36,140 | 48,598 | 55,278 | 65,345 | 68,570 |
| Electrical machinery and parts | 25,561 | 32,230 | 54,134 | 67,985 | 100,601 | 119,716 |
| Food and beverages | 6,103 | 8,022 | 10,844 | 13,488 | 16,977 | 19,443 |
| Vehicles and parts | 8,939 | 15,217 | 29,659 | 40,031 | 55,722 | 47,394 |
| Electrical appliances | 5,777 | 8,419 | 8,251* | 14,335 | 21,732 | 24,807 |
| Textile fibres | 5,638 | 8,389 | 10,025 | 13,162 | 15,715 | 18,844 |
| Fish and preparations | 7,462 | 6,881 | 14,326* | 18,274 | 19,666 | 25,565 |
| Jewellery | 4,149 | 7,073 | 12,305* | 20,625 | 29,773 | 49,580 |
| Wood | 3,501 | 5,872 | 8,164 | 14,374 | 17,747 | 20,533 |
| Total (including others) | 241,358 | 334,209 | 513,114 | 662,679 | 844,448 | 967,194 |

*Reclassified since 1987.

*Source:* Bank of Thailand, *Quarterly Bulletin,* in The Economist Intelligence Unit (EIU), Company Profile, 1992–93, Thailand.

*Note:* One US $ = 26.74 bahts as on February 1996.

**TABLE 5.4:** Employment Structure

|  | 1987 | 1988 | 1989 | 1990 | 1991 | 1992 |
|---|---|---|---|---|---|---|
| Employed | 26,940 | 28,210 | 29,250 | 29,950 | 30,580 | 31,220 |
| Agriculture | 16,640 | 17,240 | 17,590 | 17,640 | 17,830 | 18,030 |
| Total labour force | 28,640 | 29,490 | 30,340 | 31,130 | 31,930 | 32,720 |

*Source:* EIU *Country Profile,* 1992–93, Thailand, Bank of Thailand, Monthly Economic Indicators.

**TABLE 5.5:** Labour Supply

| Labour force in 1995 | | | Labour Force Participation Rate in 1995 (per cent) | | | |
|---|---|---|---|---|---|---|
| Workers in Age Group of 15–64 (in million) | | Average Annual Growth Rate (per cent) | | In Age Group of 15–64 | | In Age Group of 10–19 |
| Male | Female | 1965–95 | 1995–2025 | Male | Female | Male | Female |
| 16.54 | 13.08 | 2.66 | 0.63 | 86 | 67 | 39 | 37 |

*Source:* World Bank Book, *World Development Report,* 1995, Oxford University Press, 1995.

However, with growth in the industrial sector, there has been an increase in demand for skilled labour and the unemployment rate had fallen to around 4 per cent in the early 1990s.

Another major factor which accelerated the performance of the Thai economy was the large inflow of foreign investment. The total foreign investment from 1986 to 1991 stood at US $48 billion mainly from countries such as Japan, Taiwan, USA, Hong Kong, UK and Singapore. The major sectors which benefitted from foreign investment included engineering products, chemical products, agricultural products, hotels, resorts, industrial estates, etc.

Thailand was able to attract foreign investors by offering a highly conducive environment and relatively low government interference. Some of the features which have helped attract foreign investment to Thailand include the following:

♦ *Stable Policies* Domestic and foreign policies have remained stable despite changes in government, enabling trade and industry to expand and function in a relatively consistent environment.

♦ *Financial Stability* Monetary and fiscal policies have also ensured financial stability.

**TABLE 5.6:** Major Economic Indicators

|  |  | 1992 | 1993 | 1994 | 1995* | 1996* |
|---|---|---|---|---|---|---|
| Gross domestic product | % change | 7.9 | 8.2 | 8.5 | 8.6 | 8.0 |
| Agriculture | % change | 4.2 | −1.7 | 2.9 | 2.9 | 2.8 |
| Industry | % change | 10.0 | 10.8 | 12.0 | 12.3 | 11.0 |
| Services | % change | 7.3 | 8.7 | 7.0 | 6.8 | 6.5 |
| Gross domestic investment | % of GDP | 39.6 | 40.0 | 42.9 | 44.9 | 45.4 |
| Gross domestic saving | % of GDP | 35.7 | 35.5 | 37.2 | 38.0 | 38.4 |
| Inflation rate of CPI | % of change | 4.2 | 3.5 | 5.0 | 5.0 | 4.5 |
| Money supply growth | % change | 15.6 | 18.4 | 16.2 | 16.0 | 17.6 |
| Merchandise exports | US $ billion | 32.1 | 36.4 | 42.8 | 50.0 | 57.9 |
|  | % change | 13.7 | 13.4 | 17.5 | 16.8 | 15.8 |
| Merchandise imports | US $ billion | 36.3 | 40.6 | 47.2 | 54.7 | 63.0 |
|  | % change | 6.0 | 11.8 | 16.4 | 16.0 | 15.0 |
| Current accounts | US $ billion | −6.4 | −6.9 | −7.4 | −8.2 | −7.8 |
|  | % of GDP | −5.7 | −5.5 | −5.2 | −5.0 | −4.2 |
| External debt outstanding | US $ billion | 39.6 | 45.8 | 55.0 | 65.0 | 75.0 |
| debt-service ratio | % of exports | 14.1 | 18.6 | 11.2 | 11.8 | 12.5 |

*Estimates.

*Source:* *Asian Development Outlook, 1995 and 1996,* Asian Development Bank, Oxford University Press, 1995.[1]

♦ *Abundance of Natural Resources* The diversity in products are afforded through a wide range of investment opportunities in processing, production and marketing of products based on the abundant natural resources.

♦ *Government's Role* The government has been encouraging the private sector towards export-oriented industries and services. Procedures and regulations have been considerably minimized to support free enterprise.

♦ *Labour Potential* Thailand has the advantage of a large, fairly literate workforce with a high level of trainability and discipline. Its skilled labour force is cost competitive as compared to Korea, Singapore, Taiwan and Hong Kong. The industrial relations climate has also been generally conducive in Thailand.

**TABLE 5.7:** Foreign Investment

| Net Foreign Direct Investment (million US $) | 1987 | 1988 | 1989 | 1990 | 1991 | 1992 |
|---|---|---|---|---|---|---|
| **By Country** | | | | | | |
| Japan | 127 | 578 | 731 | 1,093 | 612 | 337 |
| Taiwan | 27 | 124 | 197 | 280 | 108 | 87 |
| Hong Kong | 31 | 111 | 223 | 275 | 454 | 572 |
| Singapore | 21 | 62 | 107 | 240 | 254 | 264 |
| USA | 71 | 126 | 203 | 241 | 232 | 463 |
| UK | 13 | 35 | 9 | 44 | 10 | 126 |
| Germany | 17 | 25 | 32 | 45 | 33 | 24 |
| Other | 45 | 46 | 278 | 230 | 316 | 239 |
| Total | 352 | 1,107 | 1,780 | 2,447 | 2,019 | 2,113 |
| **By Sector** | | | | | | |
| Financial institutions | 17 | 102 | 111 | 177 | 268 | 258 |
| Trade and services | 79 | 254 | 605 | 916 | 535 | 432 |
| Construction | 52 | 73 | 153 | 129 | 130 | 571 |
| Mining and quarrying | 7 | 19 | 22 | 45 | 81 | 123 |
| Agriculture | 11 | 12 | 23 | 30 | 23 | 6 |
| Industry | 185 | 640 | 852 | 1,213 | 935 | 686 |
| Others | 13 | 34 | 156 | 211 | 209 | 37 |
| Total | 364 | 1,134 | 1,922 | 2,604 | 2,181 | 2,113 |

*Source:* Bank of Thailand, Board of Investment, Bangkok Bank Limited, Thailand Development Research Institute Foundation (TDRI), 1993.

♦ *Market Potential*   The large domestic market itself provides a vast opportunity for consumer durables, and Thailand has the added advantage of access to neighbouring markets. The ASEAN trade agreements give Thailand preferential access to ASEAN countries. It can offer low production costs and better infrastructural facilities to make it an attractive production base.

♦ *Infrastructure*   Thailand has been making efforts to improve and upgrade its infrastructure to facilitate trade and industry.

♦ *Board of Investment of Thailand (BOI)*   The government set up the BOI to encourage and promote private investment in priority areas. It provides incentives for investment and facilitates projects by providing information, etc. The BOI also acts as a coordinating link with various government agencies to enable investors obtain necessary approvals and permits, process visas for foreigners and investigate potential business opportunities, and actively seek potential business partners.

♦ *Stock Exchange of Thailand (SET)*   Thailand has a reasonably developed stock exchange in keeping with its high growth level. Many local and international securities have been promoting investments in the Thai stock market. Thailand is viewed as one of the world's fastest emerging markets.

# Role of Government in Development

Thailand embarked upon its process of development through five-year plans starting in 1962. However, these plans were more or less an indicator of certain priorities and the corresponding direction of investment incentives and allocation of public expenditure. This is because Thailand has been relying heavily on private investment and private enterprise with minimum government regulation.

The first plan focused mainly on the development of the country's essential infrastructure. Subsequent plans stressed industrial growth through import substitution. It was only during the fifth plan period (1982–86) that the emphasis shifted to export expansion and from agro-based to industry-based economy. The Ministry of Commerce prepared a master plan to expand exports by 12 to 15 per cent per year and also for appropriate regional development of the industry.

## Government Policies for Investment and Technology Transfer

The government of Thailand established the Board of Investment (BOI) in 1960 to promote industrialization, with special focus on export-oriented industries. The BOI gives preference to certain projects and industries related to strengthening the balance of payments position, infrastructure development, employment generation, conservation of energy, contributing to technological development, etc. The BOI also tries to ensure that, to the extent possible, the projects are located in provincial areas away from the main urban centres. Special incentives are given for projects established in such areas.

In 1993 BOI started a Backward Linkage Programme to encourage full-scale industrial production of value-added products and to 'solve foreign investor's problems with shortfall in qualified subcontracting or supporting industries'.[2] The objective of this policy is not only to encourage foreign investment but also to encourage and develop existing small and medium enterprises.

For promotion of investment, both internal and external, certain guidelines have been laid down. The major thrusts of these guidelines are related to the promotion of employment-generating activities especially in rural areas, exports, technology transfer and local technological capability development to meet the challenges of international competition. The guidelines also emphasize the need to protect the environment. There are special incentives for local participation in joint ventures, technology transfer and sub-contracting, including overseas investment.

## Criteria for Foreign Investment

Thai development plans have not been the result of public debate but have been confined to a small circle of government officials. These plans serve primarily as general guidelines for government agencies and are not intended to mould the national identity or produce social transformation. Thailand's central theme of development has been its strong commitment to a free market economy. This implies opening the economy to foreign investors, facilitation of economic growth and minimal governmental interference. Because of this policy, the perception amongst foreign investors is that they can go freely to Thailand as long as the technology brought in by them is within the government's priority areas.

To protect local industries in some of the core areas, such as agriculture, animal husbandry, fishing, mineral exploration and mining, or in the service sector, the BOI insists that Thai nationals hold not less than 51 per cent of the registered capital. However, where the investment capital (excluding the cost of land and working capital) is over 1,000 million baht, the foreign investor may initially hold the majority or even 100 per cent shares, but Thai nationals must acquire at least 51 per cent of the shares within five years of starting the operations.

Thailand's licensing system is very simple. Except for some routine procedural approvals, such as commercial registration and work permits for aliens, there are no requirements of specific government approvals other than an industrial license.[3] In most cases the application for industrial license is processed within a few months through a set channel unlike other countries such as India. There are no direct negotiations between the foreign investors or MNCs and the government. The investing companies have substantial flexibility in deciding the size of the company and sophistication of technology. The government, however, does encourage the setting up of industries away from Bangkok and also assumes the responsibility of providing appropriate infrastructure in government-managed industrial estates.

There has been a further relaxation of norms regarding foreign investment during the seventh development plan period (1992–96). The foreign ownership requirements in the following areas will be considered on a case-by-case basis by the respective ministries (not by the BOI):

❑ Development of the transportation system

❑ Public utilities

❑ Environment conservation and restoration

❑ Direct involvement in technology and development

With the opening up of the economy to foreign investment, Thailand's capital stock has continued to increase as the average annual inflow of foreign investment has risen from US $ 82.5 million during 1975–80 to US $ 280.3 million during 1981–85. Initially, the focus of foreign investment was more towards import substitution. However, the liberal policy of facilitation and minimal governmental interference in the business activities of MNCs naturally resulted in a rapid export-oriented industrial growth. Some of the case studies indicate that Thailand has supplemented its location policies with heavy investment allocations in infrastructure development. The provision of infrastructure has allowed Thailand to offer investors alternative locations that are economically viable and thus in keeping with its corporate business objectives.

## Research and Development

In its effort to encourage R&D the government had set up a revolving fund for technology, research and development in 1988. The fund was initially started with 30 million baht which increased to 200 million baht by 1993. The fund is disbursed in the form of loans under the following two categories:

❑ Proposals up to five million baht at 4 per cent interest rate for 15 selected industries including rubber, agriculture, food, pharmaceuticals, micro-electronics and computers. These soft loans vary for a period from three to 10 years.

❑ Loans up to 10 million baht are available for R&D in process improvement, production, etc.

These loans are extended through quasi-government banks. A committee to evaluate and monitor these projects has been set up. From 1993 onwards some projects have been commercialized and entered successfully to meet international competition, especially in the areas of activated carbon, rubber products, etc.

Special incentives are given for R&D investment leading to improvement in production technology, productive quality, new product development, etc. In such cases the BOI can increase the tax exemption up to the total investment in R&D. For availing the exemption, the concerned organization must seek approval of the BOI with regard to machinery and equipment used in its R&D activity, the number of qualified Thai personnel employed in R&D, etc.

## Human Resource Development

With rapid industrialization and the consequent demand for skilled labour, Thailand has been facing an acute shortage of technicians, engineers and other skilled categories of workers. The Thai educational system and subsequent training and development policies have not been able to keep pace with the increasing demand for skilled personnel. Only one-fifth of the demand for technicians and engineers is currently being met. The government has therefore evolved a policy of sending students abroad for training at government expense in frontier high-technology areas, such as biotechnology, materials and micro-electronics. These students are selected and sent abroad with a job guarantee on their return after acquiring specialized training.

The government has also been encouraging expatriates in certain skilled categories and the BOI has been authorized to recommend their visas. There is no official policy of providing incentives for technology improvement or training. Most of the improvements have been brought in by the MNCs on their own, mainly to meet foreign competition in the export market.

## Industrial Relations

The industrial climate, as mentioned earlier, has been quite congenial in Thailand from the investor's point of view. Trade unions were banned by the government in 1991 because they were perceived to be playing a negative role in the industrial growth and development of Thailand which could eventually be detrimental to public interest. However, there are associations of employees, though they are not very strong. Most of the terms and conditions are settled on a tripartite basis among employers, employees' representatives and the government. There are security and welfare legislations to protect the workers' interests which normally relate to minimum wages and various other welfare and social security schemes.

## Payments for Technology Imports

There are no regulations regarding technology imports. Royalties, fees and terms of agreement between the licensor and the licensee are open to negotiation between the concerned parties. The government ensures certain guarantees against state expropriation and protection against state monopolization in industry, as in the case of a promoted firm. The BOI is also authorized to grant permission to bring in foreign technicians and expertise, to take or remit foreign currency abroad, exempt firms from export duties, etc.

## Regulations and Clearance Procedures

Earlier there used to be complaints about cumbersome clearance procedures, slow decision making, occasional changes in the liability and customs classifications, inter-government agency disputes, etc. However, efforts have been made to streamline and shorten the cumbersome process of navigating government regulations. Clearance in imported shipments, which once required over 80 signatures, now requires only around 20. There is a widespread feeling that government regulations are weak and inconsistent but not unreasonable.[4]

The government set up a Joint Public Private Consultative Committee in 1986, headed by the Prime Minister to simplify the complicated customs and port regulations and tax clearance certificates that impede exports, and to speed up the processing of applications for promotional privileges given to investors. As a result of these efforts, the procedures have been simplified to some extent. The BOI has instituted a one-stop investment centre to deal with the major complaints of investors regarding bureaucratic red-tape and tardy decision making. Any investment application to BOI now takes only one to two months for approval. If the application is approved, the firm has one month to confirm the acceptance of the approved package. Within six months of approval, the business entity must commence operation. If the application is not approved, an appeal can be made to the Secretary General of BOI. The whole clearance procedure and the time frame, etc. has been clearly laid down (see Figures 5.1 and 5.2).

With all these changes, there is appreciable increase of investment in Thailand. The criteria for granting approval to investment proposals of less than 200 million baht has been further simplified. The BOI in such cases considers only four criterion, namely, value addition, debt-equity ratio, machinery usage and environment protection cost measures. The import tax on machinery and equipment has been considerably reduced to encourage small- and medium-scale industries. However, there are still some impediments which can be streamlined.

Some of the critical areas requiring reforms and improvements are as follows:

♦ *Infrastructure* There is still considerable lack of communication among different government departments which operate in isolation of each other, with the result that the infrastructure is not fully equipped to handle the increased demands brought on by economic growth.

♦ *Critical Utilities* Electricity generation is barely sufficient to meet the current demand. It could become a bottleneck in the future if the facilities are not upgraded and expanded. Similarly, transportation and communication services need to be improved. The Bangkok area is heavily congested. The international airport also needs to be expanded and upgraded. There is shortage of water in certain geographical locations and insufficient sanitation facilities. Pollution poses a serious threat and requires immediate attention and long-term remedial measures. All these infrastructural inputs need to be looked at critically.

♦ *Wages and Salaries* One of the competitive advantages of Thailand has been the low cost of and high productivity of its workforce. However, with increasing shortage of skilled labour, the minimum wage was raised from 78 baht to 100 baht per day in urban areas in 1994. The labour costs could further rise in the years to come.

There has been a rapid increase in the wages of skilled categories, but wages in the unskilled and semi-skilled categories, especially for female and child labour in the unorganized sector, continue to be below the minimum. Even in the government, the salaries continue to be much lower than the private sector resulting in many managerial and skilled personnel, including scientists and engineers, shifting to the private sector.

♦ *Foreign Investors*  There are some restrictions and controls, on foreign ownership in Thailand, though it is estimated that foreign investment in the Stock Exchange of Thailand (SET) in 1995 was around 20 per cent. No limitations exist on the inward and outward remittances of foreign capital concerning portfolio investment.

## Conclusions

During the last few years Thailand has achieved one of the highest economic growth rates. What makes the achievement remarkable is that the country has maintained a steady growth in spite of political instability. One of the important factors has been that despite changes in government, its leaders have not tampered with economic policies. Also, the government has been gradually withdrawing its controls and has been allowing the economy to develop on its own. Owing to its locational advantage and favourable climate for investment, Thailand has been able to attract foreign direct investment. Skill development has not kept pace with industrial development, resulting in severe shortages of skilled and technical personnel. Though the Thai economy has been growing, it has not yet developed a strong policy encouraging the growth of science and technology. There is no similarly planned policy for development, assimilation and upgradation of technology. With industrial growth, the environmental and pollution problems are also becoming more acute.

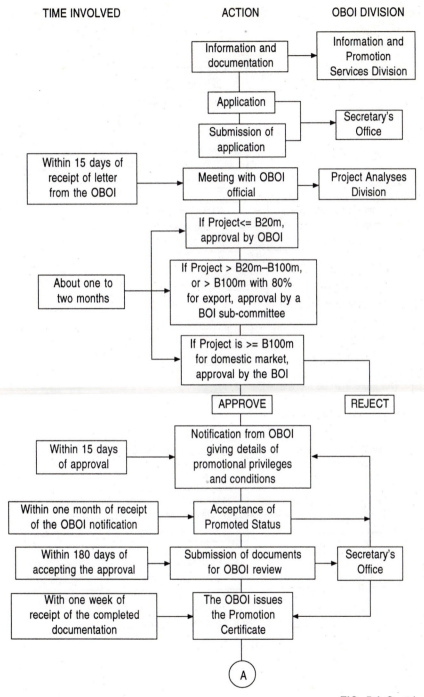

| TIME INVOLVED | ACTION | OBOI DIVISION |
|---|---|---|

Information and documentation → Information and Promotion Services Division

Application

Submission of application → Secretary's Office

Within 15 days of receipt of letter from the OBOI → Meeting with OBOI official → Project Analyses Division

If Project <= B20m, approval by OBOI

About one to two months → If Project > B20m–B100m, or > B100m with 80% for export, approval by a BOI sub-committee

If Project is >= B100m for domestic market, approval by the BOI

APPROVE    REJECT

Within 15 days of approval → Notification from OBOI giving details of promotional privileges and conditions

Within one month of receipt of the OBOI notification → Acceptance of Promoted Status

Within 180 days of accepting the approval → Submission of documents for OBOI review → Secretary's Office

With one week of receipt of the completed documentation → The OBOI issues the Promotion Certificate

A

**FIG. 5.1** Contd.

*Fig. 5.1 Contd.*

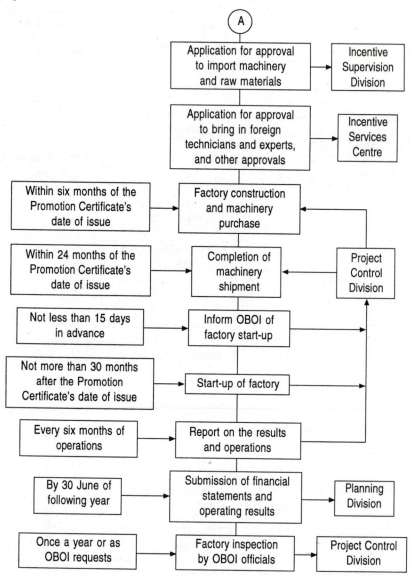

**FIG. 5.1**  BOI Application Procedure

*Source:*  The Board of Investment, Thailand, September, 1991.

## ACTIONS TO BE TAKEN TO SET UP A THAI LIMITED COMPANY
All times are estimations of government processing time after submission of complete, accurate and legal documentation

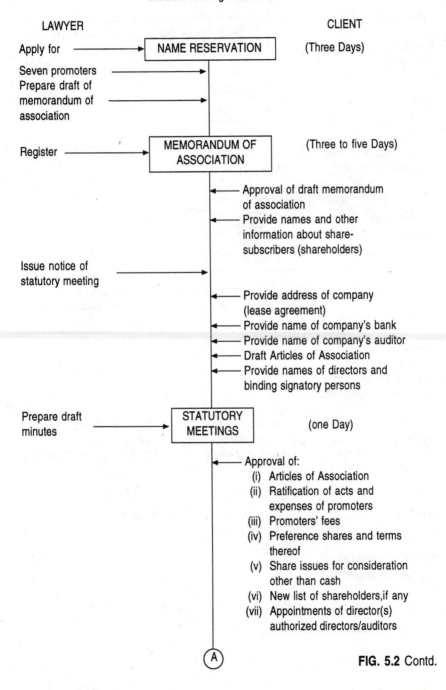

LAWYER                       CLIENT

Apply for ⟶ **NAME RESERVATION**   (Three Days)

Seven promoters ⟶
Prepare draft of
memorandum of ⟶
association

Register ⟶ **MEMORANDUM OF ASSOCIATION**   (Three to five Days)

⟵ Approval of draft memorandum of association
⟵ Provide names and other information about share-subscribers (shareholders)

Issue notice of statutory meeting ⟶

⟵ Provide address of company (lease agreement)
⟵ Provide name of company's bank
⟵ Provide name of company's auditor
⟵ Draft Articles of Association
⟵ Provide names of directors and binding signatory persons

Prepare draft minutes ⟶ **STATUTORY MEETINGS**   (one Day)

⟵ Approval of:
   (i) Articles of Association
  (ii) Ratification of acts and expenses of promoters
 (iii) Promoters' fees
 (iv) Preference shares and terms thereof
  (v) Share issues for consideration other than cash
 (vi) New list of shareholders, if any
(vii) Appointments of director(s) authorized directors/auditors

(A)

**FIG. 5.2** Contd.

*Fig. 5.2 Contd.*

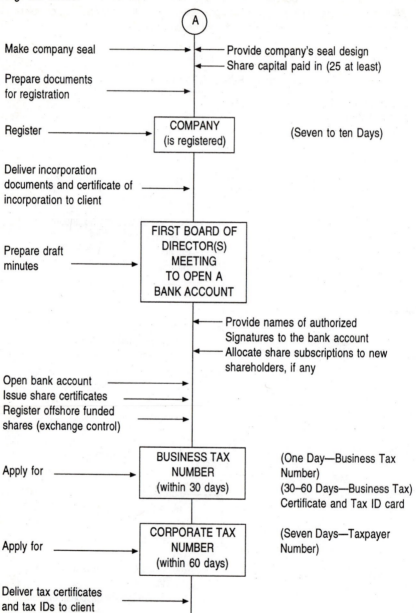

**Fig. 5.2**  Procedure to Set up a Thai Limited Company

*Source:* Tilleke and Gibbin, September, 1991.

# REFERENCES

1. *Asian Development Outlook 1995 and 1996*, Asian Development Bank, Oxford University Press, 1995.
2. Investment in Thailand, paper prepared by the Foreign Investment Advisory Services for the Board of Investment (BOI), September, 1991.
3. Alien Business Law of 1972, Government of Thailand, 1972.
4. STEWART JR., CHARLES T. and YASUMITRA NIHEI, *Technology Transfer and Human Factors*, Lexington Books Lexington, p. 65, 1987.

# 6

# INDIA

India was a British colony for more than a century. The British first came to India as traders through the East India Company, which eventually became a colonizing force and started exercising political control on various Indian territories. In 1859, the East India Company was abolished and India became a full-fledged colony of the British Empire. During the British rule, India remained an agriculture-based economy and even the few industries set up by the British were agriculture based, such as jute, tea, etc. In comparison to some of the other Asian countries, India has an abundance of natural, agricultural and mineral-based resources and a vast manpower, with the second largest population in the world (of approximately 900 million), second only to China.

Only after gaining independence in 1947 India began thinking in terms of industrialization and tapping its vast resources. Because of the domination of the East India Company that had culminated in political usurpment, India developed a fear psychosis regarding the entry of large foreign companies. This resulted in India adopting an extreme position of becoming a self-reliant and fully protected economy and adopting the socialistic model of state planning. The industrial policy initiative started with the first five year plan which focused on import substitution and domestic market orientation. Gradually emphasis came to be laid on public sector investment in heavy and basic industries. The Indian economy was highly regulated and controlled by the state. For decades it remained inward-looking and exports were confined mainly to agro-based products. Figure 6.1 shows the three main phases of economic development in India.

| PHASE I | Industrial Policy Resolution 1948, 1956 | → Import substitution<br>→ Public sector investment in core and heavy sectors |
| PHASE II | MRTP Act, 1969 | → Decentralization and emphasis on the role of small and cottage industries |
| | Industrial Policy Resolution 1973, 1980 | → Partial liberalization of licensing system<br>→ Domestic market competition |
| PHASE III | Industrial Policy Statement, 1991 | → Elimination of export subsidies and import licensing for most items |
| | New Economic Policy, 1993 | → Privatization<br>→ Free convertibility of rupee on trade account<br>→ Encouraging domestic and external competition |

**FIG. 6.1:** Process of Economic Development

The first industrial policy of 1948 and its subsequent elaboration in 1956 provided the basic framework for India's industrial growth. The main focus of the economy was on self-reliance. A major role of industry, especially heavy industry, in economic development and active participation and direction of industrial growth were the two common elements in all development programmes. The industrial policy of 1948 emphasized the need for expansion of production facilities. The first five year plan gave priority to agriculture and at the initiative of policy makers, substantial investments were made in heavy industries and infrastructural facilities. The Industrial Policy Resolution of 1956 aimed at accelerating the rate of economic growth and speeding up industrialization through development of heavy industries and expansion of the public and cooperative sector. Industrial growth, which was around 7 per cent in the 1950s, rose to 9 per cent in the early 1960s.

Within the massive overall increase in the manufacturing output, there has been a major shift in the structure of the manufacturing industry. In the early 1950s the share of the consumer goods sector was close to 60 per cent of the value added from manufacturing, within which textile production was the largest manufacturing industry group. By the late 1970s the share of consumer goods in value added from manufacturing had fallen between 30 and 35 per cent. Over the same period, the share of the basic and capital goods sectors rose from 30 to 50 per cent.

The MRTP (Monopolies and Restrictive Trade Practices) Act of 1969 drew up a list of industries which were accorded protection against competition. The industrial policy resolutions of 1973 and 1980 gave a new direction with emphasis on small and cottage industries and decentralization. The licensing system was liberalized and domestic market competition was encouraged. The 1980s recorded an average yearly increase in GDP of 5.5 per cent. Consequently, the growth rate of the per capita income more than doubled to 3.4 per cent, demonstrating the beneficial impact of higher growth on per capita welfare as there was a substantial decline in population below the poverty line.

Owing to the inward-looking approach and being an extremely protected economy, for many years foreign trade in India was insignificant and foreign investment was actively discouraged. The state took up the major responsibility of industrialization and government started public enterprises not only in infrastructure and industries but also in intermediate and even consumer industries. Some of the industries, such as coal and petroleum, were nationalized. Others were acquired to protect employment even if they were inefficient and loss making, such as textiles. Many state enterprises were inefficient and loss making, while at the same time a comprehensive system of industrial licensing throttled the private sector. Between 1965 and 1980, the India economy grew at an annual average rate of 3.6 per cent which was far lower than some of the other Asian success stories such as Malaysia, Korea and even Thailand. For example, the manufacturing sector in Malaysia accounted for 28 per cent of the GDP in 1991 from a mere 12 per cent in 1970, while in India this sector lagged behind at around 18 per cent of the GDP from 15 per cent in 1970.

During the 1980s, some moderate efforts were made to liberalize the economy, mainly consisting of a gradual shift from import substitution to export orientation, reforms in capital markets and licensing systems. Business enterprises were also given greater freedom to determine production volumes in contrast to the earlier policy of keeping production within the approved capacity limits. There was also a marginal reduction in taxes. These changes were not complemented by corresponding changes in the bureaucracy, size of government, etc. which continued to be obstructive. By and large, the performance of public enterprises, with a few exceptions, continued to be dismal, and no attention was given to privatization in the 1980s. The economy developed problems as a result of unbalanced reforms. In 1991 the growth rate was as low as 2 per cent. The crisis of increased budget deficits, staggeringly low levels of foreign reserves and rising inflation rates prompted India to implement new reforms including encouragement to private industry, foreign investment, liberalization of interest rates, elimination of import licensing, etc.

**TABLE 6.1:** Major Economic Indicators and Ratios

| Population mid-1993 | | *Income Group: Low* | | | | |
|---|---|---|---|---|---|---|
| *(millions)* | 898.2 | | | | | |
| *GNP per capita* (US $) | 300 | *Indebtedness Level: Moderately Indebted* | | | | |
| Key Ratios | | 1985 | 1990 | 1992 | 1993 | 1994* |
| Gross domestic investment/GDP | | 23.9 | 26.6 | 23.3 | 21.3 | 24.8 |
| Exports of goods and nfs/GDP | | 6.0 | 7.9 | 10.1 | 11.4 | 11.9 |
| Gross domestic savings/GDP | | 20.8 | 23.7 | 22.0 | 21.1 | 24.1 |
| Gross national savings/GDP | | 21.1 | 22.9 | 21.5 | 21.1 | 26.8 |
| Current account balance/GDP | | −2.8 | −3.7 | −1.7 | −0.3 | −0.7 |
| Interest payments/GDP | | 0.6 | 1.3 | 1.6 | 1.6 | 1.4 |
| Total debt/GDP | | 19.1 | 27.6 | 37.2 | 36.6 | 34.2 |
| Total debt/exports | | 263.7 | 314.7 | 329.1 | 287.8 | 268.2 |
| GDP: Production | | 1985 | 1990 | 1992 | 1993 | 1994 |
| (% of GDP) | | | | | | |
| Agriculture | | 33.0 | 31.1 | 30.8 | 30.3 | 30.9 |
| Industry | | 28.1 | 29.1 | 28.2 | 28.2 | 27.4 |
| Manufacturing | | 17.9 | 18.7 | 17.7 | 17.3 | 17.3 |
| Services | | 38.8 | 39.7 | 41.0 | 41.5 | 41.7 |
| | | 1985–90 | 1990–94 | 1992 | 1993 | 1994 |
| (Average annual growth) | | | | | | |
| Agriculture | | 4.7 | 2.6 | 5.3 | 2.9 | 3.4 |
| Industry | | 8.1 | 2.9 | 3.5 | 3.5 | 4.9 |
| Manufacturing | | 8.5 | 2.3 | 3.1 | 3.6 | 5.0 |
| Services | | 7.0 | 5.4 | 4.9 | 5.9 | 5.7 |

| GDP: Expenditure | 1985 | 1990 | 1992 | 1993 | 1994 |
|---|---|---|---|---|---|
| (% of GDP) | | | | | |
| Private consumption | 68.1 | 64.7 | 66.8 | 67.3 | — |
| General govt. consumption | 11.1 | 11.6 | 11.2 | 11.6 | 9.8 |
| Gross domestic investment | 23.9 | 26.6 | 23.3 | 21.3 | 24.8 |
| Exports of goods and nfs | 6.0 | 7.9 | 10.1 | 11.4 | 11.9 |
| Imports of goods and nfs | 9.1 | 10.8 | 11.4 | 11.6 | 12.6 |

| | 1985–90 | 1990–94 | 1992 | 1993 | 1994 |
|---|---|---|---|---|---|
| (Average annual growth) | | | | | |
| Private consumption | 5.4 | 4.5 | 3.8 | 4.3 | 6.4 |
| General govt. consumption | 6.6 | 2.7 | 3.1 | 7.7 | −2.1 |
| Gross domestic investment | 8.3 | 0.4 | 11.3 | −3.9 | 7.5 |
| Exports of goods and nfs | 9.6 | 11.1 | 8.8 | 17.6 | 5.6 |
| Imports of goods and nfs | 5.2 | 6.6 | 16.8 | 6.7 | 14.9 |
| Gross national product | 6.5 | 3.7 | 5.0 | 3.5 | 5.1 |
| Gross national income | 6.4 | 3.8 | 5.1 | 3.5 | 5.5 |

| Prices and Government Finance | 1985 | 1990 | 1992 | 1993 | 1994 |
|---|---|---|---|---|---|
| Domestic prices (% change) | | | | | |
| Consumer prices | 5.6 | 9.0 | 11.8 | 6.4 | 10.5 |
| Wholesale prices | 4.6 | 9.0 | 11.9 | 7.5 | 10.5 |
| Implicit GDP deflator | 7.6 | 11.0 | 8.9 | 8.1 | 8.1 |
| Government Finance | | | | | |
| (% of GDP) | | | | | |
| Current budget balance | 2.2 | −0.2 | 0.3 | 0.3 | 1.4 |
| Overall surplus/deficit | — | — | — | — | — |

| Poverty and Social | 1985–90 | 1990–94 |
|---|---|---|
| (Annual growth rates) | | |
| Population | 2.0 | 2.0 |
| Labour force | 1.9 | 1.9 |

| | Most Recent Estimate (1995) |
|---|---|
| Poverty level: headcount index (% of population) | 25.4 |
| Life expectancy at birth | 60.8 |
| Infant mortality (per 1,000 live births) | 80.0 |
| Child malnutrition (% of children under five) | 63.0 |
| Access of safe water (% of population) | 74.5 |
| Energy consumption per capita (kg oil equivalent) | 242.7 |
| Illiteracy (% of population age 15+) | 51.8 |
| Gross primary enrollment(% of school-going population) | 106.0 |

| Trade | 1985 | 1990 | 1992 | 1993 | 1994 |
|---|---|---|---|---|---|
| (million US $) | | | | | |
| Total exports (fob) | 9,463 | 18,477 | 18,789 | 22,560 | 25,605 |
| Tea | 511 | 596 | 337 | 330 | 351 |
| Iron | 473 | 584 | 381 | 371 | 359 |
| Manufactures | 5,639 | 13,781 | 14,333 | 17,550 | 18,636 |

| Total imports (cif) | 17,298 | 27,914 | 22,895 | 25,249 | 28,431 |
|---|---|---|---|---|---|
| Food | 1,321 | 690 | 702 | 787 | 1,016 |
| Fuel and energy | 4,054 | 6,026 | 5,919 | 5,762 | 5,261 |
| Capital goods | 3,503 | 5,833 | 4,531 | 5,044 | 5,270 |
| Export price index (1987=100) | 80 | 134 | 157 | 184 | 197 |
| Import price index (1987=100) | 96 | 121 | 116 | 129 | 137 |
| Terms of trade (1987=100) | 83 | 110 | 135 | 143 | 143 |
| Openness of economy (trade/GDP %) | 15 | 19 | 21 | 23 | 25 |

| Balance of Payments | 1985 | 1990 | 1992 | 1993 | 1994 |
|---|---|---|---|---|---|
| (million US $) | | | | | |
| Exports of goods and nfs | 12,773 | 23,606 | 24,478 | 28,659 | 32,137 |
| Imports of goods and nfs | 19,422 | 32,063 | 27,618 | 29,167 | 34,093 |
| Resource balance | –6,649 | –8,457 | –3,140 | –508 | –1,956 |
| Net factor income | –1,553 | –4,473 | –3,740 | –4,002 | –3,954 |
| Net current transfers | 2,207 | 2,069 | 2,795 | 3,825 | 3,852 |
| Current account balance | | | | | |
| Before official transfers | –5,995 | –10,861 | –4,085 | –685 | –2,058 |
| After official transfers | –5,636 | –10,400 | –3,729 | –315 | –1,558 |
| Long-term capital inflow | 2,280 | 4,521 | 3,049 | 8,004 | 9,029 |
| Total other items (net) | 4,168 | 3,079 | 418 | 849 | 58 |
| Changes in net reserves | –812 | 2,800 | 262 | –8,538 | –7,529 |
| Memo: | | | | | |
| in (million US $) | | | | | |
| Reserves excluding gold | 6,657 | 1,521 | 5,757 | 10,199 | 19,698 |
| Reserves including gold | 9,730 | 5,637 | 9,539 | 14,675 | 24,221 |
| Conversion rate (local/US $) | 12.2 | 17.9 | 29.0 | 31.4 | 31.4 |

| External Debt | 1985 | 1990 | 1992 | 1993 | 1994 |
|---|---|---|---|---|---|
| Export ratios | | | | | |
| Long-term debt/exports | 204.5 | 271.9 | 288.4 | 261.1 | 245.7 |
| IMF credit/exports | 31.1 | 10.1 | 17.5 | 15.4 | 11.8 |
| Short-term debt/exports | 28.0 | 32.8 | 23.1 | 11.4 | 10.7 |
| Total debt service/exports | 22.7 | 30.7 | 28.2 | 28.0 | 26.2 |
| GDP ratios | | | | | |
| Long-term debt/GDP | 14.8 | 23.8 | 32.6 | 33.2 | 31.3 |
| IMF/credit/GDP | 2.3 | 0.9 | 2.0 | 2.0 | 1.5 |
| Short-term debt/GDP | 2.0 | 2.9 | 2.6 | 1.4 | 1.4 |
| Long-term debt ratios | | | | | |
| Private non-guaranteed/long-term | 4.7 | 2.1 | 1.9 | 2.7 | 3.0 |
| Public and publicly guaranteed | | | | | |
| Private creditors/long-term | 23.8 | 29.5 | 29.7 | 30.2 | 30.8 |
| Official creditors/long-term | 71.5 | 68.4 | 68.4 | 67.1 | 66.2 |

*Preliminary estimates.

*Source:* *Trends in Developing Economies,* World Bank, 1995.

**TABLE 6.2:** Major Economic Indicators

|  |  | 1992 | 1993 | 1994 | 1995* | 1996* |
|---|---|---|---|---|---|---|
| Gross domestic product | % change | 4.3 | 4.3 | 5.3 | 6.5 | 6.5 |
| Agriculture | % change | 5.1 | 2.9 | 2.4 | 3.0 | 3.0 |
| Industry | % change | 2.9 | 3.5 | 7.6 | 8.5 | 9.0 |
| Services | % change | 4.8 | 5.9 | 5.7 | 6.5 | 7.0 |
| Gross domestic investment | % of GDP | 22.0 | 20.4 | 22.5 | 23.5 | 24.0 |
| Gross domestic saving | % of GDP | 18.3 | 18.7 | 20.6 | 21.8 | 22.3 |
| Inflation rate | % change of CPI | 9.6 | 7.5 | 11.0 | 9.0 | 8.0 |
| Money supply growth | % change | 15.7 | 18.2 | 18.5 | 16.5 | 15.0 |
| Merchandise exports | US $ billion | 18.9 | 22.7 | 26.3 | 30.9 | 35.9 |
|  | % change | 3.2 | 20.4 | 15.9 | 17.6 | 16.0 |
| Merchandise imports | US $ billion | 20.8 | 21.5 | 26.0 | 30.4 | 35.0 |
|  | % change | 10.3 | 3.2 | 20.9 | 17.1 | 15.0 |
| Current accounts | US $ billion | –2.6 | 0.6 | –1.7 | –1.3 | –1.1 |
|  | % of GDP | –1.1 | 0.2 | –0.6 | –0.4 | –0.3 |
| External debt outstanding | US $ billion | 90.1 | 91.8 | 90.5 | 89.8 | 89.5 |
| Debt-service ratio | % of exports | 29.4 | 28.4 | 24.9 | 23.7 | 23.6 |

*Estimates.

*Source:* *Asian Development Outlook 1995 and 1996,* Asian Development Bank, 1995.

# Economic Reforms—Liberalization Measures

The major impetus for the new phase of reforms introduced in 1991 came as a result of the Gulf War and the consequent balance of payments crisis. The collapse of the communist regimes all over the world also made Indian policy makers realize the inherent weaknesses of the socialist economic system where the emphasis had been primarily on state control of the economy. The third deciding factor was the change of government in India in 1991; the new government inherited an economy which was on the verge of bankruptcy.

India decided to adopt a two-pronged strategy. The first was to overcome the immediate balance of payments crisis at a time when the foreign exchange reserves were only sufficient to take care of 15 days' requirements. The second was to work out a long-term economic reform strategy on a sustainable basis. In the short term the strategy was to borrow from the International Monetary Fund (IMF) on the best possible terms. This also meant that certain conditions laid down by the IMF had to be fulfilled. These conditions were:

❑ Reducing the government deficit

❑ Taking steps to reduce inflation

❑ Disinvestment of public-sector undertakings

❑ Moving gradually towards privatization and a liberalized economy

There has been some criticism that India succumbed to IMF pressure. However, the financial situation was such that India had no choice but to borrow. If it had not done so, it would have lost complete credibility in international circles. The inflation rate may also have risen to three digit figures as was experienced in some Latin American countries. Some of the conditions laid down by the IMF and World Bank though harsh, were intrinsically sound and may have even been desirable, such as reduction of deficit, controlling of inflation and introduction of more competition in the economy.

Simultaneously, the government took the following steps towards liberalization:

❑ Industrial licensing was abolished except in the case of a few specified industries mainly for security, safety or environmental reasons. Some protection for small-sector industries was continued

❑ Taking prior approval for starting establishments, expansion of capacity, mergers, amalgamations and takeovers by large industrial houses under the MRTP Act was done away with

❑ The location policy of industries was also eased

❑ To encourage foreign investment, the government allowed up to 51 per cent of foreign equity in a number of specified industries

❑ Automatic permission was given for foreign technology agreements in high priority industries with some specified limitations

❑ The Foreign Investment Promotion Board (FIPB) was established to help collaborate with MNCs and expedite clearances of their proposals, especially in cases where equity participation was over 51 per cent

❑ Greater freedom was given to appoint foreign technicians. Also, the FERA (Foreign Exchange Regulation Act) companies were allowed to use their trademarks, borrow and accept deposits from the public, acquire and sell immovable property, etc.

❑ The role of public sector enterprises was limited to essential infrastructural areas or to the manufacture of products where strategic considerations were important. Thus, the private sector was allowed entry in almost all major industrial activities

❑ It was also decided that sick public sector undertakings would be referred to the Board for Industrial and Financial Reconstruction (BIFR) for rehabilitation or winding up. A National Renewal Fund was set up to provide assistance to industries which may have been affected by technological change or closure of sick industrial units

❑ In order to raise financial resources, a part of the government shareholding (up to 49 per cent of the total) in selected public sector units could be offered to mutual funds, financial institutions, general public and workmen

❑ The government also declared its intentions to give greater managerial autonomy to public sector undertakings through the signing of a memorandum of understanding which laid down targets of physical and financial performance, while at the same time allowing autonomy to public-sector management

❑ There was a decisive change in the thrust of trade policy towards freeing trade by reducing/eliminating qualitative restrictions, decanalizing imports and exports, bringing down customs and tariff, and simplifying export incentives

❑ To give a boost to exports, the Indian rupee was made fully convertible on trade account and partly on import and export . capital account

## FINANCIAL SECTOR REFORMS

In India, the objectives of the financial sector have all along been integrated with the priorities of the government with the Reserve Bank of India, nationalized banks and development financial institutions functioning according to the dictates of the government. However, after 1991, efforts were made to initiate major reforms in the financial sector. A special committee headed by Mr M. Narasimham was set up to examine all aspects of the structure, organization, functions and procedures of the financial system.

Some of the major recommendations of the Narasimham committee report were:

❑ Progressive reduction of the Statutory Liquidity Ratio (SLR) and Cash Reserve Ratio (CRR) in keeping with the government's intention to reduce its fiscal deficit

❑ Increase in the interest on investment under SLR and impounded money by the Reserve Bank of India under CRR

❑ Limiting priority sector lending only to the tiny sector, small farmers and weaker sections

❑ Rationalization of interest rates

❑ Strengthening other regulations relating to income recognition, uniform and transparent accounting practices and establishment of special tribunals for quick recovery of bank claims

❑ Revamping the banking system

❑ Improving operational autonomy and accountability of bank management

❑ Speeding up the computerization of banks

❑ Allowing entry of new private sector banks and liberalizing expansion of foreign banks

❑ Setting up of a board under RBI for supervision of banks and financial institutions

❑ Removing duality of control over banks and giving the RBI greater authority than the government

❑ Liberalization of capital markets by abolishing control on capital issues and pricing of issued equities

❑ Opening up to foreign portfolio investment

❑ Giving statutory powers to the Stock Exchange Board of India to regulate the capital and stock markets

❑ Establishment of asset reconstruction fund to help revive sick units under the Board for Industrial and Financial Reconstruction (BIFR)

Gradually, the financial sector reforms have been implemented. The commercial banks have been allowed to fix their own lending rates. As a consequence, the interest rate for advances was reduced to 13.5 per cent in 1993; the SLR was also cut by 2.25 per cent to 31.5 per cent. Similarly, there have been reductions on savings deposits and the ceiling of Rs 50 crore on term loan has been abolished. However, there was resistance from some of the trade unions, employers and even vested interest groups in the implementation of these recommendations.

## TAX REFORMS

With a low share of direct taxes, India's revenue structure had become both regressive and distortionary. The high incidence of excise duties was regressive and import duties of 110 per cent and above distorted investment patterns and made Indian products uncompetitive. A large number of self-employed professionals, traders and small businessmen evade income tax on a mass scale. A great part of the industrial output produced by small-scale industries was either exempt from excise duties or subject to concessional rates. The changes in the tax system since the Taxation Enquiry Commission of 1952 was of an ad-hoc nature. The Raja Chellaiah Committee was appointed to study and recommend the tax structure with the implementation being effective from 1992–93.[1]

The Committee recommended the adoption of a simple broad-based domestic indirect tax system with fewer rates of duties. The multiplicity of rates of excise duty was to be reduced to two or three rates at 10, 15 or 20 per cent, barring selective excise duty on non-essential commodities or commodities injurious to health (say at 30, 40 or 50 per cent). The tax base was to be enlarged by including services, etc. The other recommended reforms related to more specific areas of reduction in corporate taxes, changes in personal tax, agricultural income, excise duties including introduction of Value Added Tax (VAT), etc. There were also changes recommended and partially implemented in the excise and customs rules and procedures in order to simplify them and encourage foreign trade.

## THE IMPACT OF REFORMS IN THE 1990s

The foundation for economic reforms and liberalization was laid by reducing the unsustainable fiscal deficit from 8.4 per cent to around

5.7 per cent in the early 1990s. The inflation rate expressed in terms of the wholesale price index came down from over 16 per cent in 1990–91 to around 8 per cent in 1992–93 and around 5 per cent in 1995–96 as a result of the tight credit policy, lowered fiscal deficit and bountiful monsoon. The forex reserves increased from $1.2 billion to around $19 billion in 1995. The flow of foreign equity investment into India finally began to pick up. The proposals approved covered areas as diverse as oil refining, power, food processing, chemicals, transportation and tourism. The Indian industry responded to the challenge of change by entering new areas which were opened for private-sector investment. Many Indian companies entered into fruitful financial and technical tie-ups with multinationals in order to venture into new production areas.

The reform measures were brought in with much enthusiasm. However, the implementation of the various policies and measures was rather slow and did not percolate to the state level. The deficit finance, which was under some control, again begun showing a rising trend and the non-plan government expenditure also increased. The inflation rate again rose to double-digit figures in 1994 and 1995 though it came down by around 5 per cent in early 1996 thanks mainly to tight fiscal controls and credit squeeze due to higher interest rates. This was attributed to the government's short-term pre-election strategy. The exchange value of the rupee against US dollar remained steady for over three years after it was depreciated by 20 per cent in 1991. However, it suddenly depreciated by 13 per cent in early 1996. This, to an extent, inflicted a blow on corporate confidence and the foreign exchange reserves also fell. Another redeeming feature has been that with the fall of Congress government in 1996, a coalition government (United Front) of 13 parties was formed which included parties with rightist as well as leftist idealogies. All the 13 coalition parties have developed a Common Minimum Programme (CMP) of the United Front government. The programme clearly places emphasis on the continuation of economic reforms both in the industrial and agricultural sectors. The programme envisages GDP growth rate over the coming years to be sustained at 7 per cent levels, with industrial growth at around 12 per cent and agricultural output growth at about 3 per cent. However, the inevitable monetization of the large fiscal deficit of over 6 per cent of GDP in the year 1996–97; fuel prices adjustments and a hike in a wide range of administered prices, are likely to push the level of average annual inflation based on

**TABLE 6.3:** Key Indicators—India (Post-liberalization after 1991)

| 1 | 1992-93 | 1993-94P | 1994-95P | 1995-96P | 1992-93 | 1993-94P | 1994-95P | 1995-96P |
| --- | --- | --- | --- | --- | --- | --- | --- | --- |
| | | Absolute Values | | | | Per Cent Change Over Previous Year | | |
| | 2 | 3 | 4 | 5 | 6 | 7 | 8 | 9 |
| Gross domestic product (Rs thousand crore) | | | | | | | | |
| At current prices | 630.2 | 723.1 | 854.1Q | NA | 14.0 | 14.7 | 18.1 Q | NA |
| At 1980–81 prices | 224.9 | 236.1 | 251.1Q | 268.7R | 5.1 | 5.0 | 6.3 Q | 7.0 R |
| Gross national product (Rs thousand crore) | | | | | | | | |
| At current prices | 618.4 | 708.5 | 839.5Q | NA | 13.9 | 14.6 | 18.5 Q | NA |
| At 1980–81 prices | 220.1 | 230.1 | 245.6Q | 263.3R | 5.0 | 4.5 | 6.7 Q | 7.2 |
| Agricultural production (1) | 151.5 | 156.8 | 164.6 | 166.1P | 4.1 | 3.5 | 5.0 | 0.9 P |
| Foodgrain production (mill. tonne) | 179.5 | 184.3 | 191.1 | 190.4P | 6.6 | 2.7 | 3.7 | – 0.4 P |
| Industrial production (2) (1980–81 = 100) | 218.9 | 232.0 | 253.5 | 279.8 (2) | 2.3 | 6.0 | 9.3 | 12.4 (2) |
| Electricity generated (TWH) | 301.1 | 323.5 | 351.0 | 379.7 | 5.0 | 7.4 | 8.5 | 8.2 |
| Wholesale price index (3) (1981–82 = 100) | 233.1 | 258.3 | 285.1 | 299.5 | 7.0 | 10.8 | 10.4 | 4.4 |
| Consumer price index for industrial workers (4) (1982 = 100) | 243.0 | 267.0 | 293.0 | 319.0 | 6.1 | 9.9 | 9.7 | 8.9 |
| Money supply (M3) (5) (Rs thousand crore) | 368.8 | 434.4 | 531.4 | 600.5 | 15.7 | 18.4 | 22.3 | 13.0 |

*(Contd)*

| | Absolute Values | | | | Per Cent Change Over Previous Year | | | |
|---|---|---|---|---|---|---|---|---|
| 1 | 1992-93 | 1993-94P | 1994-95P | 1995-96P | 1992-93 | 1993-94P | 1994-95P | 1995-96P |
| | 2 | 3 | 4 | 5 | 6 | 7 | 8 | 9 |
| Imports at current prices (6) | | | | | | | | |
| (Rs crore) | 63,375 | 73,101 | 89,971 | 121,647 | 32.4 | 15.3 | 23.1 | 35.2 |
| (US $ million) | 21,885 | 23,306 | 28,654 | 36,370 | 12.7 | 6.5 | 22.9 | 26.9 |
| Exports at current prices (6) | | | | | | | | |
| (Rs crore) | 53,688 | 69,751 | 82,674 | 106,465 | 21.9 | 29.9 | 18.5 | 28.8 |
| (US $ million) | 18,537 | 22,238 | 26,330 | 31,830 | 3.8 | 20.0 | 18.4 | 20.9 |
| Foreign currency assets (End of period) | | | | | | | | |
| (Rs crore) | 20,140 | 47,287 | 66,006 | 58,446 | 38.2 | 134.8 | 39.6 | – 11.5 |
| (US $ million) | 6,434 | 15,068 | 20,809 | 17,044 | 14.3 | 134.2 | 38.1 | – 18.1 |
| Exchange rate (Rs/US $)ab (Period Average) | 28.96 | 31.37 | 31.40 | 33.45 | 14.9 | 14.9 | 0.1 | 6.1 |

Rs 1 crore = 10 million

*Source:* *Economy Survey,* 1995–96, Government of India.

*Note:* Gross National Product and Gross Domestic Product figures are at factor cost.

NA—Not available; P—Provisional; Q—Qick estimates; revised Advance Estimates.

1—Index of agricultural production (principal crops) with base triennum ending 1881–82 = 100.

2—April–February 1995–96.

3—As on end March, percentage change relate to point to point change in the index over the year.

4—As on March, percentage change relate to point change in the index over the year.

5—As on end March.

6—Figures relate to customs-based data compiled by DGCI&S and differs from payment based figures.

7—Per cent change indicate the rate of depreciation of the rupee vis-à-vis the US$.

**TABLE 6.4:** Exports

| Year | Export in US $ Billion |
|------|------------------------|
| 1992–93 | 18.5 |
| 1993–94 | 22.2 |
| 1994–95 | 26.2 |
| 1995–96 | 31.5⁻ |
| 2000 | 50.0ᵗ |
| 2000 | 75.0ᶜ |

*Source:*  *India Today,* 15 February 1996.

⁻estimated.
ᵗprojections by Indian Institute of Foreign Trade.
ᶜprojections by Ministry of Commerce.

*Note:*  One US $ = Indian Rupees 34.45 (as on 29 March 1996).

**TABLE 6.5:** Growth in Export and Import

(in percentage)

| Year | Imports | Exports |
|------|---------|---------|
| 1990–91 | 18.1 | 24.1 |
| 1991–92 | 17.8 | 19.4 |
| 1992–93 | 18.5 | 21.9 |
| 1993–94 | 22.2 | 23.2 |
| 1994–95 | 18.3 | 20.2 |

*Source:*  *Business Today,* April 1995.

wholesale price index at about 9 per cent from the annual average of 7.4 per cent in financial year 1995–96.

India's political stability has been a major doubt in the minds of prospective investors and the permanency of these reform measures have yet to be established. However, the fast-growing educated middle class in India has been, by and large, favourably inclined towards the process of structural reforms process. This may help in bringing about further reforms leading to greater stability and growth.

# FOREIGN DIRECT INVESTMENT

Foreign Direct Investment (FDI) contributes to economic growth through various channels—physical capital formation, technological

**TABLE 6.6:** Exports by Commodity Group
(in US $ million)

| Commodity Group | 1992–93 | 1993–94 | Apr.–Sept. 1993–94 | Apr.–Sept. 1994–95 | Apr.–March 1993–94 | Apr.–Sept. 1994–95 |
| --- | --- | --- | --- | --- | --- | --- |
| | | | | | (Per Cent Change) | |
| *1* | *2* | *3* | *4* | *5* | *6* | *7* |
| Agriculture and Allied | 3,135.8 | 3,994.8 | 1,847.7 | 1,853.2 | 27.4 | 0.3 |
| Tea | 337.2 | 311.9 | 164.7 | 141.3 | −7.5 | −14.2 |
| Coffee | 129.9 | 177.1 | 60.9 | 187.7 | 36.3 | 208.4 |
| Cereals | 343.9 | 423.6 | 193.9 | 180.0 | 23.2 | −17.1 |
| Unmanufactured tobacco | 122.8 | 118.0 | 61.0 | 34.2 | −3.9 | −44.0 |
| Spices | 135.8 | 178.9 | 85.7 | 78.4 | 31.7 | −8.4 |
| Cashew | 257.2 | 332.1 | 159.3 | 204.5 | 29.1 | 28.3 |
| Oil meals | 533.5 | 736.2 | 303.4 | 254.1 | 38.0 | −16.2 |
| Fruits and vegetables | 107.9 | 133.4 | 60.8 | 66.8 | 23.6 | 10.0 |
| Marine products | 601.9 | 808.8 | 310.5 | 438.3 | 34.4 | 41.2 |
| Raw cotton | 62.8 | 210.2 | 163.6 | 30.2 | 235.0 | −81.5 |
| Ores and Minerals | 737.8 | 888.0 | 402.7 | 435.1 | 20.4 | 8.0 |
| Iron ore | 381.2 | 432.7 | 211.5 | 188.7 | 13.5 | −10.8 |
| Processed minerals | 143.0 | 195.0 | 88.8 | 109.1 | 36.3 | 22.8 |
| Other ores and minerals | 188.0 | 232.9 | 93.7 | 129.1 | 23.9 | 37.8 |
| Manufactured Goods | 14,015.9 | 16,789.0 | 7,810.0 | 9,059.6 | 19.8 | 16.0 |
| Leather and manufactures | 867.3 | 839.9 | 410.9 | 472.4 | −3.2 | 15.0 |

*(Contd)*

| Commodity Group | 1992–93 | 1993–94 | Apr.–Sept. 1993–94 | Apr.–Sept. 1994–95 | Apr.–March 1993–94 | Apr.–Sept. 1994–95 |
| --- | --- | --- | --- | --- | --- | --- |
| | | | | | (Per Cent Change) | |
| 1 | 2 | 3 | 4 | 5 | 6 | 7 |
| Leather footwear | 410.2 | 479.8 | 202.3 | 219.4 | 17.0 | 8.5 |
| Gems and jewellery | 3,071.7 | 3,994.4 | 1,875.0 | 2,016.3 | 30.0 | 7.5 |
| Drugs, pharmaceuticals and fine chemicals | 529.3 | 642.1 | 289.1 | 346.2 | 21.3 | 19.7 |
| Dyes and coal tar chemicals | 330.6 | 366.5 | 165.5 | 214.2 | 10.9 | 29.4 |
| Manufactures of metals | 560.2 | 693.3 | 313.8 | 323.3 | 23.8 | 3.0 |
| Machinery and instruments | 541.6 | 636.4 | 304.9 | 325.8 | 17.5 | 6.9 |
| Transport equipment | 533.7 | 586.7 | 252.9 | 338.8 | 9.9 | 33.9 |
| Primary and semi-finished iron and steel | 164.4 | 432.1 | 222.7 | 174.0 | 162.9 | -21.9 |
| Electronic goods | 212.3 | 311.8 | 137.9 | 172.1 | 46.9 | 24.8 |
| Cotton yarn, fabrics, etc. | 1,350.5 | 1,542.3 | 713.4 | 1,004.9 | 14.2 | 40.8 |
| Readymade garments | 2,393.0 | 2,579.6 | 1,217.4 | 1,325.4 | 7.8 | 8.9 |
| Handicrafts | 865.2 | 928.7 | 437.4 | 481.5 | 7.3 | 10.1 |
| Crude and Petroleum Products | 476.2 | 397.8 | 236.7 | 217.4 | -16.5 | -8.1 |
| Others and unclassified items | 171.6 | 103.9 | 47.9 | 55.4 | -39.4 | 15.7 |
| Grand Total | 18,537.2 | 22,238.6 | 10,345.0 | 11,620.6 | 20.0 | 12.3 |

*Source: Economic Survey, 1994–95.*

**TABLE 6.7:** Exports to Developed and Developing Countries

| | 1989–90 | | 1990–91 | | 1991–92 | | 1992–93 | | 1993–94 | | 1994–95 | | 1995–96 | |
|---|---|---|---|---|---|---|---|---|---|---|---|---|---|---|
| | Value | % Share | Value | % Share | Value | % Share | Value | % Share | Value | % Share | Value | % Share | Value | % Share |
| **Developed Countries** | | | | | | | | | | | | | | |
| European Union | 712.3 | 25.73 | 895.1 | 27.50 | 1,189.9 | 27.01 | 1,519.6 | 28.30 | 1,818.2 | 26.06 | 1,262.4 | 25.68 | 1,505.6 | 26.18 |
| USA | 447.4 | 16.16 | 479.6 | 14.73 | 720.1 | 16.36 | 1,018.3 | 18.96 | 1,254.2 | 17.99 | 890.8 | 18.12 | 1,154.9 | 20.08 |
| Japan | 272.7 | 9.86 | 303.9 | 9.33 | 407.1 | 9.25 | 416.0 | 7.75 | 546.1 | 7.82 | 377.6 | 7.68 | 450.4 | 7.84 |
| Others | 143.6 | 5.18 | 162.4 | 4.99 | 234.7 | 5.32 | 289.4 | 5.40 | 357.0 | 5.12 | 254.5 | 5.18 | 354.4 | 6.16 |
| Total | 1,576.0 | 56.93 | 1,841.0 | 56.55 | 2,551.8 | 57.94 | 3,243.3 | 60.41 | 3,975.5 | 56.99 | 2,785.3 | 56.66 | 3,465.3 | 60.26 |
| **Developing Countries** | 1,192.1 | 43.07 | 1,414.3 | 43.45 | 1,852.4 | 42.06 | 2,125.5 | 39.59 | 2,999.6 | 43.01 | 2,130.4 | 43.34 | 2,285.0 | 39.74 |
| Total | 2,768.1 | 100.00 | 3,255.3 | 100.00 | 4,404.2 | 100.00 | 5,368.8 | 100.00 | 6,975.1 | 100.00 | 4,915.7 | 100.00 | 5,750.3 | 100.00 |

*Source:* Ministry of Commerce & D.G.C.I.& S., 1995.

*Note:* 1. The classification of developed and developing countries is based on UN Monthly Bulletin of Statistics.

2. One US $ = Indian Rupees 34.45 (as on 29 February 1996).

**TABLE 6.8:** Direct Foreign Investment

| | Actual Inflows vs Approvals | | | | |
| | 1991 | 1992 | 1993 | 1994 | Total |
|---|---|---|---|---|---|
| Approvals | | | | | |
| US $ billion | 0.2 | 1.3 | 2.8 | 2.9 | 7.2 |
| Actual inflows | | | | | |
| US $ billion | 0.2 | 0.2 | 0.6 | 0.9 | 1.9 |
| Actuals as % | | | | | |
| of Approvals | 66 | 17 | 20 | 33 | 26 |

Source: Economic Survey, 1994–95, Ministry of Finance.

transfer, human capital development and promotion of foreign trade. In India, there exists a wide gap between the actual flow of investment and approvals of FDI. During 1991 to 1994, the inflow was only US $1.9 billion against approvals of US $7.2 billion (around 26 per cent). Between 1986 and 1994, of the total FDI of $76 billion in the Asia Pacific region, India's share was only 1.76 per cent as compared to Malaysia's 9.3 per cent. The FDIs in India have been facing opposition due to fear of intense competition, takeovers, etc. despite the fact that the domestic consumer market has vast potential and is a major attraction for foreign investors. New technology and employment generation would be a natural outcome with new investment coming in and would eventually expand the capital goods sector too.

The economic growth rate, which was 1.2 per cent in 1991–92, improved to around 4 per cent in 1992–93 and 4.3 per cent in 1993–94 and further increased to 5.3 per cent in 1994–95 and around 6 per cent in 1995–96. The total exports in 1992–93 rose by over 5 per cent. There was a marked rise in exports during 1994–95 by 21 per cent. However, during 1994–95 there was again a slump in exports with growth around 12.3 per cent which picked up in 1995–96 to around 20 per cent.

There have been ups and downs in the pattern of industrial growth. In 1990–91, the growth was 8 per cent. It dipped to a negative growth rate in 1991–92, picking up somewhat to 3 per cent in 1992–93 and 1993–94. However, in 1994–95 the industrial growth increased dramatically to around 8 per cent and hovered at around 10 per cent in 1995–96. The top performers were electrical machinery, transport equipment, basic metals and alloys, synthetic textiles, etc. Some of the factors for such fluctuations in industrial growth have been frequent policy revisions, bureaucratic delays, infrastructural inadequacies,

**TABLE 6.9:** Real Per Capita Income

| Year | Increased Real Per Capita (Rupees) | Increased Real Per Capita (%) | Gross Domestic Savings (%) |
|------|------|------|------|
| 1990–91 | 2,199 | 3.0 | 24.0 |
| 1991–92 | 2,179 | –0.9 | 23.1 |
| 1992–93 | 2,238 | 2.7 | 22.3 |
| 1993–94 | 2,287 | 2.2 | 24.1 |
| 1994–95 | 2,351 | 2.8 | 24.0 |

*Source:* 'The Economy', *Business Today*, March–April 1995.

*Note:* One US $ = Indian Rupees 34.45 (as on 29 February, 1996).

especially in the power sector and, to some extent, the general recession in the economy.

In spite of changes in government in some states, such as Maharashtra, Andhra Pradesh and Karnataka, the policies regarding reforms and liberalization have not changed. Successive governments have declared their desire to encourage foreign investment and develop a conducive environment for the entry of MNCs. Even the communist government in West Bengal has been encouraging internal and external investment and streamlined clearance procedures. The Foreign Investment Promotion Board has also started clearing major proposals expeditiously. However, at the state levels, the time-bound single window concept has not yet been actualized.

A number of foreign institutional investors have been attracted by the prospect of investing in India, given its vast untapped potential. A major attraction has been the high interest rates in India, though a substantial portion of the investment has gone into the secondary share markets. Such investments have considerably improved the foreign exchange reserves of the country. However, some caution is needed here as it could create a crisis in the economy if the interest rates were to change in other countries and the funds were diverted from India, as had happened in Mexico. Therefore, some measure of control and monitoring of such investments may be desirable.

# INFRASTRUCTURE

The infrastructure development in India has not kept pace with industrial growth. There continues to be acute power shortages in most states and roads and transportation facilities are largely inadequate. Airports and seaports are not fully equipped to efficiently handle import and export requirements. The communication network is also unable to meet the growing demands imposed by industrialization. This lack of proper infrastructure is largely a result of the myopic view of earlier governments who deferred a number of projects with long gestation periods. A major portion of government resources were diverted to inefficiently run public enterprises and to non-planned expenditure mainly in the form of salaries for civil servants. There was limited private sector participation in infrastructure development.

While there were half-hearted attempts to develop and set up industrial estates, no additional facilities in terms of power, water, roads, telecommunications or housing were provided. The free-trade zones or export-processing zones in India have made little impact. The six zones that were established contribute to only about 2.5 per cent of the total employment in the manufacturing sector in 1995. The main reason is insufficiency of the incentives offered to attract investment. More recently, special benefits have been nullified due to the change-over from partial convertibility to full convertibility of the rupee.

The sharp cut in customs and excise duties on capital goods has also brought in anomalies. There have been efforts made by the government to bring in the private sector in infrastructure development, especially in power, telecommunication, road building, airport development, etc. However, clear policies on infrastructure privatization have not emerged. Some serious efforts were made to involve the private sector in the telecom industry. Unfortunately, this policy also ran into trouble because of certain allegations of pay-off and patent mismanagement.[2] There were also repeated changes in tendering norms, rejection of several bids and many after-thoughts resulting in delays. Eventually the issue was referred to the Supreme Court of India which upheld the privatization process. Obviously, proper guidelines need to be developed to avoid such delays.

Similarly, in the case of privatization of the power sector, the State Government in Maharashtra installed in 1995 cancelled the super power project contract with Enron Corporation of USA worth Rs 9,500 crore which had been committed by the earlier government. Subsequently, the new government re-negotiated the terms and signed the contract on modified conditions. This was perceived to indicate that there was lack of transparency in the national infrastructure development policy, including the role of foreign investments.

## Privatization

The socialistic pattern of growth which India adopted soon after Independence accorded prominence to public enterprises resulting in a substantial growth of state enterprises. The total investment in around 250 public sector enterprises was to the extent of Indian Rs 1,05,000 crore up to 1989–90. The average return on investment was around 1.5 per cent in the five year period of 1983–1988.

With the onset of the liberalization process in 1990–91, the government decided to partially divest its shareholdings in selected public enterprises. The primary objective appeared to be to raise financial resources and reduce the fiscal deficit. However, even the divestment process has been tardy. A major chunk of the divested portion has flowed to government-controlled financial institutions. Even the money realized on this disinvestment has not been up to the expectations. The government's approach to privatization has not been to really give the actual control to the private sector as was done in other countries such as Malaysia or Singapore. The divestment was only of a minority shareholding with the government retaining control of the enterprises. This in itself becomes a disincentive for private participation. There have been no clearly laid down policies on the extent of divestment and the price and parties to whom the shareholding will be transferred.

There has been some general opposition to privatization because of ideological reasons. It is argued that extensive government intervention in economic affairs is a necessary safeguard. More subtly, there has been some opposition from the bureaucrats who have hitherto enjoyed enormous power over public enterprises.

## SCIENCE AND TECHNOLOGY POLICIES IN INDIA

During the initial years of development after Independence, the Indian technology policy discouraged foreign collaborations. Consequently, the government policy towards import of technology was very selective. The government favoured technology transfer agreements where there was export orientation or import substitution, especially

**TABLE 6.10:** Profitability Profile of Central Public Sector Enterprises

| | 1981–82 | 1990–91 | 1991–92 | 1992–93 | 1993–94 |
|---|---|---|---|---|---|
| 1. Operation enterprise | 188 | 236 | 237 | 239 | 240 |
| (i) Profitable enterprises | 104 | 123 | 133 | 131 | 120 |
| (ii) Loss-making enterprises | 83 | 111 | 102 | 106 | 117 |
| (Rs billion) | | | | | |
| 2. Capital employed | 2,193.0 | 1,020.8 | 11,799.1 | 14,011.0 | 15,930.7 |
| 3. Gross margin | 401.2 | 1,831.2 | 2,222.3 | 2,522.7 | 2,760.0 |
| 4. Gross profit | 265.4 | 1,110.2 | 1,367.5 | 1,595.7 | 1,843.8 |
| 5. Net profit | 44.5 | 227.2 | 235.5 | 327.1 | 443.5 |
| 6. Profit of profit-making enterprises | 129.3 | 539.4 | 607.9 | 738.4 | 972.2 |
| 7. Losses of loss-making enterprises (per cent) | 84.8 | 312.2 | 372.3 | 411.3 | 528.7 |
| 8. Ratio of gross margin to capital employed | 18.29 | 17.94 | 18.83 | 18.01 | 17.33 |
| 9. Per cent of gross profit to capital employed | 12.10 | 10.88 | 11.59 | 11.39 | 11.59 |
| 10. Ratio of net profit to capital employed | 2.03 | 2.23 | 2.00 | 2.33 | 2.78 |

*Source:* 'Industrial Policy and Development', *The Economic Times*, 15 March, 1995, Bombay.

*Note:* One US $ = Indian Rupees 31.00 in 1993 and in March 1996= Rs.34.45.

in the high-technology areas. The agreements which enabled local industry to upgrade its existing technology were also selectively approved. With the objective of ensuring the implementation of its policies, the government laid down the following guidelines regarding technology transfer:

❑ Indian companies will first explore alternative sources of technology and give a detailed reasoning for selecting a particular technology

❑ There will be no restrictive clause regarding sub-licencing of know-how to other Indian parties

❑ There will be no restrictions regarding procurement of capital goods, spares, raw materials, pricing, selling arrangements, etc.

❑ No restrictions will be placed except where the collaborator had a sub-licencing arrangement

❑ There will be prohibition on the use of foreign brand names for products in the domestic market

❑ The training of Indian personnel will be a part of the agreement

❑ There will be certain restrictions on the hiring of foreign consultants

Normally, the agreements were approved for a period of five years with royalty payments ranging between 3 to 5 per cent. Most of the technology transfer agreements prior to 1991 were of the licensing type or for outright purchase of technology. An analysis of sectorwise distribution of technology transfer payments approved in the period 1981–89 indicates that the chemicals sector accounted for 36 per cent of the total technology payments approved for all the sectors (see Table 6.11). The figures for the total number of foreign collaborations approved in the period 1981–89, were nearly static, ranging between 700 to 1,000 collaborations per year. The major collaborators were from the USA, Germany, UK and Japan (see Table 6.12).

Prior to liberalization in 1991 the government had not played a facilitative role in foreign collaborations and technology transfer; it had, instead, primarily been one of exercising control. There had also been delays in getting approvals, sometimes exceeding five years. In the case of public enterprises, there had been instances where the Indian government had tried to dictate its terms to foreign collaborators. Since 1991, there have been major changes in the policies related to collaborations and technology transfers. A number of restrictions concerning import of technology have been removed. Collaborators can now invest upto 51 per cent of the equity and are allowed the use of foreign brand names. These changes have resulted in an increase in foreign collaborations including collaborations with foreign equity as is evident from Figure 6.2.

With the opening up of the economy, many large MNCs have taken advantage of the new policies and are entering into agreements with Indian companies. Owing to the low level of technology, some Indian companies are finding it difficult to face the competition with the result that they are forced to collaborate or enter into alliances with multinational corporations who, obviously, stand to gain more. Some of the examples are agreements between Coca Cola and the Parle group, Levers with Tata chemicals, Maruti and Suzuki, etc. These alliances are mainly to tap the large domestic consumer market

**TABLE 6.11:** Sectorwise Distribution of Payments Approved (1981–89)

(Rupees in Million)

| Sector | 1981 | 1982 | 1983 | 1984 | 1985 | 1986 | 1987 | 1988 | 1989 | Total | % |
|---|---|---|---|---|---|---|---|---|---|---|---|
| Alternate/renewable energy sources | — | 0.7 | 0.6 | 6.1 | 31.0 | 6.7 | 1.6 | 10.5 | 2.1 | 59.3 | 0.2 |
| Chemicals | 107.6 | 240.7 | 498.4 | 1,340.3 | 936.5 | 3,029.9 | 1,834.8 | 2,137.3 | 2,386.0 | 12,511.5 | 36.7 |
| Electrical & electronics | 72.5 | 456.5 | 262.0 | 322.6 | 1,061.1 | 1,302.6 | 682.4 | 826.7 | 475.3 | 5,461.7 | 16.1 |
| Industrial machinery | 98.3 | 211.0 | 257.5 | 325.0 | 826.9 | 127.1 | 350.3 | 1,160.0 | 325.0 | 3,681.1 | 10.8 |
| Mechanical engineering | 47.1 | 192.1 | 108.5 | 172.3 | 162.4 | 319.5 | 239.5 | 239.0 | 435.7 | 1,961.1 | 5.6 |
| Machine tools | 10.4 | 3.3 | 24.2 | 82.7 | 47.8 | 39.0 | 68.1 | 79.4 | 36.9 | 391.8 | 1.2 |
| Metallurgy | 31.4 | 123.7 | 34.8 | 92.0 | 363.0 | 428.6 | 5,14.0 | 432.3 | 2,189.3 | 4,209.1 | 12.4 |
| Textile | 116.7 | 22.3 | 19.9 | 86.2 | 317.3 | 24.7 | 12.4 | 84.2 | 14.4 | 698.1 | 2.1 |
| Transport | 35.1 | 69.4 | 131.2 | 72.0 | 144.8 | 131.0 | 106.8 | 116.5 | 79.0 | 905.8 | 2.7 |
| R&D/consultancy | — | 16.1 | 23.0 | 4.3 | 56.2 | — | 33.9 | 76.0 | 326.5 | 536.0 | 1.6 |
| Miscellaneous | 46.0 | 85.6 | 191.0 | 499.8 | 558.3 | 473.2 | 338.8 | 676.8 | 716.7 | 3,586.2 | 10.6 |
| Total | 565.1 | 1,411.4 | 1,551.1 | 3,003.3 | 4,505.3 | 5,882.3 | 4,182.6 | 5,838.7 | 6,986.9 | 55,656.7 | 100.0 |

*Source:* Ministry of Commerce, Government of India, 1993.

*Note:* One US $ = Indian Rupees 34.45 (as on February 29, 1996).

**TABLE 6.12:** Number of Foreign Collaborations

| Country | 1981 | 1982 | 1983 | 1984 | 1985 | 1986 | 1987 | 1988 | 1989 | Total | % |
|---|---|---|---|---|---|---|---|---|---|---|---|
| USA | 85 | 109 | 135 | 143 | 229 | 203 | 217 | 200 | 137 | 1,458 | 21.2 |
| FRG | 74 | 110 | 129 | 132 | 187 | 186 | 154 | 179 | 114 | 1,267 | 18.4 |
| UK | 80 | 105 | 119 | 123 | 149 | 134 | 130 | 142 | 78 | 1,060 | 15.4 |
| Japan | 27 | 51 | 58 | 78 | 111 | 111 | 82 | 98 | 63 | 679 | 9.9 |
| Italy | 18 | 37 | 30 | 37 | 59 | 58 | 54 | 59 | 42 | 394 | 5.7 |
| France | 23 | 28 | 40 | 38 | 63 | 40 | 43 | 46 | 25 | 346 | 5.0 |
| Switzerland | 26 | 41 | 47 | 30 | 43 | 32 | 32 | 45 | 25 | 321 | 4.7 |
| Sweden | 11 | 15 | 15 | 14 | 32 | 30 | 20 | 12 | 21 | 170 | 2.4 |
| Netherlands | 9 | 13 | 13 | 14 | 18 | 24 | 23 | 16 | 15 | 145 | 2.1 |
| Others | 36 | 79 | 87 | 131 | 150 | 140 | 148 | 160 | 119 | 1,050 | 15.2 |
| Total | 389 | 588 | 673 | 740 | 1,041 | 960 | 903 | 957 | 639 | 6,890 | 100.0 |

*Source:* Ministry of Commerce, Government of India, 1993.

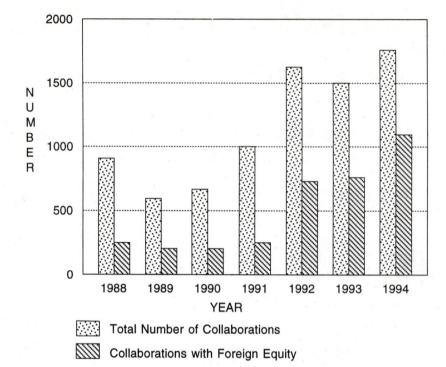

**FIG. 6.2:** Foreign Collaboration Approvals

*Source:* Directorate of Scientific and Industrial Research, 1995.

in India rather than to focus on exports. However, this is being done deliberately by the government to force Indian manufacturers to upgrade the quality of their products and meet competition.

## Research and Development (R&D)

The Government of India's policy resolution of 1958 laid emphasis on the development of infrastructure for research. It identified the following main areas—agriculture, atomic energy, space, science and technology (S&T), industrial research, and general S&T. All these were financed by the government and accounted for nearly 80 per cent of the total expenditure on S&T at that time. The major objective of the technology policy in India during the 1980s and earlier was on the development of indigenous technology and efficient absorption and adaptation of imported technology and included the diffusion of technology in use to all the beneficiaries. This involved horizontal

**TABLE 6.13:** Foreign Collaboration Approvals

(Sectorwise breakup of foreign direct investment approved
during August 1991 to November 1995)

| Sector | In Rs Million | Number of Approvals* |
|---|---|---|
| Telecommunications | 159,729 | 228 |
| Fuels (power and oil refinery) | 111,423 | 165 |
| Metallurgical industries | 40,967.0 | 306 |
| Chemicals (other than fertilizers) | 33,943.7 | 837 |
| Service sector | 31,044.4 | 267 |
| Transportation industry | 29,485.8 | 351 |
| Electrical equipment | 27,449.3 | 1,340 |
| Food processing industries | 22,987.9 | 419 |
| Hotels and tourism | 18,962.7 | 139 |
| Textiles | 15,083.6 | 284 |
| Miscellaneous industries | 70,947.7 | 3,242 |
| Total | 562,024.1 | 7,578 |

*Including both technical and finance.

*Source:* *The Economic Times,* 22 January, 1996.

*Note:* One US $ = Rs 34.45 (as on 29 February 1996).

**TABLE 6.14:** Foreign Collaborations/Automatic Approvals

| | Number of | | | | | In Rs Billion |
|---|---|---|---|---|---|---|
| | Foreign Collabora- tions | Automatic Appro- vals | Technical Collabora- tions A | With > 5% Royalty B | B as % of A | Total Lumpsum Payment |
| 1990 | 703 | — | 502 | 26 | 5.10 | 57.41 |
| 1991 | 976(634) | (188) | 678 | 171 | 25.22 | 97.98 |
| 1992 | 1,520 | 736 | 784 | 285 | 36.35 | 228.12 |
| 1993 | 1,476 | 676 | 714 | 166 | 23.24 | 369.00 |
| 1994 | 1,854 | 702 | 800 | 244 | 30.50 | 229.99 |
| 1995 | 915 | 340 | 425 | NA | NA | NA |

*Source:* *The Hindu,* 2 October, 1995.

*Note:* One US $ = Rs 34.45 (as on 29 February, 1996).

transfer of technology, technological support for ancillaries from
larger units, technological support to smaller units and upgradation
of traditional skills and capabilities. The emphasis was on self-reliance
and reduction in dependence on foreign inputs. The focus of the

technology development policy centered on giving encouragement to indigenous R&D, especially in applied research areas and commercialization of technology development in laboratories, giving certain incentives for investment in R&D by the industry.

In India there are three types of institutions and organizations contributing to science and technology development. They are:

♦ *Government Funded R&D Institutions*   The major R&D infrastructure in India consists of over 130 specialized laboratories and institutions set up under the aegis of the Indian Council of Agricultural Research (ICAR), the Council of Scientific and Industrial Research (CSIR), the Indian Council of Medical Research (ICMR), the Department of Atomic Energy (DAE), the Department of Science and Technology (DST), the Department of Environment (DOEN), the Department of Ocean Development (DOD) and the Defence Research and Development Organization (DRDO). In addition, various ministries have set up specialized research institutions which are of direct relevance to them.

♦ *Universities/Institutes of Higher Learning*   There are over 200 universities and institutes of higher learning in India. Though their primary role is concerned with education and training of students, many of them have undertaken research programmes. However, these institutions do suffer from inadequate resources and weak linkage with the industry.

♦ *In-house R&D in Industry*   A few scientific research institutions supported by industrial houses have also come up. The government too is providing several incentives and encouragement to industries to set up in-house R&D centres.

♦ *New Technology Policy*   With the liberalization of the economy, the technology policy was given a new thrust in 1993. The focus was on greater emphasis on infrastructural facilities and upgradation of human skills, including some of the traditional skills. The Policy Statement also emphasized the environmental aspects and use of safer technologies. The focus on human skills included upgrading and enlarging the base of vocational and technical institutions, improving the management of R&D institutions and also providing them with special incentives and greater freedom by reducing governmental control. The major thrust areas of technology were energy, water conservation, small-sector industries, mineral resources, agro-based industries, health services, transport, communication, petroleum products, software development, etc.

Recognizing the importance of innovative research, a far more prominent role for research, development and engineering (R&DE) was envisaged in the new policy. This included encouraging the association of R&DE laboratory systems for technology acquisition, absorption and upgradation. It also included special technological support to export-oriented sectors such as textiles, jewellery, leather, agro products, etc. The compound annual rate of GNP for the period 1988–92 was around 15 per cent, whereas the growth rate of R&D and S&T related expenditure was around 13 per cent. The government's share in R&D was to the extent of about 80 per cent while private sector contribution was only around 11 per cent in 1990–91.

**TABLE 6.15:** Expenditure on R&D and S&T Activities as Percentage of GNP

| Year | Percentage of GNP |
|---|---|
| 1970–71 | 0.44% |
| 1980–81 | 0.66% |
| 1985–86 | 0.96% |
| 1986–87 | 1.02% |
| 1987–88 | 1.06% |
| 1988–89 | 1.06% |
| 1989–90 | 1.03% |
| 1990–91 | 0.99% |
| 1991–92 | 0.99% |

Source:  *R&D in India*, Confederation of Indian Industry (CII) New Delhi, October 1993.

**TABLE 6.16:** Share of Central/State Sector and Private Sector in Total R&D

| Year | Total Central and State Sector (%) | Total Private Sector (%) |
|---|---|---|
| 1970–71 | 72.16 | 8.42 |
| 1980–81 | 78.64 | 14.83 |
| 1985–86 | 81.70 | 11.33 |
| 1990–91 | 79.29 | 11.40 |

Source: *R&D in India*, Confederation of Indian Industry (CII) New Delhi, October 1993.

In the 1993 policy statement, it was envisaged that expenditure on R&DE would reach 2 per cent of the GNP by AD 2000 against an expenditure of 0.9 per cent in 1993. It was also stipulated that to raise resources, the private sector R&DE contribution would be further encouraged by increasing incentives and other measures to stimulate contributions based on the industry turnover. Government-funded R&D institutions were to be encouraged to earn revenue by way of applied projects and their commercialization on a turn-key basis. Joint collaborations in R&DE projects between Indian enterprises/institutions and those from abroad were to be encouraged. To improve product quality, the systems and mechanisms for testing, standards inspection, etc. were to be further strengthened.

It is often alleged that many organizations do set up R&D centres, but this is done more with a view to avail tax incentives rather than make any substantive R&D contributions to technology. They find it more expedient to import the 'readymade' technology, sometimes repeatedly, without appropriate absorption, assimilation or upgradation on their own. The most often quoted example is of the Ambassador car manufactured by Hindustan Motors which continues to be produced with almost the same design and technology for over three decades. Appropriate monitoring of R&D investments and efforts remains largely ignored in India. The government's R&D expenditure has grown from Rs 11 million in 1948–49 to Rs 32,720 million in 1991–92, but it still has a long way to go before it can match the efforts of Malaysia and Singapore.

**TABLE 6.17:** R&D Expenditure by Industry (Total)

(in Million Rupees)

| | 1980–81 | 1989–90 | 1990–91 |
|---|---|---|---|
| Engineering | 1,057.4 | 3,897.8 | 4,671.0 |
| Fertilizers | 56.7 | 206.3 | 252.3 |
| Chemicals | | | |
| (other than fertilizers) | 225.5 | 827.1 | 729.6 |
| Drugs and pharmaceuticals | 196.3 | 633.8 | 768.1 |
| Textiles | 52.7 | 158.0 | 159.5 |
| (dyed, printed processed) | | | |

*Source:* *R&D in India,* Confederation of Indian Industry (CII) New Delhi, October 1993.

*Note:* One US $ = Indian Rupees 34.45 (as on 29 February, 1996).

**TABLE 6.18:** Industrial R&D Expenditure Classified by Leading Industry Groups, 1990–91

| Industry Group | Public Sector | | Private Sector | | Industrial Sector | |
|---|---|---|---|---|---|---|
| | No. of Units | R&D Exp. (Rs mill.) | No. of Units | R&D Exp. (Rs mill.) | No. of Units | R&D Exp. (Rs mill.) |
| Electronics and electrical equipments | 29 | 708.4 | 179 | 797.8 | 208 | 1,506.2 |
| Defence industries | 7 | 1,134.9 | — | — | 7 | 1,134.9 |
| Metallurgical industries | 26 | 712.4 | 66 | 224.4 | 92 | 936.9 |
| Drugs and pharmaceuticals | 8 | 66.1 | 100 | 701.9 | 108 | 768.0 |
| Transportation | 5 | 29.3 | 43 | 703.2 | 48 | 732.5 |
| Fuels | 10 | 707.8 | 10 | 22.7 | 20 | 730.5 |
| Chemicals (other than fertilizers) | 9 | 126.3 | 173 | 603.3 | 182 | 729.6 |
| Telecommunication | 16 | 471.9 | 40 | 69.3 | 56 | 541.2 |
| Industrial machinery | 9 | 12.7 | 82 | 405.1 | 91 | 417.9 |
| Fertilizers | 6 | 164.8 | 7 | 87.4 | 13 | 252.3 |
| Food processing industries | 1 | 0.8 | 32 | 219.2 | 33 | 220.0 |
| Rubber goods | 1 | 2.9 | 18 | 217.1 | 19 | 220.1 |
| Other goods | 28 | 302.1 | 233 | 1,074.8 | 261 | 1,377.2 |
| Total | 155 | 4,440.7 | 983 | 5,126.6 | 1,138 | 9,567.3 |

*Source:* Ministry of Commerce, Government of India, 1993.

*Note:* One US $ = Rs 34.45 (as on 29 February 1996).

In terms of sectorwise expenditure on R&D, electronic and electrical equipment was the major beneficiary. The defence sector has the largest government R&D investment. In the public sector, defence alone accounted for over 25 per cent of the total R&D expenditure.

## Human Resource Development (HRD)

India has a large base of qualified manpower with a number of technical and non-technical educational institutions. Unlike some of the other developing countries such as Thailand and Malaysia, India has a surplus of technically qualified persons which is the cause for unemployment even among engineers and other technical professionals. However, paradoxically, there is a shortage in certain specialized skills. Industries also complain that the technical institutions do not produce properly skilled and trained professionals to meet the challenges posed by the latest technology. This is possibly owing to the fact that while there is a reasonably good basic educational infrastructure, the efforts in terms of skill upgradation are not commensurate with new and emerging technologies.

The onus of skill upgradation is thus left to the enterprises with the government playing a marginal role in this process. The efforts on the part of the enterprises is also half hearted, with the result that in the event of any change in technology little effort is made to retrain personnel. Instead, the organization resorts to new recruitment, and owing to trade union pressures, they are unable to retrench the existing employees. Most organizations are, therefore, faced with this dual problem of surplus staffing on the one hand and shortages in certain skills on the other.

To overcome the problem of surplus staffing, organizations are clamouring for an Exit Policy so that they can retrench some employees as and when the situation demands. At present, there are restrictions on retrenchment and government approval is required under the Industrial Disputes Act. The government has created a National Renewal Fund with a view to retrain employees as well as compensate the retrenched workers under various schemes. However, the Fund has been mainly used for retrenchment compensation in the public sector. There is still no clear policy regarding skill upgradation, training and retraining.

With over 200 government-supported universities and 9,000 colleges, there exists a reasonably good educational infrastructure—both for technical and non-technical education in India. In addition, there are a number of private educational institutions. However, much of the education imparted is not job-oriented. The situation is further aggravated by a lack of proper equipment and trained instructors. The private sector industries, in recent years, have been spending a substantial part of their resources primarily on management training programmes. As a result, training of workers for skill upgradation remains a neglected area.

Owing to language and other cultural disparities, there are also constraints on the mobility of labour which prevents proper utilization of available skills in the country. The problem of skill shortage is further accentuated by the migration of skilled professionals to other countries. With the entry of MNCs, who are able to attract many of skilled and trained professionals by offering them higher compensation packages, the dearth of qualified skilled professionals among Indian companies has been further aggravated.

While transferring technology, there is a tendency, especially on the part of MNCs, to also transfer the management practices of the parent organizations. These are often alien to the Indian culture and ethos. For example, in India, exclusive reliance on merit devoid of seniority may not be acceptable since the employees prefer to seek a long-term career in their organizations. These problems of dissonance do result in low employee morale and poor industrial relations. In a country such as India one cannot transfer in to the managerial techniques of foreign companies and appropriate blending is found to be necessary. Similarly, the manning norms in India may have to be different, taking into account the lower base level qualifications of the labour, climatic conditions and blending of the old and new technologies.

## SUGGESTED MEASURES FOR INDIA

It may be argued that India cannot be compared to Malaysia, Singapore or Thailand owing to vast differences in terms of size, resources, culture, etc. However, the basic fact remains that these other countries have been able to bring in structural reforms in all the relevant sectors and have ushered in faster economic growth. These countries have also brought in major changes in their market structure to become globally competitive and export-oriented, which has given a tremendous boost to their economies. Export-oriented manufacturing, especially in Singapore and Malaysia, has enhanced their capabilities enabling them to compete in international markets. This is a pointer to the need for faster technological development to keep pace with global changes. India has taken steps in this direction almost two decades later. It could draw useful lessons from the experiences of its neighbours by suitably adopting and modifying some of their strategies in order to improve the effectiveness of its policies in key areas.

## Market Competition and Financial System

For boosting industrial growth and bringing in competitiveness, the veil of protection given to industries in some sectors should be removed so that they can be subjected to the rigours of market competition. Private sector growth is essentially dependent on the existence of an efficient financial sector. Many countries now realize that excessive government intervention in credit allocation has an unfavourable impact on both financial and industrial development. Countries such as Japan, Malaysia, etc. which have successfully reformed themselves were all market-oriented economies. Intervention of the government through the Central Bank in the financial system is a prominent feature of developing economies. This policy is defended on the grounds that it helps redressal of imbalances, divergence between private and social optimality, etc.

The money market and the banking system need to be restructured to meet the challenges offered by the new economic policy. The secondary market investment at times resulted in a buoyancy in the stock market index which does not truly reflect the performance of the industries. The primary market investment should be supported by the financial institutions and care should be taken that funds are not diverted to secondary market speculation. The taxation structure should also be reviewed to encourage primary market investment through proper incentives.

## Role of Multinational Corporations (MNCs)

To increase competitiveness and meet the quality requirements of the global market, it is necessary that the latest technology is available, even though it may have to be imported. Even to manufacture *swadeshi* (Indian-owned and produced) products there is always a high component of import content, the cost of which has to be met by exports. Many oppose the entry of MNCs into India on ideological grounds. The reason is partly the fear that MNCs will threaten the emergence of local industries/entrepreneurs. There is also the East India Company fear psychosis that MNCs may acquire a dominating political face and take over the country's economy. There is also the subtle opposition from existing enterprises in India which have all along enjoyed monopolistic markets under a regime of government controls and protection.

The experiences of countries such as Malaysia or Singapore indicate that they have not lost their sovereignty. On the contrary, there has been heavy external investment, emergence of new enterprises, generation of increased employment even a shot in the arm to internal and external competitive advantage and exports as many of the MNCs have brought in the latest technologies. What is possibly needed is to ensure that one or two MNCs alone do not monopolize the domestic market. One needs to also perhaps ensure that part of their products are meant for exports. Some linkages of MNCs with exports will also ensure that these companies bring in the latest technology to meet external competitiveness (as in the case of Malaysia), which can eventually improve the quality of goods not only for exports but also for the Indian consumers. At present there is an unfortunate trend where superior quality goods are shipped abroad and the inferior ones are sold in the domestic market. Indian consumers should also have access to quality products and this will eventually give a competitive advantage and boost exports. Some degree of protection to Indian industries could be maintained to ensure that the MNCs do not simply take over existing units but also invest in new ones, expand and diversify established units, in order to generate employment and contribute to the economic growth.

In one of the studies conducted by Associated Chambers of Commerce and Industry (Assocham) in India, it has been pointed out that a number of benefits could be derived from allowing MNCs in the country. The major benefit would be the transfer of the latest technology which they possess. It is the MNCs which control up to 85 per cent of the global patents and 33 to 53 per cent of the world trade is conducted among MNCs or their affiliates on an entry-firm basis. The study also pointed out that India lags far behind other countries, not only in terms of the number of foreign affiliates in the country, but also in the number of 'parent corporations' or local firms in India which have equity stakes in enterprises abroad.[3] The Assocham study indicates that in Singapore there are 10,709 foreign affiliates, in China 15,966 affiliates, while India has only 926 foreign affiliates (see Table 6.19).

**TABLE 6.19:** Multinational Operations

| Country | Parent Corporations* Based in Country | Foreign Affiliates Located in Country |
|---|---|---|
| Brazil | 566 | 7,110 |
| China | 379 | 15,966 |
| India | 187 | 926 |
| Republic of Korea | 1,049 | 3,671 |
| Hong Kong | 500 | 2,828 |
| Singapore | NA | 10,709 |
| Taiwan | NA | 5,733 |

*Local firms which have equity stake of 10–100% in enterprises abroad.

NA—Not Available.

*Source:* *India Today,* 31 January, 1996.

## Tariffs on Imports

Malaysia and Singapore manufacture and promote the high-tech and value addition type of production activities. This has resulted in a boom in the electrical and electronic industries which are basically · assembly-type operations with a high degree of value addition. These units are also primarily export-oriented units and the raw material/ components are mostly imported.

These industries have created massive employment opportunities. In order to support the industrial reconstruction strategy, government support continues in industrial rationalization in basic industries in India. The tariffs and tax incentives provided by the government should be able to protect the Indian market to a reasonable extent. The import of finished goods so far have attracted the least duties compared to the tariff on import of raw materials and components. However, the system of evaluating value-addition by manufacturing processes need to be strengthened. Manufacturing technology should be accorded high priority to bring in maximum gains through value addition. On the other hand, selective restrictions on raw material and import of components would enhance assembling, manufacturing and marketing skills.

## Banking System

The policies in Singapore, Malaysia and Thailand on foreign direct investment, banking and exchange control have been instrumental in accelerating their economic growth. Government financial institutions and nationalized banks have played a major role in their industrial development. In India, however, the state-controlled financial institutions, banks, etc. continue to exert a critical control over industrial investment and extension of financial credit. The post-liberalization euphoria and spurt in private sector investment received a serious setback during the stock exchange scam of 1994 when the banking sector funds were diverted to secondary markets with the intention of artificially fluctuating the stock market for making quick speculative profits. The monies raised through public issues for expansion, diversification, etc. were, as a result, adversely affected. Drawing lessons from the scam, future policies should ensure proper channelization of resources to production and employment-generation activities and not to secondary market investments as had happened during the scam. In this connection some of the suggestions given in the Narasimham Committee Report on reforms as mentioned earlier need to be implemented. There is also an urgent need to constitute proper machinery to implement and monitor the new liberalized financial systems. The Security Exchange Board of India (SEBI) and the Reserve Bank of India (RBI) will have to develop self-controlling mechanisms and guidelines for financial institutions and banks to ensure that the bulk of the finances are used for production and employment-generation activities.

## BOO, BOT, BOOT Strategies

Malaysia follows the build-operate-transfer (BOT); build-own-operate-transfer (BOOT); build-own-operate (BOO); strategies in high-priority industries and core sector areas such as power, roads, buildings, etc. The government makes the initial investment in these sectors requiring long gestation period and then hands over operations to the private sector. A similar strategy with substantial guidance, support and finance could perhaps be undertaken in India to give an impetus to the high-priority sectors and infrastructural development.

## Political Interference and Instability

Owing to lack of political stability in India, political parties often interfere and exercise an unnecessary influence on local investments in industry. As a result, long-term employment opportunities are often sacrificed for short-term gains. The terms and conditions as well as procedures for investment at the state level are largely influenced by political pressures. This has led to lopsided development in some states in terms of the type of industries that have been set up, their size and the infrastructure facilities available, depending upon the incentives for investment in each state. Ideally, the policies should benefit the nation as a whole instead of being designed to protect a few million employees or some vested interest groups.

## Clearance Procedures

The bureaucratic style of functioning was most apparent when it came to giving approvals for industrial licenses. The inherent delays in the earlier system were major deterrents to industrial growth in India. With some of the new measures, the Indian government has ventured to simplify clearance procedures. The policy responses to the changed economic scenario have resulted in the constitution of the Foreign Investment Promotion Board (FIPB), an automatic approval channel and a modified existing channel for industrial approvals.

India has a lot to learn from Malaysia which has completely restructured its science and technology administrative framework. The Ministry of Industry in India has a cell for technology transfer approvals. The approvals take two weeks and all clearances are centralized except in cases with specific requirements or clarifications. India could improve upon the system by introducing a real single-window system as it exists in Malaysia, where all clearances are given at the same time. In India, for obtaining any approval there are far too many levels through which the papers must move. There is an urgent need to reduce or eliminate some of these levels which would eventually mean a reduction in the size of the bureaucracy. Without this the structural reform process would have very little impact. There is also a need to streamline the internal handling procedures in order to hasten the movement of documents/papers and reduce delays. This also implies that the government will have to work out an exit policy for the bureaucracy at all levels. This will result in a reduction in government spending on non-developmental activities.

## Continuity of Policies

In order to attract investments in the industrial sector, the government may need to plan for protection against nationalization. Malaysia has entered into investment-guarantee agreements with several countries to protect foreign investors against nationalization and has also given assurances on equity ownership (that is, there is no restructuring of approved equity). Similarly, India could introduce some measures to create confidence among foreign investors by signing bilateral investment-guarantee agreements and allay their fears on future policy changes. Some moves in this direction have already been initiated.

## State-level Measures

Though the reform process has been initiated at the central government level, its percolation to the state level has been rather slow in some cases with the result that the impact of liberalization has not been fully felt by the entire industrial sector. It may be advisable to set up a committee to review the percolation of the reform process at the state levels and develop broad guidelines which the states could follow to hasten the process of liberalization and industrial growth.

## Modernization

Industrial growth has also been adversely affected by the hitherto short-range planning and policies. Many industries failed to adopt suitable measures for long-term growth. This is most apparent in the case of textile mills. The textile industry had enjoyed protection and the larger mills had a monopoly in the marketing of speciality products. Lack of timely modernization, diversification and innovation drastically affected the mills, resulting in the closure of some and consequent redundancies of labour. These mills failed to upgrade and revamp their facilities in order to enjoy the benefits of increased production, better quality products, etc. and face the competition offered by new entrants.

## Research and Development (R&D)

R&D investment is critical for sustained growth. India has done reasonably well in terms of basic R&D. However, the country needs to prioritize its requirements for applied research, especially in the manufacturing process technology and design engineering areas. Private sector investment in R&D so far has been minimal with short-term gains being the major consideration. The government had set up a Technology Development Fund in 1995 earmarking Rs 200 crore for it. It is expected that the fund will be used for encouraging research and updating technology. It is also stated that the disbursement of the Fund could be through commercial banks. In most cases it is found that these banks do not have the requisite expertise to assess the existing technology or to project future technology needs to meet competition. There is always the danger of the Technology Development Fund being used to finance the purchase of machinery and equipment and not necessarily to upgrade or bring in the latest technology. Therefore, it is important that an appropriate agency should carry out an industrywise/sectorwise need assessment of technology on the basis of which the Fund could be utilized.

The government has passed a Research and Development Cess (Amendment Bill) in 1995 under which the Technology Development Board has been created. This is an amendment to the R&D Cess Act of 1986, as it was found that though an R&D Cess was collected at the rate of 5 per cent of all payments in foreign exchange made towards import of technology, the objective of using the amount for promoting indigenous industrial R&D was not being properly met. This amount was to be credited into the Venture Capital Fund (VCF) of the Industrial Development Bank of India (IDBI) which in turn, was responsible for funding industrial R&D. However, the capital amount transferred to the IDBI was a small fraction of the amount collected. Even the amount collected was inadequate for really encouraging the indigenous R&D (see Table 6.20).

Subsequently, the Department of Science and Technology started operating the R&D Cess Fund and all applications for funding were expected to be processed through the Technology Development Board.

The coalition government in 1996 released a document 'Technology vision for India 2020', an action plan to transform India into a

**TABLE 6.20:** Collection and Utilization of Technology Development Fund

| Year | R&D Cess Collected at 5 % (Rs in Million) | Amount Credited to VCF of IDBI |
|------|------|------|
| 1988–89 | 163.2 | 8.84 |
| 1989–90 | 272.0 | 5.00 |
| 1990–91 | 301.2 | 1.00 |
| 1991–92 | 327.7 | 10.00 |
| 1992–93 | 448.9 | 3.00 |
| 1993–94 | 607.4 | NA |
| 1994–95 | 710.0 | NA |

VCF—R&D Venture Capital Fund; NA—Not Available.

*Source:* *The Economic Times*, 7 December 1995.

developed country by the year 2020. This document indicates what India can achieve, rather than what it will achieve. It has drawn contribution from 500 experts from 17 areas in various sectors of the economy. However, to translate this into reality, some hardcore planning is required with regard to the role of the government, private sectors and the MNCs in technology transfer and upgradation, in addition to the financial resources required for investments in R&D and other sectors of economy. In the absence of such concrete planning, there is always a danger of the vision remaining a paper exercise.

## Monitoring of Financial Resources

The revival of sick units was taken up by the government to help out the thousands of mill workers rendered jobless due to the closure of sick mills. The problem of siphoning off of critical financial resources meant to revive these units had further deteriorated the situation. The monitoring of the sick units needs to be further strengthened as the industries declared sick enjoy some incentives (mainly financial). It is often alleged that under the cloak of revival, vital financial resources are being diverted to secondary market investments, other ventures, etc. With reduced government control in the new climate of liberalization, industries will need to establish a definite code of ethics to ensure growth and development. The various chambers of commerce and trade and industries' associations have to play a major role in ensuring that unfair practices are discouraged. If this is not done there is always the chance of the government re-imposing controls and regulations.

## Labour Laws

In India, the labour laws are not very encouraging from the industy's point of view. The redressal/grievance handling procedures are cumbersome and result in delayed decisions. In view of the on-going liberalization programme, the labour legislation also needs to be reviewed. Here India could draw useful lessons from the industrial relations situation in Malaysia, Singapore and Thailand which is conducive and encourages investment in industry. In these countries the labour laws are such that the basic framework is laid down to ensure a fair deal to employees. Matters relating to promotion, transfer, dismissal, reinstatement and allocation of duties are excluded from the collective bargaining machinery.

## Exit Policy and National Renewal Fund

One aspect of structural reforms relates to the development of the exit policy for the industry. The term 'exit policy' is a bit of a misnomer. Most employers interpret it as having an unconditional right to hire and terminate employees if they find them surplus or not of use to the organization due to technological change or any other reason. However, the origin of the exit policy in India started with the right of the organization to close their unit in case they did not find it economically viable; just as they have the right to start a unit. This has an indirect implication for employees as their services have to be terminated. According to the existing law under the Industrial Disputes Act, any closure or termination requires the prior approval of the government. It is hoped that the exit policy will dispense with the approval provision.

In India, most sick units are not interested in closing down; instead they are more interested in obtaining funds for rehabilitation under the provisions of the Board for Industrial and Financial Reconstruction (BIFR) or some other similar plan. However, at the same time, they want to retain the right to terminate the services of their employees. Given the prevalent situation, such an unconditional right is not possible; it is not in existence in advanced countries. In most countries some legal protection is given to employees through appropriate rehabilitation plans or social security. In India a National Renewal Fund was set up by the government in 1992 to protect the interests of the workers affected by industrial restructuring.

However, it is still not clear how best this Fund can be used. The major portion of the Fund needs to be used for training and retraining of employees in the newer skills rather than merely provide compensation for voluntary retirement or retrenchment. For an exit policy to be effective, each organization needs to work out both its short-term and long-term strategies as well as their implications. Retraining and redeployment within the existing organization to meet the needs arising out of expansion or upgradation at the micro level, and estimating the emerging skills and organizing training for these cases at the macro level could be one strategy. Another strategy could be to encourage these displaced persons to set up ancillary units on a cooperative basis with proper incentives including training by the organizations and the government. For those who are untrainable, voluntary retirement schemes could be worked out with adequate compensation. In Malaysia and Singapore, Skill Development Funds have been created which are primarily used to subsidize retraining in courses that have been approved by the government through a tripartite forum comprising representatives from government, employers and the unions.

## Conclusions

There is no doubt that the liberalization process begun in 1991 has resulted in the faster growth of the economy as compared to earlier years. The GDP growth rate during 1994–95 was over 6 per cent. Similarly, per capita income in real terms was estimated at Rs 2,401 during 1994–95 as compared to 2,292 in the previous year, a rise of 8.5 per cent. Similarly, the gross domestic saving at current prices has also increased to around 24 per cent in 1995 as compared to 21 per cent during earlier years.[4] Industrial growth has also picked up to around 10 per cent.

On the external front, exports registered an increase of over 24 per cent in 1995. Imports increased by around 29 per cent. In spite of these increases, there are other areas which require acceleration in reform processes. Good monsoon and consequent increase in agricultural output was a major constituent of the increased GDP.

The share of industrial growth could have been greater. The fiscal deficit increased to 6.6 per cent of GDP in 1994–95. Privatization of the infrastructure is being delayed due to various administrative hassles. The value of the rupee against US dollar declined considerably in 1996. There was also a corresponding decline in foreign exchange reserves. In the financial markets also there have been price rigging scandals exposing regulatory defects in the capital markets. In the World Competitiveness Report for 1995 prepared by the World Economic Forum and International Institute of Management Development, India was ranked 34th among the 48 countries, in comparison to Singapore having the second rank, Malaysia 22nd rank, Thailand 27th rank.[5] Most of the countries also concentrated on reforming their civil services and the bureaucracy during the reform process. Not much importance has been given to civil service reform in India, which many claim continue to be an obstacle in the liberalization process. Foreign investors feel that the pace of liberalization was not as fast as many would like it to be. In fact, in many areas the reform process has slowed down. There is also a feeling that reforms have accentuated the disparities in income levels and that reforms are helping a tiny minority of Indians.[6]

The development policies in India have so far focused on growth, reduction of poverty, industrialization, etc. The initial motivation behind the structural adjustments stemmed from the problem of repayment of external debts and restoring balance of payments position. The trade, fiscal and monetary policies aimed at enhancing domestic production and stimulating exports. However, to maintain the tempo of growth, it is important for India to further accelerate the reform process at all levels.

# References

1. Malhotra, R.N., 'Economic Reforms: Retrospect and Prospects', Foundation Day lecture at ASCI, December, 1992.
2. *Business Today*, 6 January, 1996.
3. *India Today*, 31 January, 1996.
4. *The Economic Times*, 22 February, 1996.
5. *Business Today*, 7 October, 1995.
6. *Business Today*, 22 October, 1995.

*part three*

# **O**RGANIZATIONAL CASE STUDIES

The macro-level country cases given in Part Two were meant to provide a broad understanding of the policy initiatives that each of the four countries have taken to achieve accelerated development and growth. This part attempts to analyze the impact of the various policies, environmental constraints, the role of the government and the initiatives taken at the organizational level. Four organizations in India were selected and a detailed analysis of the different approaches to technology development adopted by them was made. These cases are presented in the following chapters.

All the selected four organizations belong to the high-technology sectors—two are in the public sector and two belong to the private sector. The selection was made in order to understand and compare the responsiveness of these organizations to technology development belonging to both the sectors. The case studies attempt to illustrate the importance and need for technology development strategies, team efforts, responsiveness to environmental changes and efforts made to prepare human resources for change. The four case studies highlight the successes and failures of strategies adopted for growth and development. To maintain confidentiality, the actual names of the organizations have been changed.

# 7

# PROCESS INDUSTRIES LTD

## INTRODUCTION

Process Industries Ltd (PIL) is one of the large chemical process industries in India in the public sector with a sales turnover of Rs 227.9 billion in 1993. In 1989, PIL was rated as one of the best performing chemical companies in the world. In 1991 it was placed among the top ten.

The major PIL products consisted of petrochemicals (plastics, synthetic rubber, synthetic fibre and industrial chemicals), advanced engineering plastics, catalysts, adsorbents, wire and cable compounds, corrosion consultancy and external training contracts. In 1994, it had around 30 plants spread over three locations employing over 11,000 staff. Its R&D facilities were manned by 72 full-time scientists. Most of these plants were set up with technology transfer agreements with some of the largest technical firms in the world. Till 1995, it had almost 30 technology transfer agreements—mainly from USA and Europe. In addition, PIL had joint venture agreements with leading MNCs in the areas of vaccines and advanced engineering plastics. It has also entered into a joint venture with large Indian companies for development of port facility. PIL is also in the process of setting up a joint venture in the Middle East and has an agreement to train technical personnel from one of the countries in the Middle East.

In the initial stages of establishment, as a matter of policy PIL bought the technology on a lumpsum payment basis without any equity participation with a view to subsequently develop the technology themselves. In most cases, the technology was bought as a package deal. No reverse engineering was undertaken, and the agreements had restrictive clauses with regard to technology upgradation. The period of agreements were for a long duration, ranging from six to 15 years. Before 1991, investment through equity participation of the foreign partner was discouraged except in very specialized sectors. However, after 1991, the situation changed and PIL entered into alliances based on 50 per cent equity participation. Recently the company has gone in for equity participation with appropriate transfer technology alliances with foreign companies.

The development of technical capability within PIL and also its past performance have been able to attract foreign investments which, in turn, have helped PIL obtain the latest technology from its counterparts. Most of the earlier technology transfer arrangements were packaged agreements where the licensors would set up only the production facilities and provide training in plant operations. The setting up of various plants was contracted out to engineering consultants by PIL. Training of personnel was confined to operational aspects and not to the process know-how. Therefore, the adaptation and setting-up skills have been missing. The documentation of various technology agreements has been weak; therefore, accessibility of available data for upgradation and improvements have been limited.

## NATURE OF THE LATEST JOINT VENTURE IN PIL

In its most recent alliance, PIL is attempting to bring in a totally new work culture and has tried to rectify some of the problems mentioned earlier. This new alliance was entered into on the premise that the very latest technology in advanced engineering plastics would be accessible to the Indian partner. The foreign partner, on its part, was able to enter the Indian market which had hitherto been a highly protected one. PIL has been in this field for a long time using different raw materials and technology. The new plant was set up with a totally separate identity and every facility was independent of the existing plants.

The Head of the Unit is one of the Directors of PIL and the head of manufacturing has been recruited on the basis of his earlier experience in similar technology. The head of manufacturing and the quality assurance manager along with the other key personnel were given extensive training at the foreign partner's plant. The training combined both plant operations as well as courses in general management, marketing, human resource development, etc. They were given access to the latest technology available with the foreign partner. The operations and quality departments in the new unit were encouraged to bring in process modifications, product improvements, etc. This has resulted in very major savings in terms of enhanced productivity, energy conservation, and product acceptability owing to the innovative practices introduced in the new plant.

The manning norms have been decided with an emphasis on on-the-job flexibility. There is a noticeable blending of Indian and foreign cultures to keep the manning levels to the absolute minimum. Personnel have been selected on the basis of their technical competence and innovative skills. There is a considerable amount of flexibility built into each job. For example, the entire plant personnel are referred to as a manufacturing team and all operators/technicians handle both operation and maintenance jobs. The concept of multi-skilling has been introduced. This culture is in total contrast to PIL's earlier work culture where operations and maintenance were treated as two distinct jobs. This alliance has provided the Indian partner with the latest technology, though there are some restrictions imposed on the market, inputs, etc.

The market for the products of the new plant is restricted to the Middle-East, Southeast Asia, India and the neighbouring countries. The present process adopted also requires that almost 80 per cent of the raw materials and components need to be imported from the foreign partner. This is owing to the nature of technology introduced which requires totally new grades of raw material inputs available only with the foreign partner. An R&D centre is being set up at a different location to undertake application research and is headed by an expatriate. This centre plans to take up various product applications research, raw material alternatives, etc.

The new venture has been set up with the intention of introducing a more informal work culture. Creativity and innovation are encouraged. The work practices take into consideration the cultural background and attitudes of employees towards the new working style and transplanting does not take place in isolation from these larger social conditions. A common uniform has been designed for all employees as is the practice in the foreign partner's plants. Indigenous managerial capability in the plant is also being promoted to achieve the desired performance standards.

This alliance has sought to overcome some of the technology-related problems by adopting more well-defined strategies. The level of absorption of technology has been quite high though it is too early yet to assess the actual extent of assimilation. There are no immediate plans for expansion as other possible markets are yet to be explored.

# FACTORS THAT HELP OR HINDER TECHNOLOGY ASSIMILATION

## Assessment of Technology

For any assimilation or transfer of technology, the recipient organization should have the capability to adequately assess the technology which they intend to import. This calls for proper assessment of technology gaps by developing an institutional mechanism and use of appropriate data bases. This also entails upgrading the skills of human resources who can analyze such information. In the initial stages, PIL did not possess sufficient technical competence to assess the technology being negotiated for. Over a period of time, PIL has gained sufficient experience in the area to enable it to bargain for the best available technology. The earlier agreements were biased towards the licensor. Many restrictive clauses had been incorporated which were not conducive to upgrade the technology.

## Internal Technology Development and Marketing Strategies

In PIL, the process of assimilation was not focused on product upgradation, nor were proper marketing strategies devised. PIL operated in a protected market and thus overlooked the need for forecasting technology development and suitable upgrading of skills. Now, with the opening up of the economy and entry of MNCs, PIL is under tremendous pressure to explore new markets.

## Negotiating for Technology Alliance

The choice, evaluation and negotiation mechanism are very crucial for any technology alliance. PIL's team for negotiating technology was based on expertise. However, at times, there were pressures from the government or the company's top management to select persons on expediency rather than expertise. There were also limitations imposed regarding the number of persons who could be sent abroad for negotiations. For instance, in a negotiation with a US-based licensor, the negotiating team faced major problems in obtaining clearances for their visit to the US. The government was willing to allow only two representatives and insisted on the Director being one of them. After a lot of follow-up, a three-member team was granted permission.

During the course of negotiations, the US company tried incorporating restrictive clauses in its agreement according to the American Anti-Trust Law (Section 302). It was the presence of the technical expert that helped avoid the inclusion of this clause. It was offered that PIL could obtain the technological know-how documents through another licensee of the American firm located in Asia. In earlier practices, PIL had scrupulously observed the restrictive clauses imposed by the licensor. It is worth noting that the constitution of the negotiation team and process are at times constrained by the rules and regulations in the public sector. The private sector, on the other hand, has the freedom to select the best possible teams based on their expertise with the result that they are able to take faster decisions and get better terms.

# ISSUES OF ASSIMILATION

Though PIL has been successful in developing and commercializing certain technologies, it has not been successful in marketing its technological know-how. It has been PIL's experience that the Indian market is biased towards foreign tie-ups for the brand name even though indigenous technology is available and is both proven and cheaper. Also, the company has not been aggressive in selling its technology.

## Incentives for Assimilation/Upgradation of Technology

In the earlier years, the emphasis was on getting readymade technology without real attention being given to internal assimilation and upgradation. In many cases due to the weak negotiating position, such upgradation was also restricted. Because of the monopoly enjoyed by PIL, there was little incentive to upgrade technology even after the expiry of the agreement and restriction period. It was only after 1991 that with increased competition the company started introducing CAD and CAM technologies for simpler controls and better document-ation and data retrieval systems. For any assimilation and upgradation of technology, the understanding of the process aspect of technology is important. However, in PIL, initially owing to the restrictive clauses and later due to lack of initiative, the transfer of technology and even the training given to the employees was confined to the operational level. Since R&D had a limited role in PIL, for any upgradation the company repeatedly went in for further technical collaboration, even though it meant paying high professional charges.

## INTERDEPARTMENTAL COORDINATION AND ROLE OF R&D

Another noticeable feature in PIL was that even after the transfer of technology, the interaction between R&D and operations was not intensive. There was a noticeable lack of coordination and a reluctance to share information and documentation. PIL had a technology department which acted as a coordinating agency between the R&D wing and the operations department. The role of the technology department included monitoring the production process, identifying areas for improvement and involving R&D in bringing in the necessary changes or modifications. The role of R&D was therefore restricted to some trouble-shooting, a few attempts at indigenization of certain raw materials, enhancing/optimizing consumption levels, etc. The role of the technology department could be made more intensive at the time of technology transfer and gradually the R&D department could play a greater role along with the operations in order to constantly improve and upgrade technology through closer monitoring. In future the technology and R&D departments could perhaps be merged so that the R&D does not operate in isolation and can also take up more applied research activities.

To some extent, R&D had made some significant contributions in terms of developing certain catalysts and process modifications. PIL is now able to offer certain advances and improvements in technology and also show greater potential for assimilation. The technical back-up and R&D inputs available within the organization have helped PIL in entering into alliances with larger firms.

## Human Resources

Another factor hindering the proper assimilation process is the evolution of the manning pattern in PIL. In a study, it was found that around 30 per cent of employees, both at the managerial and workmen level, were surplus and also a number of them had overlapping responsibilities. During the project implementation stage, proper caution was not observed in matching the persons and skills required. Further, identification of personnel and transfer decisions were delayed, leaving limited time for adequate preparation for the new job. The selection of persons sent for training, especially those sent abroad, was based on the seniority principle rather than competence or potential for utilizing the new expertise. For instance, one of the senior managers in the Personnel Department was sent abroad for training in advanced welding technology with the collaborators simply because he was the senior-most person and it was his turn on the basis of his seniority to undergo technical training. On his return, he was put back in the Personnel Department and within a year of his return he retired from service. The entire training effort was therefore a waste. While selecting people for handling new projects, the criteria applied does not necessarily include previous training and experience in a particular line. This is again partly due to the organizational culture that provides more people the opportunity to handle new projects and undergo training. There were many such instances which indicate that there is lack of proper career planning, training and placement policies in the organization.

Trade unions and the officers' associations hamper upgradation and technological change by putting up overt pressures. In case of technology change and minor process modification, the PIL trade unions do not allow redundancies to be declared. This indicates a lack of appropriate redeployment policy in the organization.

## CONCLUSIONS

Being a public sector company, PIL is at times dependent on the government for its various policies and strategies, including direct R&D funding. Its technology development strategy is also very much influenced by the corporate strategic plan, R&D budget, foreign technology developments and intellectual property policies. PIL has an excellent manufacturing base and a large, highly skilled and experienced manpower. Though the company has not consciously taken up technology development and upgradation activities, it has built up considerable expertise in operations. The existing core competency and vast investment need to be profitably managed to realize their full potential. The new joint venture has, to some extent, tried to overcome some of the existing restrictive practices. PIL has undertaken massive expansion projects in new locations as well as diversification projects. At the same time, changes in import tariffs have also considerably affected PIL's market share. All this calls for the consolidation of efforts to improve the efficiency of the projects to meet competition. The overheads, manpower, utilities, etc. need to be reduced to improve the margins and cost effectiveness of the products to meet new challenges and competition.

# 8

# XYZ (ELECTRONICS) LTD

## INTRODUCTION

XYZ Ltd was established in 1967 in order to develop indigenous know-how and manufacturing capability in electronics, primarily to meet the requirements of strategically important areas such as defence. Its primary objective was to develop indigenous technology for the manufacture of control systems for power plants and space centres. Since the scientists also came from power and space establishments initially, XYZ Ltd was put under the overall charge of the Ministry of Energy. As a policy, it was envisaged that the country would need an increasing number of power plants. Therefore, there would be a continuous need for control systems in the plants. XYZ Ltd was expected to meet indigenous requirements and reduce its reliance on imported components and control instruments.

The initial aim of the organization was to be self-reliant and hence any foreign collaboration was discouraged. Accordingly, indigenous new product development was considered to be the main mission with R&D playing an important role. Considerable freedom was given to new product development as long as it led to import substitution. Commercial viability was not given due importance and the functional areas of marketing, finance, costing, etc. were also neglected. Thus, while one did see new products, their development became an end in itself.

During 1970–76, XYZ Ltd was able to develop 250 products, some of them new and sophisticated. All these products were developed as independent projects without any cohesive organizational focus or examining their commercial viability. In many cases the costs of products developed was high as compared to other international competitors and in some cases the reliability was also poor. The result was that XYZ Ltd ended up making losses by the late 1970s as can be seen from Table 8.1.

**TABLE 8.1:** Highlights of Corporations Performance Since Inception

(Rs in Million)

| Year | Net Sales | R&D | Net Profit Before Tax | No. of Employees |
|---|---|---|---|---|
| 1967–68 | 0.8 | 0.2 | 2.5 | 928 |
| 1968–69 | 2.7 | 0.8 | 3.5 | 1,278 |
| 1969–70 | 7.0 | 1.4 | 1.5 | 1,396 |
| 1970–71 | 16.6 | 0.9 | 1.3 | 1,618 |
| 1971–72 | 28.4 | 0.6 | 6.8 | 2,403 |
| 1972–73 | 49.3 | 1.1 | 11.3 | 3,350 |
| 1973–74 | 98.6 | 4.6 | 15.1 | 4,196 |
| 1974–75 | 162.6 | 11.4 | 15.8 | 4,912 |
| 1975–76 | 225.7 | 8.4 | 17.4 | 5,538 |
| 1976–77 | 243.3 | 11.9 | 13.7 | 5,884 |
| 1977–78 | 259.7 | 12.0 | 10.5 | 6,088 |
| 1978–79 | 306.9 | 11.2 | 14.5 | 6,437 |
| 1979–80 | 354.0 | 8.8 | 1.1 | 6,617 |
| 1980–81 | 305.4 | 10.4 | 35.8 | 6,755 |
| 1981–82 | 504.5 | 10.2 | 16.2 | 6,975 |
| 1982–83 | 582.5 | 8.7 | 21.3 | 7,178 |
| 1983–84 | 662.7 | 14.9 | 25.1 | 7,498 |
| 1984–85 | 733.9 | 19.1 | 24.0 | 7,484 |
| 1985–86 | 1,114.1 | 18.2 | 99.4 | 7,535 |
| 1986–87 | 1,458.9 | 24.6 | 107.9 | 7,651 |
| 1987–88 | 1,588.9 | 29.6 | 97.6 | 7,774 |
| 1988–89 | 1,878.8 | 22.3 | 31.8 | 7,863 |
| 1989–90 | 2,729.0 | 31.4 | 39.2 | 7,879 |
| 1990–91 | 2,333.0 | 33.5 | 103.7 | 7,892 |
| 1991–92 | 2,071.4 | 41.8 | 275.8 | 7,768 |
| 1992–93 | 2,860.7 | 55.9 | 105.0 | 7,653 |
| 1993–94 | 3,289.4 | 63.3 | 694.0 | 7,395 |
| 1994–95 | 3,871.9 | 70.0 | 410.0 | 7,328 |

There was a change in the top management in the late 1970s and early 1980s. The focus shifted from the earlier policy of total self-reliance to foreign collaboration in selected areas, especially in areas where quick customer response was needed. It was felt that with foreign collaboration, the technological base of the company could be strengthened. The earlier policy of unrestricted freedom to develop new products was also curtailed in that any new products now must have commercial viability. R&D efforts were also centred around three major areas, namely computers and communication, control systems and home electronics. The company also entered the computer market, both in mainframe and micro computers. All these policies did show immediate benefits, with XYZ Ltd making a profit of Rs 2.3 million in 1979–80. Sales also increased from Rs 282 million in 1977–78 to Rs 390 million in 1979–80.

A repercussion of the new policy was that the R&D professionals felt demoralized because of curbs on their freedom and the perception of reduced importance of R&D. This resulted in a heavy turnover of technical personnel in the early 1980s and the emergence of new competitors. Some of the divisions such as television and computers, had lost their pre-eminent positions. In spite of its efforts the company could not bring in any real marketing orientation or a conducive research atmosphere. Hardly any new products with substantive commercial viability were released in the market through their own R&D efforts after 1978 till the mid-1980s.

## Organizational Structure

In the early 1980s XYZ Ltd made an effort to reorganize itself into business groups. The company was divided into seven business groups in addition to the service groups. Each group was treated as a profit centre with its own set of officers and workers. Each group was responsible for developing its business, its own R&D, product range and even the marketing of its products. Mobility between groups was also limited and was normally discouraged. Rigidity in group-based working was partly explained by the fact that each group required its own specialization and expertise, especially in technical skills, and therefore, mobility was not desirable in certain areas.

At the corporate level, certain services were common, such as personnel, finance and accounts. Even though there was a separate central marketing and R&D division, the role of marketing was largely for gathering business intelligence rather than entering specific market segments and building them. This role was left to the individual business groups themselves. Similarly, the centralized R&D too had a limited role which was more in the nature of trouble-shooting. The total number of personnel in R&D were around 30 in 1996, which is insufficient to conduct meaningful research in all the activities of the groups. The central R&D had again no role to play during negotiations for any major technology transfer/ collaboration.

The structuring of XYZ Ltd into groups had its own merits and demerits. The advantage was that each group become a profit centre and could give exclusive focus to its limited activities in a coordinated manner as they were fully responsible from R&D and manufacturing to marketing. However, the disadvantage, as observed in XYZ Ltd, was that they had a short-term focus with the objective of ensuring immediate viability. Although each group had some design capability, they were unable to foresee new technology or process for the future as they too were involved in their day-to-day work, rather than concentrating on futuristic development. XYZ Ltd had a Corporate Marketing Division but this was treated more as a staff activity primarily handling Public Relations (PR) aspects. Subsequently, they were also involved in export activity. The relationship between corporate marketing and groups was not very clear.

## Dynamics of a Public Sector Undertaking (PSU)

Most PSUs find themselves working under tremendous constraints, with the result they are unable to be proactive in a competitive environment. For example, XYZ Ltd could not obtain clearance from the government for the purchase of a particular component, 'Rapiscan', for more than 18 months. Another classic example of bureaucratic delays was that of the proposal of the Mainframe Computer Division to manufacture mainframe computers with foreign technical collaboration under the aegis of the government. The idea was conceived in 1979, wherein XYZ Ltd was identified as the agency to import and develop technology. Based on the proposal prepared by XYZ Ltd the Department of Electronics formed a Committee in 1982 to draft the technology specifications of the project which was to be treated as a national project. At that time, it was estimated that there was a market for 400 mainframe computers.

Subsequently, on the basis of the Committee's recommendations, global tenders were called for in 1983 in accordance with government rules. After the receipt of tenders, the actual evaluation and finalization was delayed up to the end of 1985. In 1985, an American company was identified as the technology source by the Committee of Parliamentary Affairs and XYZ Ltd was asked to carry out further negotiations. In the meantime, a ban was imposed on the export of this technology from the USA till the end of 1986. Initially, 20 technical personnel were sent to the USA for training on products and specifications. After the ban was lifted, the EXIM Bank took one year (till 1987 end) to give the loan clearance. The Secretariat for Industrial Approval (SIA) took another year to give their approval for the project.

It was only in 1989 that all the clearances were obtained. By this time the technology had become obsolete. Moreover, the same technology was available internationally at one-tenth the original cost estimate. In the meantime the company had started the manufacture of the estimated 400 pieces. XYZ Ltd was able to sell only 28 machines. With rapid change in technology, there was no further demand for mainframe computers and the manufacturing activity had to be stopped. However, the department and employees had to be retained at heavy cost as the maintenance and support service wing. This amply illustrates how a bureaucratic system was unresponsive to competitive environment and technological changes resulting in erroneous and delayed decisions and losses.

There is another example of a major project which did not take off owing to delays, inappropriate technology and poor negotiations resulting in loss to the company. XYZ Ltd was approached by a government transport company for an 'automatic technical protection system'. The proposal was initially discussed with technical experts from the government transport company, the R&D personnel of XYZ Ltd, members of the Department of Electronics (DOE) and some academicians. They estimated a project cost of Rs 0.38 billion and an advance of Rs 0.15 billion was paid to XYZ Ltd. However, the procedures took two years to be completed. Subsequently, XYZ Ltd supplied a prototype to the transport company which was rejected on technical grounds and the order was cancelled.

The project lay dormant for six years. The DOE requested the government transport company to import the system through a global tender and also involve XYZ Ltd to help in evaluating the technology and also its subsequent transfer to India. Two companies submitted their proposals/bids—one American and the other British. Though the technical personnel from the transport company preferred the British company, the DOE preferred the American company because it proposed the use of futuristic digital technology. All these negotiations took another five years. The American company then asked for a 40 per cent hike in the cost of the project, which after initial hesitation, was accepted.

For technology transfer, XYZ Ltd paid Rs 8.6 million as the first instalment. In the meantime, the American Company increased the cost of technology transfer by a further 20 per cent which XYZ Ltd refused to accept. Subsequently, the American company reduced the items of technology transferred to XYZ Ltd at the original negotiated cost. This was again found unacceptable by XYZ Ltd since they felt that manufacturing the system would be difficult without all the components.

This lead to another technical evaluation of the entire project by the DOE and the government transport company. It was now felt that there was really no necessity of installing the 'automatic technical protection system' as they did not foresee much traffic in the transport system in the near future. This was in total contradiction of the initial forecast on which the whole project was conceived and negotiated upon. Based on the latest assessment, XYZ Ltd was asked to drop the entire technology transfer project. The American Company claimed damages and threatened a legal suit. In order to recover the first instalment of Rs 8.6 million XYZ Ltd used the plea of the American company increasing the price twice over. After prolonged negotiations, XYZ Ltd managed to retrieve the Rs 8.6 million without interest.

This case highlights incorrect forecasting of market demand and need for technology, poor assessment of appropriate technology, procedural delays and weak negotiation, resulting in a major waste of resources.

## Technology Development

The company has been adopting different approaches in the area of technology development, partly because of its own initiative and partly because of government pressure and also because of its ideological bias towards import substitution. In certain areas, XYZ Ltd has been acquiring technology from the Council for Scientific and Industrial Research (CSIR), National Chemical Laboratory (NCL), and Bhabha Atomic Research Centre (BARC) laboratories, which according to the perception of many officers was not commercially proven technology and was also expensive. There were certain delays in production for commercial purposes in the transfer of such technology as compared to foreign technology from the existing manufacturing set-up.

The second approach subsequently adopted by XYZ Ltd in technology development was value addition. In some areas, such as in the control system group, the business was developed jointly either with foreign partners or even Indian partners whereby part of the product was supplied by the partner and XYZ Ltd contributed to value addition. Normally, the approach in such cases was that the customer was first identified and then the process for selection of partners begun. This was sometimes based on the preferences given by customers themselves and others where the government itself specifies the joint venture/working partner. On some occasions XYZ Ltd itself tried to find out the best available collaborating partners and then, after preliminary negotiations with the customer, worked out the detailed arrangements.

The negotiation team normally consisted of the project manager and his team and the finance representative. At times, the marketing representative was also involved. However, as mentioned earlier, the central R&D was never involved in the negotiation process. While the teams were usually competent, the major accent was on somehow getting the projects without giving due consideration to the cost and marketing aspects.

## Research and Development (R&D)

As the groups were not able to concentrate on futuristic R&D, a separate corporate R&D wing was set up. It was to focus on process development and provide training. Its primary objectives were:

- ❑ To build competence
- ❑ To examine emerging technology/future scenario
- ❑ To support other groups in problem solving

The company started with a small number of professionals and plan to increase this number gradually. The R&D wing has been concentrating on instrument-related products/process, software, etc.

Since each group was also responsible for its own R&D, there was a certain lack of clarity with regard to the role of R&D vis-à-vis the business groups. The groups normally depend upon the help of the corporate R&D, which also technically evaluates proposals before the management takes a decision.

Though the company had an R&D base, it did not have an appropriate technology development strategy. The corporate R&D wing was expected to coordinate activities of the different divisions while at the same time each division was considered to be independent with their own R&D expertise and facilities. The corporate R&D was perceived more as a control mechanism in terms of seeking approval for projects costing more than Rs 0.5 million. There was no linkage between corporate R&D and divisional R&D in terms of designing or implementing the project. Similarly, there was ambiguity about the roles of marketing and R&D. It was perceived that marketing does not play a substantive role in identifying customers. Apart from developing technology, the R&D was also compelled to find its own customers. The following example illustrates this anamoly.

The R&D division of XYZ Ltd developed a networking system to indicate the price indices of state-level commodities and was to be controlled from the state capital. This system, which was proposed to be installed at 200 locations, was duly approved by the state government. Later, the marketing department cancelled the order on the plea that the system was not suitable for local market needs. The entire project was suddenly dropped in spite of the fact that the related technology capability had been developed and could have been sold to other states.

XYZ Ltd had developed core competencies in some areas of electronics, and had pioneered the development of consumer electronic products. Initially, they enjoyed full government support and protection which enabled them to develop their own technology and establish themselves as leaders in this product category all over the country. However, later, with the entry of competition and the necessity to import some components for upgradation, the company lost its competitive advantage. The ideology of self-reliance adopted by XYZ Ltd prevented it from importing any technology or components for upgradation, unlike its competitors. The company was also slow in developing a competitive marketing strategy owing to the market protection offered by the government. The situation reached a stage whereby XYZ Ltd was contemplating the closure of the entire division.

The company thus lost the opportunity of developing core competency in this emerging area.

Wherever the company has been able to develop core competency and pursued it, it was successful in assimilating, transferring and marketing the technology. A typical example is of an electronic security system which it developed where it had some technical competence. The company initially imported the technology, giving up its qualms regarding self-reliance. It was able to modify the technology to suit customer specifications and successfully market the product. However, it was not able to fully harness and develop the core competency in the same product because of the slow response and bureaucratic bottlenecks typical of a public enterprise. To some extent, the company had also been able to transfer and export technology in its other core competencies to some developing countries such as Saudi Arabia and Uganda as well as to some state-level enterprises within the country. However, export or sale of technology was not strongly pursued as a business strategy.

The company was allotted the maintenance contract for the system imported by the government and gradually able to negotiate the transfer of know-how in a phased manner. The company started with importing around 80 per cent of the components which were indigenized to the extent of 50 per cent. Meanwhile, the transferors of technology asked for 50 per cent equity participation. The decision remained pending with the Cabinet for a number of years. The company had built up technical competence but was unable to meet the competition due to higher costs, poor marketing strategies and time over-runs. With increasing pressure to minimize losses and become profitable, the company took up short-term profitable peripheral ventures (such as preparing laminated identification cards) which were completely unrelated to its core competencies.

## Human Resource Development

For any high technology based organization, the constant development of human resources is crucial. XYZ Ltd had an abundance of highly qualified workforce at all levels. But in the absence of a long-term human resource strategy, it could not take full advantage of its skilled workforce. The company did impart training, but this was done on a piecemeal project-to-project basis. When any project was abandoned or modified, the personnel continued to remain with their original competencies, and the company made no serious effort to retrain them. Moreover, the reorganization of the company into groups inhibited the movement of personnel from one group to another which resulted in surplus staff in some groups and shortages in others. The company did not have any formal training centre of its own. Subsequently, in 1996, it was contemplating establishing a full-fledged training centre at an estimated cost of around Rs 0.5 billion as a long-term HRD strategy.

The training and redeployment efforts of the company had met with strong resistance from workmen as well as officers because they feared loss of seniority. There was an exodus of highly skilled and qualified people. Some of them had even set up their own enterprises in the field of electronics and become competitors of XYZ Ltd. There was also a widespread belief in the company that a number of employees had maintained parallel businesses while remaining in the organization. They preferred the status quo and resisted further training or redeployment so that they had ample time for their own private business. The situation was the result partly also because of the government's policy of not retrenching surplus employees.

## CONCLUSIONS

This case highlights the fact that though the organization may have technical capability, there are still no proper strategies for technology transfer, forecasting, assimilation and development. With no market forecasting and appropriate human resource strategies, the company cannot survive for long. The case is a pointer to what can happen if an organization does not quickly respond to a changing environment. If the company has to develop an edge in a competitive environment, then most of the government procedures and bureaucratic delays will have to be removed to enable long-term growth and profitability This indicates the need for organizational autonomy in public enterprises.

# 9

# ABC (INFORMATION) COMPANY

## INTRODUCTION

The ABC Company is a diversified integrated private sector corporation dealing with information technology, consumer products, health care, systems engineering, lighting, financial services, etc. The information technology division of the ABC Company is its largest wing with a total sales turnover of about Rs 3,000 million (total sales turnover of the company was Rs 6,000 million) and a profit of Rs 80 million in the year 1993–94. The information technology division is divided into two wings—one dealing with computers and the other with systems. The technology division is considered to be one of the fastest growing software companies in India including exports to the tune of Rs 340 million in 1993–94. The company offers the widest range of products in this line.

The company's strategy has been to invest in R&D apart from entering into alliances with global leaders and technology providers, such as AT&T, Tandem, Sun Micro systems, Intel, etc. It ventured into the field of information technology in the early 1980s and gradually expanded its operations from services to technology and products.

It started with the import of hardware and software from two separate large MNCs for the assimilation and upgradation of these technologies. It then progressed from adopting industry standards to implementation of sophisticated networking systems.

The ABC Company has positioned itself as a mediator between the various technology providers and technology packagers. It customizes or modifies the technology to suit the requirements of its customers or end-users and also provided the necessary support services. For example, it imported around 50 per cent of the hardware components and now manufactures the end product by integrating the system with suitable user packages.

## Technology Alliances

The ABC Company has entered into different types of arrangements to suit its diverse business needs, such as forming alliances for marketing and technical know-how, providing qualified design engineers and subsequently an equity partnership with a MNC to promote and sell its products. The marketing alliances were entered for the benefits of distribution and economies of scale. The exchange of qualified personnel was in terms of the training and experience-sharing of the latest technological developments in the organizations run by technology providers. This kind of arrangement began on a project-tied basis to establish an initial business relationship, which eventually resulted in the development of mutual trust and further collaboration. For example, in one such arrangement, the company was able to negotiate for the import of tools and basic technology for substantial value addition in its local unit. There has been a considerable build-up of the knowledge and skill base as a result of this exchange. The engineers trained in specific areas abroad return to the organization and, in turn, train specific groups in the usage of systems, packages, etc.

## Human Resource Development

The ABC Company employs around 1,700 employees, 80 per cent of whom are qualified technical personnel. The organization professes to give utmost importance to HRD and constant skill upgradation. It has developed a well-integrated system of internal and external training through both the annual performance appraisal report as well as the assessment done by an external agency employed specifically for this purpose. The organization claims that because of its emphasis on HRD, the turnover of its employees is around 12 per cent as compared to the industry average of 18 to 20 per cent. It believes in internal growth and career planning of its personnel. Even in the case of new projects in diversified areas, the first priority is given to the placement of existing employees with appropriate training rather than through external recruitment. This also contributes to a lower turnover of employees in the organization.

The organization believes that the technology cannot only be purchased but can also be brought and assimilated by the personnel who are sent abroad for training. These foreign-trained personnel, in turn, also bring in the expertize to develop similar technology indigenously. The organization has a well-developed system of job rotation in keeping with the interests, aptitudes and career planning needs of its employees. Personnel with even four to five years' experience are also sent on projects abroad to provide them with opportunities for outside exposure.

## R&D

In the ABC Company, R&D is considered an important ingredient in the process of technology absorption. The total expenditure on R&D during the year 1993–94 was about Rs 65 million which was around 2 per cent of the total sales turnover. This increased to Rs 140 million in 1994–95 constituting more than 3 per cent of the sales turnover. The ABC Company's R&D investment ranked among the top 50 R&D investments in India, which focused on frontier areas of technology. This has enabled the company to build a creditable skill and knowledge base which, in turn, facilitated its entering into strategic alliances with large MNCs. Its R&D had the inherent strength and capability for developing micro and mini computers incorporating the latest technology. As a result, the company was able to design and launch several new products, some especially designed for international markets. It gave R&D equal importance in relation to other departments. The member of R&D professionals in the company was around 450 in 1994–95 as compared to 300 in 1993–94. They work in close collaboration with the marketing division and are also intensively involved right from the inception stage of negotiations with clients and partners in technology.

The information technology industry faced intense competition and technological obsolescence owing to rapid and phenomenal changes. To keep pace with the changes, the ABC Company has been importing technology for value addition and sale with not much accent on technology assimilation.

# FACTORS THAT HELP/HINDER TECHNOLOGY ASSIMILATION

## Assessment of Technology

The ABC Company follows a systematic procedure for continuous assessment and upgradation of technology keeping in mind its market potential. The company has been investing in upgrading human skills through research and training in the frontier areas of technological development. Because of the constant upgradation and investment in R&D, the company is in a better position to assess the global competitiveness of technology and approach the technology developers.

## Internal Technology Development and Marketing Strategies

The ABC Company operates in a highly competitive market environment which has necessitated the adoption of aggressive and innovative strategies to retain and expand the market. There is constant upgrading of technology and product features to suit customer needs and specifications with the back-up of support services to enhance the marketability of its products.

## Negotiating for Technology

The ABC Company builds the team for negotiations for alliances with persons having the best expertize. Competence, experience and position are not the only criteria for selection. The process of negotiation for any tie-up or alliance with another organization is initiated gradually after building rapport and creating goodwill. For example, the ABC Company first provided only design experts to a US-based company to help them in design and programming. Over a period of two years, after establishing a definite level of confidence and a positive working relationship, the ABC Company approached the organization for an alliance to operate from India.

## Issues in Assimilation

The nature of technology and products dealt with by the ABC Company require a high level of assimilation and upgradation of technology. The products and processes are imported with the intention of marketing them after suitable value addition and customization. This, in itself, has been an incentive for constant upgradation of technology. Access to technology has been through training in organizations abroad and continuous involvement of R&D in all areas of business activity for gaining better terms and conditions for technology transfer.

## Role of R&D and Interdepartmental Coordination

One noticeable feature is the role of R&D in the mainstream activity of the company and its involvement in all the major activities including negotiations. Marketing and R&D are treated at par and work in very close coordination. R&D is actively involved in technology development and applications research to improve product lines and features.

## Marketing of Technology Capability

The ABC Company has established a reputation for trustworthiness and quality in global R&D and marketing capabilities. The technology, products and systems such as the UNIX operating system developed by the company have been accepted in the international and domestic markets.

## Human Resource Related Issues

The ABC Company believes in proper training and development of personnel. However, its high turnover remains a major problem which, although lower than the industry average, does present certain constraints. Career planning and growth paths are reviewed periodically to overcome problems in succession planning. There is a systematic training need identification process to help individuals in the organization upgrade their skills. The selection process for initial recruitment tried to maintain a balance between experience and newly acquired skills. With the opening up of the economy and the entry of MNCs into the market and the consequent shortage of skills, the compensation packages are very high to attract the best available talent. This has added to the overall manpower costs considerably.

## Manufacturing Activities

The country's economic liberalization and changes in customs and import duties has drastically affected the manufacturing operations in the information technology industry. The ABC Company has had to substantially reduce its own basic manufacturing activity since importing the bulk of the components had become simpler and cheaper. The company naturally decided to take advantage of the economies of scale afforded by larger manufacturers. This has affected technology assimilation to some extent.

## CONCLUSIONS

ABC Company has been able to retain its entity since most of its collaborations have been through licensing agreements with royalty payments requiring no equity participation. There have been, however, certain restrictive clauses in these arrangements relating to the entry of the ABC Company into certain markets. Recently, owing to severe national and international competition, the company did enter into equity partnership with a large MNC to promote their products, especially in India.

R&D plays a major role in the ABC Company and 45 per cent of its business is stated to be R&D driven. About 10 per cent of the company's R&D is being financed through government contracts, while the balance is financed by the company itself.

The ABC Company has evolved strategies for technology development with a span of two to three years. Interestingly, the organization does not perceive the government as having any major influence on their internal technology strategy except in areas such as export, R&D-related funding by the government and technology-oriented procurement policies. The major factor affecting the strategy is the import tax for tools and equipment. On the whole, the ABC Company does not foresee a major role of the government in developing their human resources. They acknowledge a marginal role in the areas of educational policy related to technical and managerial education, including funding by government in training of scientific personnel. The government policies about redeployment and retraining can also affect them.

The ABC Company gives importance to employee training and had spent Rs 350 million, i.e. around 1 per cent of the sales turnover, on employee development in 1994. Around 40 persons were engaged in the training function. 70 per cent of the training budget was spent on technical and equipment-specific training. Approximately 5 per cent of the staff underwent training with various collaborators. There is no employees' union in the organization, nor have there been any redundancies as a consequence of technological changes. The company has been able to absorb the displaced employees through internal retraining.

The ABC Company has developed its strengths through major R&D efforts and by trying to retain its independent status. The investment in R&D and training has helped in consolidating its technology base and sustaining its market share to a large extent.

# 10

# COMPUTER COMPANY LTD

## INTRODUCTION

Computer Company Limited (CCL) is a joint venture company between a large industrial house in India and a private limited company in a Southeast Asian country. The major activities of CCL have been in the design, development and marketing of software for projects. The company also has a sales and service tie-up for one of the products of a leading foreign company based in a fast developing country in Southeast Asia. CCL is also diversifying into corporate training and education services in information technology.

The company employed around 215 persons in 1995, 85 per cent of whom were technically qualified. It operates through marketing zonal offices in major cities in India and area offices in other big towns. The company has an extensive R&D set-up employing 86 professionals specializing in design and development. The company has indigenously developed certain systems and greatly enhanced the value of imported systems. The value addition in the company for all imported systems is to the extent of 30 to 40 per cent. The company operates primarily on large projects. The project team consists of experts from marketing, finance, R&D and technical departments right from the negotiation stage.

## R&D

CCL has a strong R&D base and spent around Rs 0.65 million in the year 1993–94 which represented 5.4 per cent of its total revenue. R&D plays a prominent role in the development of customized solutions and software for its clients. It was also involved in developing other products and enhancing utilities of the available systems and packages. In order to upgrade its skills and sustain earnings, the company's R&D personnel were sent on a contractual basis to R&D laboratories abroad, on offshore projects, etc. This has helped them build competencies in handling technical projects. The company's R&D efforts are also channelled towards frontier areas of technology development, such as multimedia to keep pace with the changing technology.

## Human Resource Development

The company recruits highly qualified professionals and has an internal system of training through job rotation and specialized training. The career progression is based on a two-path system, that is, one can either advance through the managerial/administrative channel or as a specialist. Employees are regularly sponsored for training within India and abroad. In spite of the company's efforts to retain trained persons, the employee turnover is high, ranging around 20–25 per cent which also happens to be the average turnover rate in the industry.

As a result of the high turnover, the company is constantly engaged in recruitment of personnel and the planned HRD aspects get less attention. However, to minimize the adverse effects of high turnover, the company has insisted on proper documentation of all design and development activities. It also ensures that every job/project has a team of persons working to maintain continuity and minimize the impact of the sudden departure of one person. CCL also has to increase its compensation packages to keep pace with the market demand for professionals.

# FACTORS THAT HELP/HINDER ASSIMILATION OF TECHNOLOGY

## Assessment of Technology

CCL has not been able to develop a very systematic approach to assess the sources of technology. It depends primarily upon the information collected through the latest journals and product requirements from its customers.

## Internal Technology Development and Marketing Strategies

CCL has a reasonably strong internal R&D set-up and has been successful in developing products/software indigenously. However, it has been unable to firmly establish its product image in the market.

## Negotiating for Technology

For any negotiations with collaborators, CCL follows a team approach. Its negotiating team comprises experts from R&D, marketing and finance. The major areas of negotiation have been for larger projects, sales and support services.

## Issues in Assimilation

CCL's main focus has been on software development, specifically for customer-driven solutions, development and upgradation of other packages. Though efforts are being made for technology development, with the high rate of technology obsolescence in this industry, CCL has only managed to keep pace with the existing technology developments.

## Incentives for Assimilation and Upgrading Technology

CCL has been concentrating on value addition to imported products and processes, which has resulted in a higher level of technology assimilation. However, this has been confined to existing levels of technology with less emphasis on its upgradation and further development. Periodically, the company sends people abroad on projects and training, but has not been able to derive the maximum benefit from this exercise because of the high turnover of such personnel.

## Documentation

CCL has made considerable efforts in institutionalizing the document-ation system of all design and development activities, especially in the R&D wing, to minimize the adverse effects of high turnover. This has the added advantage of information sharing within the organization.

## Role of R&D

CCL has given tremendous importance to R&D within the organization by treating it as a separate cadre. This has facilitated the growth of employees as specialists who are at par with managers in other departments or sometimes even slightly better off. R&D also plays a lead role in identification of technology, its selection and suitability as well as in the negotiation process for its transfer.

## Marketing of Technological Capability

Being a comparatively new organization in this field, CCL is yet to establish a strong market image for technological capability both in India and abroad. However, it has been able to develop and market some systems, such as terminal concentration and 3D graphics.

## Manufacturing Capability

CCL has been concentrating mainly on value-addition activities, especially in software, as the liberalization process has eased import restrictions on hardware. This has considerably reduced its manufacturing activity and affected the assimilation of technology to some extent.

## Technology Development Strategy

CCL has a well laid out technology development strategy based on corporate plans, internal R&D capability, foreign technological developments and the government's research policy. While CCL does not have a formal technology development or planning cell, a team of four to five senior managers are involved in strategy development. The R&D group is treated as the main organ to understand and transfer technology. The time span for technology development in CCL is usually between three to five years. So far CCL has mostly entered into licensing type of arrangements based on royalty payments with certain restrictive conditions related to purchase of capital goods, raw materials, etc.

CCL believes that the government's influence on its technology strategies is primarily on technology-oriented procurement policies, results from government research facilities, direct R&D funding by the government and monetary policies. The company also feels that the government can develop joint R&D programmes in collaboration with scientific research laboratories such as CSIR and Indian Institute of Science. The high rates of duties on imports is considered to be one of the policies of the government that has had a major negative influence on CCL's technology policy.

CCL also perceives that the government plays a substantial role in the development of manpower, especially in the scientific and technical fields. It also believes that the government could play a major role in improving linkages between scientific institutions and the industry. Around 5 per cent of the CCL staff is engaged in training activities. Nearly 70 per cent of the training programmes are in technical and equipment-specific areas. The organization has no formal employees union nor has it faced any redundancy problem arising out of technological changes.

## CONCLUSIONS

CCL has the technical ability and expertise to assimilate and develop technology which it could actively pursue. At the same time, instead of relying on foreign brand images, it could try to develop, build its own independent identity and image in the market. For this the company could develop appropriate short and long-term marketing strategies. CCL has a good cadre of specialist technicians. However, retraining them continues to be a problem. They need to develop a long-term HRD strategy with appropriate incentives to reduce the high turnover of personnel. As compared to other industries, CCL has developed a good documentation system which could be further strengthened. CCL had a strong R&D base. However, it may be desirable if the R&D and marketing departments are able to work in closer coordination. There could, perhaps, be even a planned job rotation policy between the two, keeping in mind the core competencies and development of the technical professionals.

# part four

# Lessons and Directions for the Future

# 11

# WHAT DO WE LEARN?

## INTRODUCTION

The four country and organizational cases have clearly demonstrated the importance of technology development, foreign investment and building of human resources for economic growth and development. The cases indicate certain common features that determine the efficacy of technology transfer and human resource development. Here the creation of a conducive business climate for attracting the much-needed foreign investment assumes significance. At the same time the cases reveal that there are certain differences and peculiar features that are relevant to each country. The process and stage of reforms in each of the emerging nations is measured according to various parameters to assess their competitiveness (see Table 11.1). The similarities and dissimilarities in approaches to development, the strategies adopted by each of these countries and the experiences bring forth some guidelines which emerging countries could perhaps adopt with appropriate adjustments.

As indicated in Table 11.1, Singapore tops the list in all the considered factors except science and technology where it ranks second. Malaysia ranked fourth, followed by Thailand while India was placed eleventh in 1992.

**TABLE 11.1:** Emerging Nation's Competitiveness in the World

| Overall Ranking | | | A | B | C | D | E | F | G | H |
|---|---|---|---|---|---|---|---|---|---|---|---|
| (1) | 1 | Singapore | 1 | 1 | 1 | 1 | 1 | 1 | 2 | 1 |
| (4) | 2 | Taiwan | 3 | 3 | 4 | 7 | 6 | 3 | 1 | 3 |
| (2) | 3 | Hong Kong | 5 | 2 | 3 | 2 | 3 | 2 | 4 | 5 |
| (5) | 4 | Malaysia | 6 | 5 | 2 | 3 | 5 | 4 | 6 | 4 |
| (3) | 5 | Korea | 2 | 6 | 6 | 8 | 2 | 5 | 3 | 2 |
| (6) | 6 | Thailand | 4 | 4 | 5 | 6 | 12 | 6 | 7 | 6 |
| (7) | 7 | Mexico | 9 | 7 | 7 | 5 | 8 | 8 | 10 | 7 |
| (—) | 8 | S. Africa | 12 | 10 | 10 | 4 | 7 | 7 | 5 | 14 |
| (—) | 9 | Venezuela | 11 | 8 | 9 | 9 | 9 | 9 | 11 | 8 |
| (8) | 10 | Indonesia | 7 | 13 | 8 | 12 | 11 | 12 | 9 | 11 |
| (10) | 11 | India | 8 | 14 | 11 | 11 | 13 | 11 | 12 | 9 |
| (9) | 12 | Brazil | 13 | 12 | 14 | 10 | 4 | 10 | 14 | 12 |
| (—) | 13 | Hungary | 14 | 9 | 12 | 14 | 10 | 14 | 8 | 10 |
| (—) | 14 | Pakistan | 10 | 11 | 13 | 13 | 14 | 13 | 13 | 13 |

Rankings based on:
A—Domestic Economic Strength; B—Internationalism; C—Government; D—Finance; E—Infrastructure; F—Management; G—Science and Technology; H—People.
Overall Ranking in: (1991) 1992.

*Source:* *World Competitiveness Report,* World Economic Forum, 1992.

Another *World Competitiveness Report* prepared in 1995 by the World Economic Forum and the International Institute for Management Development indicates that India's ranking in fact dropped five places from the 34th position it held in 1994. In comparison, Singapore was ranked 2nd, Malaysia 21st, China 24th, Thailand 26th and India 39th among the 48 major countries of the world. This was in spite of the fact that India ranked 4th in terms of management competence and 6th in terms of entrepreneurship and innovation. Therefore, this indicates that there are various other economic and policy factors which can play a crucial role in development. (see Table 11.2)

Some of the major conclusions that can be drawn from the case studies discussed in previous chapters are given below.

# POLICIES AND STRATEGIES

## Similarity in Initial Policies

In all the four countries studied, i.e. Singapore, Malaysia, Thailand and India, the initial approach to economic development was inward-

**TABLE 11.2:** Competitiveness Ranking of Selected Asian Countries on Major Economic Indicators

| | Singapore | Malaysia | Thailand | China | India |
|---|---|---|---|---|---|
| GNP per capita | — | 27 | 33 | 46 | 47 |
| Economic risk | — | 4 | 9 | 41 | 35 |
| International influence | 1 | 2 | 10 | 13 | 23 |
| Trade to GDP ratio | 1 | 3 | 10 | 38 | 45 |
| State interference | 3 | 16 | 25 | 38 | 41 |
| Cost of capital | 2 | 4 | 18 | 34 | 30 |
| Credit flow | 3 | 6 | 18 | 47 | 25 |
| Support from political system | 1 | 2 | 28 | 45 | 33 |
| Financial risk | — | 19 | 24 | 34 | 39 |
| Intellectual property protection | — | 24 | 32 | 44 | 41 |
| Air transport | 1 | 27 | 36 | 45 | 40 |
| Effectiveness of distribution system | 3 | 26 | 30 | 48 | 32 |
| Power supply | 1 | 37 | 31 | 48 | 47 |
| Price/quality ratio | 3 | 21 | 29 | 47 | 44 |
| Customer orientation | — | 25 | 29 | 33 | 43 |
| Managerial rewards | 1 | 6 | 11 | 46 | 20 |
| In-company training | — | 14 | 23 | 45 | 38 |
| Time market | 2 | 18 | 25 | 47 | 43 |
| Competent sr. managers | — | 9 | 35 | 48 | 4 |
| Worker's motivation | — | 32 | 34 | 36 | 37 |
| Entrepreneurship and innovation | — | 30 | — | 48 | 6 |
| Values of society | 1 | 4 | 14 | 37 | 15 |
| Competitiveness overall ranking among 48 countries | 2 | 21 | 26 | 34 | 39 |

—Data not available.

*Source: World Competitiveness Report*, World Economic Forum, 1995 and the International Institute of Management Development, Geneva, 1995.

looking with emphasis on import substitution and development of indigenous technology to minimize external reliance. However, Singapore and Malaysia soon realized the pitfalls of self-reliance and import substitution, while in the case of Thailand and India the realization came much later. Singapore adopted an export-oriented policy owing to the small size of its domestic market. It realized that development and growth was possible only through export orientation, which necessitated foreign investment and technology transfer. India, Malaysia and Thailand being agrarian economies, the industrial and manufacturing activities in these countries were initially largely agro-based.

## Timing of Reforms and Export Orientation

All the four countries in the process of development felt the need to change their philosophy of import substitution and self-reliance to export orientation and encouragement of foreign investment. In the case of Singapore, Malaysia and Thailand the formation of regional blocs such as ASEAN also played an important role in changing their orientation from being totally inward-looking to outward-looking economies. Trade within the ASEAN countries was encouraged and some common approaches were adopted. Though India was also invited to be one of the founder members of ASEAN, it declined the offer owing to ideological and political reasons. The reforms and liberalization processes started much earlier in the three other countries—in 1965 in Singapore, in the late 1960s in Malaysia and in the late 1970s in Thailand. The process in India started only in the early 1990s triggered by the balance-of-payment crisis after the Gulf War and the break-up of the erstwhile Soviet Union and its socialistic pattern of development.

As a result, at about the time the reforms were initiated in India, the four countries, which were almost at par in the late 1950s, showed drastic differences in terms of growth (see Table 11.3). Singapore showed a high level of consolidation of resources and a resultant dramatic growth. Malaysia and Thailand succeeded in attaining more than a moderate rate of growth. India too has shown an improved performance since 1991, but it has yet to contain the problems of a booming population, unemployment and illiteracy. India has also been unable to bring down its inflation rate to more manageable levels.

Another factor which has influenced the attitude of developing countries is their philosophy of import substitution rather than export orientation. The *World Development Report 1995* indicates that with the protection of local industry and encouragement of import substitution, labour is adversely affected. The data given in the *World Development Report* indicates that the increase in real wages in the past two decades has been lower in India, as compared to some of the outward-looking economies such as South Korea or Singapore. Even the rise in employment in India has been much lower in

**TABLE 11.3:** Comparative Economic Indicators of Growth in Malaysia, Thailand, Singapore and India

|  |  | *Malaysia* | *Thailand* | *Singapore* | *India* |
|---|---|---|---|---|---|
| PER capita GNP (US $) 93 |  | 3,160 | 2,040 | 19,310 | 290 |
| Growth rate of |  |  |  |  |  |
| GDP (1992–96) |  | 8.22 | 8.24 | 8.74 | 5.3 |
| Agriculture % per annum |  | 2.8 | 2.22 | 0.18 | 3.28 |
| Industry |  | 9.92 | 11.22 | 9.26 | 6.3 |
| Services |  | 15.08 | 7.26 | 8.46 | 11.41 |
| Gross domestic investment |  | 35.86 | 42.56 | 41.24 | 22.48 |
| Gross domestic saving |  | 35.76 | 36.96 | 56.22 | 20.34 |
| Inflation rate |  | 4.14 | 4.44 | 2.94 | 9.02 |
| Money supply growth |  | 19.52 | 16.76 | 10.36 | 16.78 |
| Merchandise exports | US $ billion | 58.8 | 43.84 | 90.7 | 26.94 |
|  | % change | 19.8 | 15.44 | 16.7 | 14.62 |
| Merchandise imports | US $ billion | 56.04 | 48.36 | 99.78 | 26.74 |
|  | % change | 19.12 | 13.04 | 17.24 | 13.3 |
| Current accounts | US $ billion | – 3.72 | – 7.34 | 5.54 | – 1.22 |
|  | % of GDP | – 5.04 | – 5.12 | 7.86 | – 0.44 |
| External debt |  |  |  |  |  |
| outstanding | US $ billion | 24.66 | 56.08 |  | 90.34 |
| Debt-service ratio | % of exports | 6.04 | 13.64 |  | 26 |

*Source:* *Asian Development Outlook, 1995 and 1996,* Asian Development Bank, 1995.

*Note:* The above figures includes estimates for the year 1995 and 1996.

comparison to other developing countries. Though efforts are being made in countries like India after 1991 to remove import substitution, some internal resistance still persists which needs to be tackled for the overall growth of the economy (see Table 11.4).

## Long-term Policies

The case studies indicate that a long-term vision for the country rather than ad-hoc or, at times, sporadic attempts to introduce changes plays a vital role in hastening the process of development. In Malaysia, Vision 2020 has clearly laid down the targets to be achieved and all the agencies for development have been working towards attaining the status of an industrialized nation by the year 2020. Similarly, Singapore's Vision 2000 clearly defines the goals to be achieved. In the case of Thailand, though there are no specific long-term plans, there is a general consensus that free enterprise will be encouraged

**TABLE 11.4:** Relative Earnings in Selected Countries

| Country | Average Annual Growth (%) | | Index (1980 = 100) | | |
|---|---|---|---|---|---|
| | 1970–80 | 1980–92 | 1990 | 1991 | 1992 |
| India | 0.4 | 2.5 | 134 | 130 | 129 |
| Indonesia | 5.2 | 4.3 | 164 | 171 | 172 |
| Philippines | − 3.7 | 5.2 | 161 | 180 | 181 |
| Malaysia | 2.0 | 2.3 | 129 | 135 | 138 |
| South Korea | 10.0 | 8.4 | 209 | 231 | 237 |
| Singapore | 3.0 | 5.1 | 176 | 187 | 200 |

*Source:* *World Development Report, 1995,* as quoted in *India Today,* August 1995.

*Note:* Figures are for the manufacturing sector.

mainly through private sector investment. India, on the other hand, has yet to define a concrete long-term vision which clearly lays down future goals and targets to be achieved in specific terms.

## Strategies for Reform

There were certain commonalities as well as differences in the reform processes adopted in the four countries. Singapore, right at the beginning of its reform process, opened up its economy with the removal of major state-control measures. Malaysia adopted a planned development approach through various government measures which encouraged investment in a formal manner through legislation. The primary objective of all these legislative measures in Malaysia was to offer incentives for domestic and foreign investment, streamline procedures, provide a conducive industrial relation's climate, etc. Thailand's growth began in a rather unplanned manner, except that its economy was opened up to private sector investment, both domestic and foreign, with the removal of certain restrictions. India pursued a policy of self-reliance and import substitution for almost four decades after gaining independence from colonial rule. The liberalization process in India began only in the early 1990s with partial deregulation and gradual opening up of the economy. The process has yet to percolate fully throughout India's cumbersome bureaucracy and down to the various states.

# INVESTMENT CLIMATE

The investment climate in any country is influenced, to a great extent, by the existence of conducive factors which encourage investors to set up industries.

Some of the characteristics of the investment climate in the four countries in the context of the above factors are discussed below.

## Development Philosophy

In Thailand, the philosophy of growth is based on economic development and it is assumed that this will lead to social change. In Singapore, the economy has been opened up for growth which has resulted in economic and social change. The living standard of people in Singapore is now comparable to advanced countries in the West. There is hardly any illiteracy and people are provided with adequate social security for old age, etc. In Malaysia, the emphasis is on restructuring the society to bring about both social and economic change. India has also followed a policy of simultaneous economic and social change. Considerable resources have been spent on social projects in non-productive sectors, with the objective of providing relief to the weaker and unemployed sections of Indian society.

## Policies for Industrial Investment

♦ *Key Expected Benefits to the Nation*   In Thailand, the emphasis is on the export-earning potential of the industry, in addition to economic growth. In Singapore, the expected investment is in high-technology industries with export-earning potential. In Malaysia also, industrial investment is expected to bring in technology and export earnings, leading to economic growth. Industrial investment in India is basically expected to support technology, provide self-sufficiency and satisfy export and domestic demand. In India, the thrust so far had been on import substitution but is now gradually shifting to export-led production.

♦ *Government Intervention*   One of the contributory factors that encourage investment is the role played by the government. In Thailand, the government's role is to facilitate the entire investment process and provide necessary help in overcoming the obstacles wherever feasible. In Singapore, the government actively encourages industrial investment, even taking the initiative of bringing in the latest technology and foreign investment. The Malaysian government also facilitates industrial investment. Government intervention in India is more to do with regulating and monitoring industrial investment. Recent moves to reduce government intervention have yet to percolate down the line.

♦ *Extent of Government Intervention*   In Thailand the government does play a role initially in terms of issuing operating licences and offering incentives for industrial investment. There is, however, minimal government intervention after the initial licensing formalities are completed. Singapore also offers incentives for investment and government intervention is low. In Malaysia, after the initial formalities of licensing and incentives are over, government intervention is limited to the extent of ensuring the implementation of various protective legislations. In India, government intervention is initially high with several restrictions and permit quotas to be met. The quotas and restrictions in certain sectors are being gradually reduced though government intervention continues in terms of approvals.

♦ *Location Policies*   To reduce congestion in and around Bangkok, the government of Thailand encourages industries to be located away from urban centres by providing the necessary infrastructure. Singapore provides the infrastructure for industrial investment in Singapore, but is now encouraging industrial investment outside Singapore, as it has reached saturation due to space constraints. Malaysia encourages regional development within the country and industrial investment is encouraged by providing the necessary infrastructure. Similarly, in India also there is emphasis on promotion of regional development, especially in backward areas, by providing special incentives in terms of tax concessions. However, the Indian government has not taken much responsibility for providing infrastructure facilities in these backward regions.

♦ *Environment*   The need for obtaining environment clearance for industries located in Thailand has only recently received attention. Singapore, on the other hand, has a high level of government regulation for environmental factors with stringent statutory requirements to be fulfilled by the industry. In Malaysia, industrial investment requires clearances from the environment

| Countries | Thailand | Singapore | Malaysia | India |
|---|---|---|---|---|
| **Factors Affecting Investment** | | | | |
| **Development Philosophy** | Thrust on economic growth to bring about social change | Open economy for faster growth | Accelerate restructuring of society to correct social and economic imbalances | Simultaneous social and economic change |
| **Policies for Industrial Environment** | | | | |
| (a) Key expected benefits to nation | Economic growth and export earnings | High tech and export earnings and economic growth | Export earnings and technology | Technological self-sufficiency and satisfying domestic demands and export |
| (b) Government intervention | To facilitate | To facilitate and encourage | To facilitate | To regulate and monitor |
| (c) Extent of intervention | Low initially, minimal after licensing | Low | Low initially and medium subsequently to ensure implementation of protective legislation | High initially and continues |
| (d) Instrument | Operating license | Incentives and approvals | Operating license and incentives | Operating license, permits and quotas |
| (e) Location policy | Relieve urban congestion and provide infrastructure | Provide Infrastructure, encourage investment outside Singapore | Provide infrastructure and encourage regional development within the country | Promotion of regional development within the country |

(Fig. 11.1 Contd.)

| Countries | Thailand | Singapore | Malaysia | India |
|---|---|---|---|---|
| **Factors Affecting Investment** | | | | |
| (f) Environment | Recent awareness and incentives being introduced | High government regulations statutory norms | Clearance required along with operating license | Separate approval for environment and pollution control |
| **Other Issues Affecting Investment** | | | | |
| (a) Direct negotiation | Minimal | Intense for high technology by government | Minimal | Intense |
| (b) Time taken for clearance | Months | Months | Weeks | One to two years with exceptions (weeks/months) |
| (c) Location | Industrial estates | Industrial estates encouraged | Industrial estates encouraged | Backward regions encouraged |
| (d) Infrastructure | Government responsibility | Government responsibility | Government responsibility | Companies are on their own |
| (e) Joint ventures | Required in some cases and otherwise encouraged (outside Singapore) | Encouraged specially for units located outside Singapore | Required in some cases | Encouraged and required in some cases |
| (f) Employment quotas | Not an issue | Not an issue | Some reservations for *bhumiputras* (son of the soil) | Reservations in public and government organizations |
| (g) Sophistication of technology | Encouraged through incentives | High technology encouraged (special incentives) | Encouraged through incentives | Encouraged |

(Fig. 11.1 Contd.)

| Countries | Thailand | Singapore | Malaysia | India |
|---|---|---|---|---|
| *Factors Affecting Investment* | | | | |
| **Human Resource Development (HRD)** | | | | |
| (a) Skill development and upgradation | Company's major responsibility | High government incentive and subsidy for skill upgradation | Partly government incentive for skill upgradation | Company's sole responsibility |
| (b) Labour protection measures | Trade unions not allowed | Trade unions exist but concentrate on nonbargainable activities | Good protective legislation, control on direct action, union role minimal | Politically affiliated and fragmented trade union movement. Accent on bargaining machinery |
| **Fiscal and Monetary Policies** | | | | |
| (a) Currency convertibility | Full convertibility with some restrictions on repatriation | Full convertibility and free exchange regulations | Free exchange regulations with some restrictions on repatriation | Partially convertible currency and restrictions on repatriation |
| (b) Interest rates* | High (10.7%) | Very low (3.4%) | Low (3.9%) | Very high (12.9%) |

*The interest figures relate to 1994, *The Economic Times*, 4 September, 1995.

**FIG. 11.1:** Investment Climate of the Four Countries

ministry, along with the operating licenses. In India, a separate approval is required from the State Pollution Control Boards under the Ministry of Environment. The Pollution Control Board also monitors environmental and pollution control measures on a continuous basis.

## Other Issues Affecting Investment

♦ *Direct Negotiation* Foreign investment requires negotiations, not only at the enterprise level but also at the government level. This in itself can facilitate or hinder investments. In Thailand, direct negotiations at the government level are minimal. In the case of Singapore, the government does play an active role in negotiating for investment, specially in the high-technology areas. In Malaysia, in contrast, the government plays a minimal role except in regulating the licensing and royalty procedures. In India, the government role in negotiation is high with a lot of bureaucratic red-tape which often delays investment decisions.

♦ *Time Taken for Clearances* There is a time-bound clearance procedure laid down in Thailand and any approval for industrial investment is made within two to three months. The clearance procedure in Singapore is fairly simple and no approvals are necessary except a formal registration of the company including compliance of environmental regulations. In Malaysia, everything is cleared through the single-window system and all the clearances are given by the Ministry of Trade. Normally the effort is made to grant clearances within two to three weeks. In India the time taken for clearance could vary from two weeks to three years depending upon the complexity of the project and its political repercussions. However, in most cases there is a considerable delay in getting clearances from various departments and ministries.

♦ *Location* In Malaysia, Singapore and Thailand, the industrial estates are well-equipped with all the necessary infrastructure for the location of industries. The industries are thus encouraged to be located in these industrial estates where the government takes the responsibility for providing the infrastructure. In India, though there are taxation incentives for industries to be located in backward areas, the companies themselves are responsible for meeting the infrastructural requirements.

♦ *Joint Ventures* To facilitate the development of indigenous industry and at the same time obtain the latest technology, the governments encourage joint ventures between the host country and foreign investors rather than relying purely on an exclusive ownership by foreign investors. In Thailand, foreign investment in most industries can be made through joint ventures with some exceptions relating to infrastructure industries. In Singapore, joint ventures are mainly encouraged in the case of investments by local entrepreneurs in countries outside Singapore. In Malaysia, joint ventures are required in certain specified industries. In India, joint ventures are encouraged in most industries and required in some cases such as public sector units. Recently, there has been a conscious policy in the Indian public sector to have joint ventures with both foreign and domestic enterprises.

♦ *Employment Quotas* To reduce social disparities, the government in certain cases insists on employment of certain categories of persons, such as 'sons of the soil' in the case of Malaysia, or persons belonging to backward regions or deprived classes/castes in India. In Singapore and Thailand, there are no such restrictions. In India, these restrictions are confined to mainly the public/government enterprises. In Malaysia, there are certain reservations for persons of Malay origin who are called the *bhumiputras.*

# HUMAN RESOURCE DEVELOPMENT (HRD)

## Skill Development and Upgradation

For any appropriate assimilation and absorption of technology, as we have seen, basic education and continuous skill upgradation play a significant role. In fact, availability of skilled personnel can be an incentive for investors to set up an enterprise. In this respect, Singapore is a classic example where the state plays a major role in ensuring education as well as constant upgradation of skills on a continuous basis. The state subsidizes the skill upgradation programmes through the Skill Development Fund which has been specially created for the purpose. In Malaysia also, the government has set up a Human Development Fund along the lines of the Singapore model. In India and Thailand, to a large extent, skill upgradation continues to be the company's responsibility. Though there are a large number of technical institutions in India for imparting technical education, the level of technical skills in relation to sophisticated technology continues to be poor.

As the developmental process gains momentum, the experience of developing countries suggests that shortages of highly skilled personnel is inevitable though there may, simultaneously, be a surplus in the unskilled categories. The Singapore government took a major initiative in continuous skill upgradation through a separate fund created for the purpose. Malaysia also emulated the Singapore model. By adopting proactive policies, these countries have been able to reduce the adverse effect of redundancies. Thailand is facing acute shortages of skilled labour and the government has to define long-term strategies in terms of training and retraining its technical personnel. Though India has a surplus of overall manpower resources, there are shortages of skilled labour, especially in the high-technology areas.

## Labour Protection Measures

The government regulation of industrial relations and trade union movement in each country has a role in developing a conducive industrial relations climate. One of the important reasons for the heavy inflow of foreign investment into Singapore, Malaysia and Thailand is the favourable industrial relations situation. In Thailand, trade unions are banned and the formal associations of employees concentrate primarily on non-bargainable activities, such as welfare measures for its members, worker's education, training, etc. In Malaysia, though unions are allowed, there are controls on direct action by the trade union in an organization and a good protective legislation. New ventures enjoy protection from strikes during the initial years of establishment. In India, the situation in the industrial relations front is not very encouraging. Trade unions are fragmented and politically affiliated. There is a lot of emhasis on collective bargaining, direct action and legal machinery which hampers industrial activity and investment in industry.

# Fiscal Policies

The fiscal policies relating to repatriation, fiscal guarantees, etc. play an important role in encouraging foreign investment. Thailand,

Singapore and Malaysia offer full currency convertibility and there are very few restrictions on repatriation. In contrast in India, only recently has the Indian rupee been made fully convertible on trade account and partially convertible on current account. Certain restrictions still exist on repatriation.

## Availability of Finance and Interest Rates

This is crucial for any industrial investment or technology transfer process. An oft-expressed fear in developing countries is that open-ing the economy to MNCs can affect the competitiveness of local enterprises since finance is available at much cheaper rates of interest in most developed countries in comparison to developing countries. But, the Singapore and Malaysia experiences suggest that with appropriate incentives and availability of various financial schemes, local industries can come up and be competitive, more so when many large industries use local enterprises as their outsourcing suppliers or even ancillaries. Easy availability of finance, especially in Singapore, for upgrading technology and human skills has also contributed to instilling competitiveness among local enterprises.

It may be worth noting that easy availability of funds, especially to rehabilitate sick units, can also result in the units not even attempting to improve their performance. In India, there is always an effort on the part of enterprises not doing well to get incentive under the Board for Industrial and Financial Reconstruction (BIFR) schemes. Often these resources get used more for the revival of sick units whose problems in the first place arose due to mismanagement. Thus, there is reduced availability of funds for upgradation of technology or starting new ventures.

Availability of finance for investment is also dependent upon the interest rate. Some believe that lower interest rates lead to greater Investment. In 1994, the average interest rate in Malaysia was 5.9 per cent, in Thailand, it was 10.75 per cent, while it was the lowest in Singapore at 3.44 per cent. On the other hand, in India it was much higher at 12.97 per cent. A complaint that is often made by Indian industrialists is that the foreign MNCs are in a better position because they can raise funds at cheaper rates as compared to Indian investors. However, there is another view that holds that availability of easy money can trigger inflation and raise interest rates but may not lead to growth as is evident from Figure 11.2.

| | Inflation | Interest Rate | GDP Growth Rate |
|---|---|---|---|
| MALAYSIA | 5.90 | 5.90 | 9.90 |
| SOUTH KOREA | 4.50 | 15.90 | 9.90 |
| THAILAND | 5.40 | 10.75 | 5.40 |
| SINGAPORE | 1.70 | 5.44 | 7.20 |
| TAIWAN | 4.70 | 5.75 | 7.00 |
| INDONESIA | 10.00 | 15.00 | 5.50 |
| INDIA | 10.50 | 12.97 | 5.50 |
| HONG KONG | 5.90 | 5.77 | 5.10 |
| PHILIPPINES | 5.50 | 9.50 | 4.70 |

**Fig. 11.2**  Relationship between Inflation, Interest Rate and GDP Growth

*Source:  The Economic Times*, 4 September, 1995.

## Incentives for Investment

The four countries have developed various incentive schemes to encourage investment. Thailand, Singapore and Malaysia have set up industrial estates with proper infrastructure facilities which act as incentives for investors. Thailand gives additional incentives for location of industries outside its urban centres. India is also giving taxation benefits for locating an enterprise in undeveloped or backward regions. However, in India infrastructure still continues to be the primary responsibility of the companies themselves. Having reached its saturation level owing to shortage of space as well as labour, Singapore gives additional incentives for entrepreneurs to set up their plants outside the country. All the countries have earmarked priority industries for which special taxation and monetary incentives are given. Singapore has taken the lead in identifying industries which suffer from low productivity and then helping them through consultancy, technology guidance and training to enhance productivity. All the countries offer some incentive or the other for export-oriented industries.

## Clearance Procedure

A simple clearance procedure for setting up of an industry, especially where foreign investment is involved, can act as an added incentive. Malaysia has greatly simplified its entire clearance procedure under a single-window system, where in normal cases, the clearance is given within two or three weeks. Singapore has also developed a quick institutionalized system. Thailand had a complicated clearance system, but during the last few years this has been simplified. The Board of Investment, apart from giving clearance, also assists the investors in approaching other ministries or departments to get quicker clearances. In India, till recently the clearance procedure was considered obstructive rather than facilitative. The government has set up a Foreign Investment Promotion Board for speedy clearance of proposals. However, the experience is that even after receiving clearance from the Board, the investors have to approach various ministries and departments for other approvals.

# LOCAL INDUSTRIES AND MNCs

The four case studies indicate that MNCs have brought in the much-needed capital for investment, latest technology and employment opportunities during the critical stages of economic development of each of the countries. MNCs have also brought in new management techniques including training of personnel. The indirect benefit of technology transfer by MNCs is the development of skills through the setting up of training institutes. Many MNCs in Singapore and Malaysia have set up technical training centres with the help of local governments to train not only their own employees but also extend facilities to other local companies and even new entrants in the job market.

The Malaysian industrial sector has been dominated mostly by large industrial enterprises and a few small-scale industries. The large industrial concerns are controlled by foreign interests either as subsidiaries of foreign-owned MNCs or as joint ventures. The bigger establishments, especially the subsidiaries, have no technological problems. Joint venture companies also benefit from having their own R&D and foreign technical back-up services. The foreign-owned companies may have similar manufacturing operations elsewhere and operate in Malaysia to take advantage of labour and marketing benefits along with the other incentives. In India, though the industrial sector has a few large industrial units, the medium- and small-scale units form a substantial part of the industry. They face a host of technological problems and are non-competitive both in terms of cost and quality.

There has been an apprehension that with the advent of MNCs, local industries, especially those in the small-scale and medium-scale sector, would be adversely affected. However, the case of Singapore suggests that it need not be so. The experience of large MNCs suggests that they would like to outsource their components to local industries as long as their stringent quality requirements are met. In fact, they are in many cases willing to transfer technological know-how and develop the expertise of local industries as long as they have the capability to receive and absorb the new technology. In this respect, the government in Singapore has played a prominent role in developing the technological capabilities of local companies including skill upgradation of the workforce. This includes providing various types of financial incentives for local industries. As a result in the last few years local industry has grown by around 20 per cent per annum. This is also being emulated by Malaysia to some extent. In India, however, the fear still persists that opening up the economy will eventually be detrimental to the growth of small-scale and medium-scale indigenous units.

## Research and Development (R&D)

In the initial stages of development, Singapore, Malaysia and Thailand did not give much importance to internal R&D investment. The major reliance was on technology transfer mainly through foreign investment and MNCs. However, in the case of India, the government took the initiative in setting up R&D laboratories in critical industries. Yet R&D efforts in India have been far from satisfactory. The investment by the private sector in R&D in all four countries has been marginal in spite of the financial incentives offered by their respective governments. After the signing of the GATT agreements there have been efforts to invest in R&D, but most of the countries suffer from a shortage of qualified scientists and researchers.

# At THE MICRO ORGANIZATIONAL LEVEL

The case studies of a few organizations at the micro level focused on eliciting data on the interpretation of the macro level policies at the micro level, especially with regard to the investment pattern, technology transfer arrangements, technology assimilation and upgradation, and the strategies to prepare human resources within the organization. Some of the major conclusions emerging from the micro level studies are given below.

## Assessment of Technology

For any assimilation of technology, the recipient organization should have the required capability to assess the technology they intend to import. In Singapore, the government itself plays a leading role in helping organizations assess the technology gaps and then transfer the required technology. Malaysia has a conducive investment climate, which enables companies to bring in the latest technology on their own to raise their quality standards to global requirements. In India, it was found in certain cases that owing to an incorrect assessment of technology, the project had to be abandoned after substantial investments had been made.

## Internal Technology Development and Marketing Strategies

Owing to lack of government pressure in India to upgrade technology, unlike Singapore and to some extent Malaysia, the Indian organizations which operated in a protected market environment did not invest in technology development and upgradation. However, wherever there was a competitive environment in India, organizations such as the ABC Company had adopted systematic procedures for acquiring information on the latest technological developments and market potential. They had also invested in upgrading human skills through research and training in the frontier areas of technology development. In Singapore and Malaysia, the government provides additional financial incentives to upgrade technology. It was found that in certain cases, though the local industry has been successful in developing and commercializing certain technologies, it has not been successful in marketing its technological know-how. Organizations in developing countries are often biased against foreign tie-ups because of their known brand name, even though an equivalent indigenous technology may be available which may be both proven and cheaper. But these indigenous companies have not been aggressive in selling their technologies.

With the lifting of trade barriers and market globalization, most developing countries have been prompted to change their policies from import substitution to export orientation. However, owing to limited availability of resources and the need to meet the demands of global competitiveness, the trend in organizations has been towards building core competencies in selected areas and developing products that meet stringent global quality standards.

## Negotiations for Technology

The choice, evaluation and negotiation mechanism are very crucial for any technology transfer arrangements. In contrast to countries such as Singapore where the government plays a facilitative role, in India, government role has some times been restrictive as was found in the cases of PIL and XYZ Ltd. There were pressures from the government or even the top management of the companies to select certain persons to negotiate technology transfer arrangements on the basis of expediency rather than expertise. Often, the constitution of the negotiation team and process are constrained by the rules and regulations in the public sector. On the other hand, the private sector has the freedom to select the best possible teams on the basis of their expertise, with the result that they are able to take faster decisions and get better terms.

## Interdepartmental Coordination and Role of R&D

Another noticeable feature found in organizations in some developing countries such as India and Thailand was that close interaction and coordination between R&D and operations was often lacking. At times, there was even a reluctance to share information and documentation between the two departments. However, wherever R&D was involved in technology transfer right from the negotiation stage and its operationalization and training of human resources was given due importance, the assimilation of technology was faster and had a noticeable effect on improving the product lines.

## Government Influence on Technology Development Strategy

All the six company's studied were asked to indicate the manner in which government policies influence their technology development strategies. The responses indicate that in most cases the government does not have a major influence on their technology development strategy (see Table 11.5). The factors which do affect their technology development strategy were R&D and tax credit. In the case of Malaysian companies, political stability in the country helped. A private sector organization in Malaysia indicated that technology-oriented procurement policies, investment tax credit, labour policies and export policies of the government also helped in developing positive technology development strategies. In the case of Indian companies, the factor which affected their policies were procurement policies, results from government research facilities, national technology ventures, R&D related loans and export policies. The political situation, labour policies and export policies in the case of one Indian public sector organization were perceived to have had a somewhat negative influence on the organization's technology development strategy.

## Skill Upgradation and Redeployment Policies

In Singapore and Malaysia organizations are compelled to constantly upgrade their human resource skills because of the export thrust and external competition. On the other hand, in India and Thailand, training of workers and their skill upgradation is given less importance in comparison to managerial training. Many organizations in India end up with surplus staff whenever there is technology transfer and upgradation. This is partly because of the lack of government policy on employee exit and also because of pressures from trade unions. Companies do not have proper retraining and redeployment policies. As a result, there have been situations where, on the one hand, companies have wished to get rid of certain categories of employees and on the other hand, have gone in for recruitment of additional manpower for the new technology. This eventually ends up in surplus staffing.

The entry of MNCs owing to increased technology transfers have created large anomalies in the compensation packages. MNCs are often willing to pay high salaries in order to attract the best available professionals. Local companies are therefore forced to increase their compensation packages adding to the overall manpower cost

**TABLE 11.5:** Government Influence on Technology Development Strategy

| | Negative | | | | Somewhat Negative | | | | Has No Influence | | | | Somewhat Positive | | | | Positive | | | |
|---|---|---|---|---|---|---|---|---|---|---|---|---|---|---|---|---|---|---|---|---|
| | Indian | | Malaysia | | Indian | | Malaysia | | Indian | | Malaysia | | Indian | | Malaysia | | Indian | | Malaysia | |
| | Pvt | Pub | Pvt | Pub | Pvt | Pub | Pvt | Pub | Pvt | Pub | Pvt | Pub | Pvt | Pub | Pvt | Pub | Pvt | Pub | Pvt | Pub |
| 1. R&D tax credit | | | | | | | | | 1 | | | | 1 | 1 | 1 | | 1 | | | |
| 2. Technology-oriented procurement policies | | | | | | | | | | 1 | | | | | | | | | 1 | |
| 3. Agency-level research policy | | | | | | | | | 1 | 2 | 1 | | 2 | 1 | | | | | | |
| 4. National science and technology policy | | | | | | | | | 2 | 1 | | | | | 1 | | | | | |
| 5. Results from govt. research facilities | | | | | | | | | 1 | 1 | | | | 1 | | | | | | |
| 6. Results from facilities operated by and for the govt. | | | | | | | | | 1 | 2 | | | | 1 | | | | | | |
| 7. Major national technology ventures | | | | | | | | | | 1 | | | 2 | 2 | | | | | | |
| 8. Direct R&D funding by govt. | | | | | | | | | | 1 | | | 1 | 1 | | | | 2 | | |
| 9. Investment tax credits | | | | | | | | | | 1 | | | 2 | 1 | | | | 1 | 1 | |

*(Contd)*

|  | Negative | | | | Somewhat Negative | | | | Has No Influence | | | | Somewhat Positive | | | | Positive | | | |
|---|---|---|---|---|---|---|---|---|---|---|---|---|---|---|---|---|---|---|---|---|
|  | Indian | | Malaysia | | Indian | | Malaysia | | Indian | | Malaysia | | Indian | | Malaysia | | Indian | | Malaysia | |
|  | Pvt | Pub | Pvt | Pub | Pvt | Pub | Pvt | Pub | Pvt | Pub | Pvt | Pub | Pvt | Pub | Pvt | Pub | Pvt | Pub | Pvt | Pub |
| 10. Monetary policy |  |  |  |  |  |  |  |  | 1 | 2 |  |  | 1 |  | 1 |  |  |  |  |  |
| 11. R&D related loans |  |  |  |  |  |  |  |  |  |  |  |  |  |  |  |  |  |  |  |  |
| 12. Political situation |  |  |  |  | 1 |  |  |  | 1 | 1 | 1 |  | 2 | 2 |  |  | 1 |  | 1 | 1 |
| 13. Labour policies |  |  |  |  | 2 |  |  |  |  | 2 |  |  |  |  |  |  |  |  | 1 |  |
| 14. Export policies |  |  |  |  | 1 |  |  |  |  |  |  |  | 1 | 2 |  |  |  |  | 1 |  |

Pvt—Private sector
Pub—Public sector

N = 
4 Indian organizations (2 public sector and 2 private sector)
2 Malaysian organizations (1 public sector and 1 private sector)

considerably which at times they can ill afford. Thus, there is a flight of trained manpower and skilled professionals from local companies to MNCs.

## Manufacturing Activities

The import and export policies as well as the duties levied can, at times, affect manufacturing operations. In Malaysia and India, because of the initial thrust on import substitution, there were a number of restrictions on imports, in addition to heavy duties. However, subsequently, the imports have been liberalized and duties considerably reduced. In India, this has affected, to some extent, the reduction in manufacturing activities as in the case of the ABC Company since importing the bulk of the components has become simpler and cheaper. Reduced manufacturing activities have affected technology assimilation as well. In the case of Singapore and Malaysia, however, there has been a shift in manufacturing activities to boost value added activities, especially in the re-export sector.

## Documentation

The assimilation and absorption of technology is much better in cases where there is proper documentation of the entire process of negotiation, transfer, technical details, including any upgradation/ modifications made from time to time. In Singapore, apart from proper documentation at the micro level, the National Productivity Board (NPB) and Singapore Institute of Standards and Industrial Research (SISIR) maintain macro-level documentation of industry-wise technology. At the micro level, a few cases studies indicated that there is continuity in assimilation with proper documentation as in the case of the ABC company. In the absence of proper documentation there is less assimilation and absorption of technology even where there is low turnover as in the case of PIL.

## Privatization of Public Enterprises

Privatization of public enterprises is considered to be an important part of the liberalization process. Each of the four countries studied adopted specific strategies for privatization.

There were a number of public enterprises in Malaysia that were incurring losses and were being supported by public funding. To reduce their financial and administrative burden, the government developed a privatization Master Plan under which 246 organizations were identified for privatization by independent consultants. The programme was to be implemented in a phased manner with 69 enterprises to be privatized within two years, 107 within two to five years and the remaining after five years. Accordingly, a Privatization Action Plan (PAP) was prepared which was based on the following premises:

- ❏ The private sector to build-and-operate a new project (BO)
- ❏ The private sector to build-operate-and-transfer to the government (BOT)
- ❏ Transfer of management responsibility of an existing entity to the private sector
- ❏ Management buy-out
- ❏ Sale of assets
- ❏ Sale of equity

The other objectives of privatization were greater efficiency, lessening the crowding of private investment, reducing the size of the public sector and assisting *bhumiputras* to acquire equity. Singapore started its privatization efforts in 1986 with the establishment of the Public Sector Divestment Committee. Its main objectives were:

- ❏ Gradual withdrawal from commercial activity
- ❏ Expanding the Singapore stock market by releasing more shares
- ❏ Avoiding or reducing competition with the private sector

The Divestment Committee recommended that of the 90 government-linked companies, nine should be wound up and in another 40 there could be divestment of the shareholding. In all the others, only minority shares were to be held by the government. However, some of the larger organizations still continue to be under majority public sector holding, such as Singapore International Airlines and Singapore Port Trust. Though these are public enterprises they are efficiently managed since they are largely allowed to operate independently as commercial enterprises with little government interference.

The privatization efforts in Thailand started in the 1980s with the decision that fewer public enterprises would be set up in Thailand in the future. The government also expressed its intention to privatize some of the existing public enterprises with the following objectives:

- ❏ To stabilize the external debt of public enterprises and encourage them to finance their own investment
- ❏ To improve their efficiency
- ❏ To strengthen the stock market

However, in actual practice privatization in Thailand has not made much headway. Recently, efforts are being made to privatize some of the larger enterprises such as Thai Airways and Electricity Generating Agency of Thailand. In Thailand, there is still a strong group opposed to the idea of privatization.

In India, privatization efforts were contemplated only after 1991 The major reasons were to raise funds for the government, reduce budgetary deficit, divert funds for the development of infrastructure rather than subsidizing loss-making public enterprises and improve their overall efficiency. However, owing to strong opposition, mainly on social and ideological grounds, privatization has been rather slow in India. A beginning has been made by divesting a small percentage of shares of profit-making public enterprises. Only in very exceptional cases such as the Maruti-Udyog Ltd has the government divested its share to the extent of 50 per cent.

## Cultural Diversities in Technology Transfer

While transferring technology, there is always a tendency to also transfer some of the managerial practices and systems to the developing countries in the belief that these management concepts are universal and can be grafted to all the countries. However, whenever such grafting is enforced it is found that it does not work. In such situations, the organizations are forced to adopt an indigenous approach by arriving at various compromises and adaptive changes, at times resulting in frustration. This also produces a distinct hiatus between the professed policies and the actual practices followed in the local environment.

The Indian case could be a classic example of such a hiatus. On the basis of theories that are suited to the essentially western industrial infrastructure, policies are evolved and plans made on the assumption that foreign or western management practices would work in Indian conditions too. The enforcement of such policies results in a strange dualism in Indian management practices, one which is professedly western on paper and the other which is actually followed. Figure 11.3 outlines the situation in Indian management (Virmani and Guptan,1992):

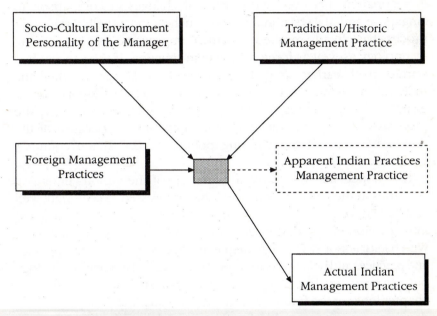

**FIG. 11.3;** Dualism in Indian Management

While transferring managerial technology, it may be necessary to do an appropriate blending of management practices taking into account cultural peculiarities.

## Conclusions

It is hoped that some useful lessons can be drawn from the case studies for the benefit of some of the newly emerging countries such as India and help them in evolving their policies. These lessons should also help organizations to prepare themselves better, not only to receive, but also to absorb, assimilate and upgrade their technology. However, it must be pointed out that these lessons, drawn as they are from the experiences of countries such as Malaysia, Thailand and Singapore, cannot be applied in toto to a large country such as India, where the scale of the problems is entirely different. It must be recognized that one set of policies which succeeded in a smaller country such as Singapore cannot be exactly replicated in a large country such as India.

Also, countries such as Malaysia and Singapore had a fairly stable political environment in comparison to India. However, on reflection it is apparent that even with marginal changes in comparison to Singapore and Malaysia, in a country such as India the liberalization process has already resulted in marked improvement in investment, technology as well as foreign exchange situation. If the process had started much earlier, as it did in Malaysia or Singapore, then the Indian situation too may have been different. Thailand presents another example where, although there has been political instability, the processes of economic development is continuous because of the non-interference of the differing political forces in the country's economic development.

It is hoped that the foregoing analysis of the various emerging countries in the Asian region who have progressed exceedingly well and have developed a clear-cut vision for the future may evoke some introspection on the part of developing countries and provide them with useful lessons. This may help in further sharpening their policies and practices and help in the appropriate blending of not only technology but also managerial practices while undertaking transfer. The following chapter looks at the future scenario and the possible policy initiatives developing countries could take in the years ahead—both at the macro level and also at the organization levels.

# 12

# POLICY INITIATIVES: WHERE DO WE GO FROM HERE?

## INTRODUCTION

As we have seen in the four countrywise case studies, during the last few years there has been a definite trend for the economies of developing countries to gradually integrate themselves with the world economic system. Most developing countries have initiated the process of economic liberalization, developing global corporate strategies and ushering in technological changes. To hasten this process of growth, each country needs to develop its own short-term and long-term strategies relating to economic and structural re-adjustments, technology policies and human resource strategies. A conducive climate for investment for growth needs to be created internally with special emphasis on building infrastructure, technological capabilities and human resources.

Along with globalization, a parallel movement of regionalization too has gathered momentum. This simultaneous growth of two disparate movements has sometimes created conflicts of interest. World trade has been moving in a direction where clear-cut distinctions between free trade on the one hand and protectionism on the other are becoming increasingly blurred, thus bringing in a paradoxical trend. All this means that developing countries need to develop well thought-out structural re-adjustment policies for economic reform.

Till the late 1950s, world economy was fragmented and divided into a number of unintegrated or loosely integrated groups that included the sterling areas, the franc zones, the US dollar and the Council for Mutual Economic Zones, mainly linked to the erstwhile Soviet Union and the socialist economies of Eastern Europe. There were high tariffs, strict quotas and lots of barriers. However, recently there has been a gradual reversal of this process and the world is now moving towards economic and financial integration. In many cases tariffs have been reduced, international trade has been revived and the volume of world trade has increased more rapidly than world production. In the labour field also there is an emerging international labour market, particularly for managerial, professional, technical and highly skilled labour.

In the 1980s the trend towards globalization gained a new impetus. The contributory factors were the growth of offshore financial markets, the explosion of mergers and acquisitions, both nationally and internationally, and the growth of MNCs. Rapid technological changes and the trend towards deregulation has, however, broken down the barriers and strengthened perceptions of globalization, resulting in internationalization of production. Because of global competition, many organizations, especially MNCs, have been compelled to use newer technologies to adopt product characteristics to suit different regional and local markets. All this has resulted in a reduction in state control and forced states to view their policies from the global rather than national angle.

The internationalization of currency markets has further limited the role of central banks in controlling the supply of money. The ability of large firms to locate their fixed investments in any part of the world has further reduced the role of the state in regulating interest through taxation or minimum wage legislation, environmental control or any regulatory mechanisms. All these trends have weakened the controlling ability of the state, which is in danger of disappearing completely unless they learn how best to manage a truly global economy.

It may be argued that any generalized recommendation and conclusion drawn from the four different types of countries—Malaysia,

Singapore, Thailand or India—may not be applicable to all types of developing countries because of the vast differences among them in terms of size, resources, population, culture, etc. However, it must be admitted that there was also some commonality in the policies which these countries adopted that led them to faster growth. Some lessons can surely be drawn from this and keeping in mind individual requirements, be applied in other countries with suitable modifications. One common feature in these countries was the acceptance of the need for structural reform. Following from this realization they brought in major changes in their market structure to become globally competitive and export-oriented, which gave a tremendous boost to their economies. Export-oriented manufacturing, especially in Singapore and Malaysia, enhanced their capabilities to compete in international markets and highlighted the need for faster technological development to keep pace with global changes. India, however, took these steps much later, with the result that it has lagged behind in economic development.

As we have seen, one of the important variables in any structural economic reform and technology transfer process is appropriate availability and development of human resources. An important reason for the success of Singapore, and recently Malaysia and South Korea, is their heavy investment in constant development of human resources right from the school stage to their on-the-job upgradation. Another contributory factor to the development of these countries has been the free flow of human resources from one country to another. Countries such as Singapore and Malaysia have relied heavily, at the initial stages of development, on the import of manpower from other countries, in addition to heavy investment in training and development for full upgradation of indigenous manpower. The ultimate objective of any economic reform and technology transfer process is to raise the living standards of the people, who are not only contributing to its development, but are also its beneficiaries. It is in this context that the economic reforms process, technology transfer and human resource development are very much interlinked.

In the previous chapters, the issue of economic restructuring and reforms, technology transfer, assimilation and development and the substantive role of human resources has been discussed in detail with special reference to Singapore, Malaysia, Thailand and India. Many developing countries can draw certain lessons from these experiences. In this chapter, some general suggestions are made which could possibly help the developing countries both at the macro and micro level, in streamlining their economic development, technology transfer and human resource development policies.

# Economic restructuring

## Forward Vision

There is an old adage that says, 'where there is no vision the people perish'. For faster development a long-term vision on the part of the nation's leadership can play a significant role. The former Prime Minister Lee had a vision of Singapore becoming a 'developed' nation by the year 1999. Today it is close to achieving this target. Similarly, in Malaysia, Prime Minister Mahatir Mohammad had spelled out his long-term vision of seeing Malaysia achieve a developed nation status by the year 2020. All the sectors of the Malaysian economy are gearing themselves to achieve the targets set for Vision 2020.

It is also important that the vision about the future is very specific and not given in general terms. For example, Malaysia's Vision 2020 clearly stipulates that the country has to achieve an average growth rate of around 7 per cent per year and all the sectors of the economy have to make an equal contribution to achieve these growth targets. In contrast, India has only spoken in general terms about removal of poverty and overall development. But specific targets and efforts required for each segment of the economy on a long-term basis are either weak or missing. Thus, a clear articulation of a long-term vision is needed for developing countries to formulate their short-term and long-term plans and targets for growth.

## Opening up of the Economy

The primary objective of any economic development process is to raise the living standards of the masses. This can be achieved by ample production and availability of goods and services at affordable prices and increasing the purchasing power of the people through proper employment. Industrial development is crucial to produce goods and services and generate employment. This also requires heavy investment. Developing countries do not have adequate financial resources for investment, especially in the initial stages of development.

Therefore, they have to rely on investments from other countries and MNCs. Thus, one of the basic prerequisites for any economic development is the encouragement of investment in industrial activity.

Foreign investors, especially the MNCs which have the requisite technology and resources, will only invest in countries where there is a congenial investment climate, appropriate infrastructure facilities and where they can get adequate return on their investment. The experience of the countries studied indicates that free market economy is more conducive to investment rather than a state-controlled one. The opening up of the economy to domestic as well as foreign investment thus becomes essential. Some of the strategies which could be adopted are outlined below.

♦ *Development Philosophy* Any investment made should be more in the productive sector rather than in social projects which are non-productive and provide only short-term temporary relief to weaker or unemployed sectors. For example, during the recession period both the governments in Malaysia and Singapore, in order to sustain the levels of employment, took up massive construction projects (both housing and roads). This served a two-fold purpose: one, it offered employment opportunities; and two, it resulted in the development of better infrastructure. In contrast, in India some of the subsidies have been in the shape of doles and huge amounts were spent on social projects in non-productive sectors. It may be more prudent for developing countries such as India, Pakistan, Bangladesh, Nepal, etc. where there is more unemployment, to identify specific projects which can help in building infrastructure or are productive and, as a temporary measure, also provide much-needed employment to the population. At the same time, investment could be concentrated on long-term employment-generation ventures.

♦ *Export Orientation* The world is moving towards a borderless market and a global economy with the gradual removal of trade barriers. Countries need to adopt export-oriented policies rather than ones based on import substitution. This entails liberalized imports especially for items that are meant for value addition and re-export. Singapore and Malaysia allow imports freely. This has not only resulted in value addition for export but has also generated internal competition resulting in better quality of products. While helping in meeting the external competition for exports, this ultimately benefits the internal consumers as well.

♦ *General Agreement on Trade and Tariff (GATT)* With the trend towards globalization, trade barriers among different countries are getting reduced. More and more regional blocs are being formed whereby the movement of goods is freely allowed and most favoured nation treatment is accorded to countries within the regional blocs. Almost all the major countries in the world have recently signed the GATT which imposes some binding commitments to reduce/eliminate special tariffs on certain items to encourage merchandise trade. There are also certain limitations imposed under the GATT agreement to reduce subsidies on the goods meant for exports. There are also provisions for protection of intellectual property and patent rights on certain original invention processes and design, etc.

Under the GATT, the World Trade Organization (WTO) has been formed with a view to oversee the operation of the agreement on a regular basis. The WTO will also be responsible to help in settlement of disputes arising out of the agreement. All these indicate that gradually, in terms of trade and movement of goods, the world is moving towards a borderless world and regional/country barriers are likely to get further reduced. Therefore, each country will have to develop certain core competencies and export orientation in those areas and, in turn, import other goods to meet its requirements.

♦ *Government Withdrawal and Privatization* One of the common features in some of the developing countries is the active role played by the government in running enterprises directly. This has resulted in heavy investment in these industries and also at times subsidizing the losses. It is suggested that the governments withdraw gradually from the manufacturing sector and concentrate in the development of infrastructure as well as health and education. In a country like Malaysia, the government had initially started industries in sectors where private investment was not forthcoming and then as a policy transferred it to the private sector on the principle of Build-Own-Operate-and-Transfer (BOOT) or Build-Own-and-Transfer (BOT). Some of the finances raised through divestment could be used for development of infrastructure.

In some developing countries such as India, Bangladesh and Nepal, the socialistic ideology of the role of the state in running the industries still persists. Also, in public enterprises, there is much greater security for the workers even if the industry is not doing well. Often, this can result in complacency and lower production. There is also strong opposition from the labour unions and political parties to any major economic restructuring and privatization efforts owing to the fear of employees losing their jobs as a result of privatization. In such circumstances, it is important to have a safety net which will, to some extent, reduce the feeling of insecurity. This has also to be linked with the policies related to retraining and redeployment of the work force. This has been discussed in detail later in this chapter.

## Financial Sector Reforms

Normally, there are two types of inflow of foreign investment into developing countries—one is Foreign Direct Investment (FDI) and the other is investment made by Foreign Institutional Investors (FII) who normally invest in financial markets. FDI in most cases is through equity participation in industries or services which ultimately results in production of goods and services. Therefore, FDI is normally a long-term investment. On the other hand, investments by foreign institutions in financial markets is often used in the secondary market and can, at times, result in short-term buoyancy in the stock markets—as had happened in both India and Mexico during 1993–94. Environmental uncertainties can affect financial markets and result in sudden withdrawals of FII which can, in turn, precipitate a crisis not only in that country but in other countries also. For example, as we saw in Mexico, the financial crisis in 1993–94 resulted in a crash in the financial market not only in Mexico but its repercussions were felt in a number of developing countries in the Asian region as well. Therefore, it is desirable to attract FDI in productive sectors rather than in the secondary share markets. A certain amount of regulatory control therefore on FII may be necessary to prevent a Mexican type of financial crisis. While opening up the economy to foreign investors, some checks can be maintained to oversee the foreign investments and their utilization.

♦ *Funds for Investment* The interest rate mechanism has come to play a vital role in investment decisions—both domestic and foreign. Any minor fluctuation in the interest rate, especially in the developed countries, has an immediate impact on the world financial market. Easy availability of funds for proper investment is necessary for any industrial development. It is often observed that while the interest rate in developed countries is low, it is fairly high in developing countries mainly with a view to increase savings. An often-voiced complaint by local investors is that they do not have a level playing field since foreign investors have easier and cheaper availability of funds. In these circumstances, it is important that at the initial stages of development the government controls the interest rate meant for investment purposes or provides special financial incentives to local entrepreneurs as is being done in Singapore and Malaysia.

♦ *Convertibility*   Another financial aspect which attracts foreign investment is the free convertibility of the currency so that there are no restrictions on earnings and repatriation of funds. While in the long run this is a desirable objective, in the short run certain amount of regulatory mechanism may be necessary for a developing country till the economy has reached a take-off stage. Sometimes, the sudden free convertibility of currency can also result in the flight of capital out of the country. Therefore, at the developing phase it may be advisable to have convertibility on trade account while on capital account certain checks and balances may be desirable as was done in India during 1994–95.

## Continuity of Policies

In the developing stage of a country economic stability is necessary— both for internal and external investment. Even if there is political instability, it is important that there be some consensus and understanding among all the politicians about the country's economic policies and development. Thailand is a good example where there have been major political changes from time to time but the economic policies have not changed. This has built up confidence amongst the investors. In fact, in Thailand the government is gradually withdrawing from practising a regulatory role, thus attracting more foreign investments into the country.

## Reforms in the Civil Service

With the intention of bringing in social justice in the initial years of development, the bureaucracy is generally given a prominent role in regulating the economy. In due course, however, it degenerates into procedural clearances and delays, thus hindering the process of growth. This, in turn, discourages investment especially by foreign investors from developed countries. For example, the Indian and Singapore governments agreed to jointly set up Technology Parks in India. While the proposal was cleared at the central government level, there were still a large number of cumbersome clearances that had to be obtained—both at central and state government levels—which caused considerable delays.

Most developing countries have realized the significance of bureaucratic and procedural reforms. We have already seen how in Malaysia with the introduction of a single-window system for clearances, approvals are obtained within two to three weeks. Each civil servant in Malaysia is required to enlist his responsibilities and time-frame for critical jobs which are prominently displayed. In case of any delay or if a civil servant is not following a set procedure, a complaint can be registered in the specially set-up cell for action against such delays. For example, telephone operators in government departments are required to answer the telephone within two to three bells. This has improved the overall efficiency of the entire civil service.

Similarly, in Singapore no clearance is required, except where it comes to adhering to environmental laws and completion of the registration formalities with the Registrar of Societies, customs, etc. Thailand has also recently streamlined its clearance procedures. Considering the importance of timely clearances for investment in developing countries, Thailand has not only hastened the procedure but also reduced the number of approvals/clearances required. This will, of course, entail a reduction in the size of the bureaucracy for which appropriate human resource redeployment policies within the public services need to be developed.

Though the reform process has been initiated at the central government level in some countries such as India, its percolation to the state level has been rather slow with the result that the impact of liberalization has not been fully felt by the industrial sector. It may be advisable to set up a Committee to review the percolation of the reform process at the state levels and develop broad guidelines which the states could follow to hasten the process of liberalization and industrial growth.

Civil services need to bring in greater professionalism in their work so that they can play a more facilitative role. In most structural re-adjustment programmes such as the one in Malaysia and Singapore, simultaneous attention has been given to reforms in the civil service including development of human resources within the government. The major objective of such reforms is to enhance the capability of the government to implement and facilitate economic development and introduce human resource development programmes. Some of the major areas which may require attention could be the following:

♦ *Reduction in Size and Levels of Governmental Machinery* A major chunk of the government's expenditure often goes towards maintaining a large number of employees. Very little resources are left to provide actual services to the people. In countries such as Singapore and Malaysia, it has been found that reducing the level of hierarchy in the government can also lead to a simplification of procedures. This results in providing faster services to the public and improving the overall efficiency of government officials.

♦ *Clarity of Missions and Performance Standards* As a part of the reform process, Malaysia has recently embarked upon the task of clarifying the mission of each government department or agency and its goals. Each functionary is also expected to develop one's own performance standards in qualitative or quantitative terms. These are made transparent to the public who, in turn, demand the services as a matter of right. This has resulted in the introduction of the concept of 'total quality management' within the civil service. Such experiences are worth emulating by all the countries.

♦ *Facilitative Role of the Government* There has been much debate all over the world on the subject of the regulatory role of the government and the extent to which it should withdraw and play a more facilitative role. Extreme withdrawal can sometimes have an adverse effect; for example, in Thailand, the environmental aspects have been neglected resulting in major pollution problems. On the other hand, Singapore has opened up its economy but at the same time retained stringent regulatory mechanisms by various government statutory bodies. It is therefore important for developing economies to review various regulatory rules, laws, etc. The government could consider withdrawing those which are restrictive, while at the same time bring in those rules and norms which facilitate investment and development.

Public enterprises can also be run efficiently, as mentioned earlier in the cases of Singapore International Airlines and Singapore Port Trust. These have been run as commercial enterprises with minimal governmental interference. Competition can also ensure efficiency even in public enterprises, provided it is made abundantly clear that if an enterprise is not running efficiently or goes bankrupt, the government will not come to its rescue.

## Infrastructure

It is found that investment is directed at those countries which offer the best infrastructure facilities in terms of power, roads, transport, port facilities, etc. Singapore excels in this regard. Singapore believes in constantly upgrading its facilities with the government playing a catalyst role. The governments in developing countries should concentrate their efforts and resources on infrastructure development rather than engaging in commercial activities. The private sector can also be involved in developing infrastructure. In Malaysia, for example, the major road network is developed and maintained by the private sector with appropriate government controls over toll charges.

## Incentive for Local Industries

It is observed that a major source of employment generation in most countries is by local industries and through MNCs. There has been a recent trend for many MNCs to outsource their products to local industries who have the appropriate technological capability, especially with regard to human resources. It is often believed that opening up of the economy to MNCs will retard the growth of local industries as they cannot compete in terms of investment or technology. However, the Singapore experience suggests that while initially local industries were affected, subsequently they picked up momentum by adopting conscious policies of encouraging local industries through availability of funds and facilitation of latest technology by the government along with incentives.

Many MNCs are even willing to provide the appropriate know-how provided local industries have the basic capability to absorb and assimilate the technology. In Singapore, the government has played a major role in such capability-building through government statutory bodies such as the National Productivity Board (NPB). The result is that local industries have, in recent years, shown an annual growth of around 20 per cent. What is important for the government in developing countries is to do an assessment of local industries, their current level of technology, the availability of skills and resources in the local market and then formulate appropriate incentives and remove some of the factors that obstruct development.

# TECHNOLOGY

## Strategic Alliances in Technology Transfer

In the present context, technology is the key to the growth and development of any nation. Some countries, because of their innovative practices and inventions, have been able to develop technology at a much faster pace, resulting in better living standards for their people. However, there are a vast number of less developed countries who, for various historical reasons, have not been able to keep pace with technological developments. Also, with changes in income patterns, communication among the nations of the world and their people, it has become a futile exercise if each country were to develop its own technology from scratch. While some countries develop their expertise and technology in certain areas, others have different kinds of skills and resources to offer. Therefore, it is imperative that technology is shared for achieving better living standards worldwide.

With globalization, competitiveness has increased and many organizations lack the resources to develop all the requisite technologies on their own. There is always need for continuous innovation, especially in high-technology industries. Here, strategic alliances help to fulfil the technological gaps, increase the inter-connected product range, tap new markets, meet competition, service the customers better and above all save time and resources in developing new products and process technologies.

Many companies today are entering into strategic alliances for mutual advantage. The success of these alliances are dependent upon the core competencies and strengths the parties can offer to each other. Alliances often degenerate to a sell-out if one partner is either weak in negotiation or has not developed core competencies. One partner is normally the MNC who has inherent strengths and is in a better bargaining position unless the local companies can consolidate their offers. For example, countries such as India can offer the following major benefits:

❑ Large domestic market

❑ Wide distribution network

❑ Reasonable manufacturing base/excess available capacity

❑ Reasonable level of manpower, skill and expertise

❑ Relatively cheaper labour

❑ Outsourcing of components at lower costs

Smaller countries such as Singapore and Malaysia have been able to offer a better industrial relations climate, good infrastructure, simpler procedures and special financial incentives.

On the other hand, the recipient organizations/countries look towards the MNCs/foreign partners to bring in:

❑ The latest technology

❑ Capital for investment

❑ Evidence of increased profitability

❑ Continuous access to the latest technology

❑ Avenues for specialized training of manpower

❑ Prospects of joint ventures in third-world countries; and

❑ Marketing and services outside their own countries

## Assessment of Technology

As we have seen earlier, for any assimilation or transfer of technology, the recipient organization should have the capability to appropriately assess the technology which they intend importing. This calls for proper assessment of technology gaps through the data base and developing an institutional mechanism for such an assessment. This also entails constant upgradation of human resource skills to analyze and update their information. The assessment of technology should include internal R&D efforts, global competitiveness of the technology, latest market developments, customer preferences, etc.

## Negotiation

The choice, evaluation and negotiation mechanism are very crucial for any technology transfer. The team constituted for negotiation should comprise experts from different areas—technology, R&D, marketing, finance, etc. The government also plays a role in the negotiation process, which can either be constructive or negative. For example, in Singapore the government agencies keep themselves abreast of the latest information on technological developments and help organizations in the negotiation process. On the other hand, in India there are often pressures on the enterprises in terms of team selection and number of persons to be sent for negotiation, which at times are based on expediency rather than expertise. With the requisite international information and documentation systems in place, governments can play a positive role. Alternatively, they should leave the enterprises free to select their own teams. Many local organizations do not negotiate technology transfer packages for the purposes of assimilation to their advantage. It is desirable that these organizations gradually develop their own capability for equitable alliances rather than enter into pure technology transfer arrangements.

## Long-term Planning for Technology Development

For any organization to survive on a long-term basis, it is important that the short-term and long-term technology development policies are clearly defined and the strategies worked out accordingly. This helps in focusing the assimilation efforts on technology for the long-term growth and development of the organization. In many cases, technology assimilation is not defined by companies as one of their missions or objectives. Often organizations concentrate mainly on technology transplants and meeting production targets as a result of which development of a conscious long-term strategy for technology assimilation gets neglected.

Local organizations, especially in developing countries, often try to get foreign brand names which could have a better saleability. This is always to the disadvantage of local organizations because there are conditions attached to any such arrangements with regard to purchase of technology. Instead, these organizations should develop short-term and long-term technology assimilation policies which can also go a long way in building their image.

## Research and Development

Given their limited resources, it is not feasible to undertake major R&D investments in developing countries. Therefore, it is important to first identify a few core sectors where there is scope to develop competence and then make a major investment in these areas. One of the drawbacks found in R&D investment in India is that owing to the initial thrust on import substitution, investments in R&D were spread across a large number of areas with inadequate funding for any one sector in particular. This has resulted in a poor output in terms of major innovations or developing commercially-viable products and processes that can be patented. It would perhaps be better to concentrate on a few selected areas, develop one's own patents, and even export technology outside. This will also attract equitable strategic alliances with MNCs in core sectors. With the signing of the GATT agreements it has become all the more necessary to develop one's own patents through R&D efforts.

Owing to limited resources for R&D investment, the accent in many newly developing countries is on import of technology. However, as the economies reach a stage of positive growth and stability, the resources should gradually be directed towards R&D. Also, the R&D efforts should be in applied research rather than in basic research. The encouragement towards reverse engineering, though considered unethical at times, is widely practised by some countries. Reverse engineering entails detailed breakdown and study of already manufactured components with the objective of under-standing its manufacturing process. This does not involve major R&D investment in starting the related research right from scratch and results in substantial savings of time and money. However, the GATT agreements may not allow uncontrolled reverse engineering. It has therefore, become all the more necessary now for developing countries to first earmark core competency areas in order to concentrate their R&D efforts.

Proper coordination among the various functional areas, such as operations, R&D, marketing and human resource development, is essential for total assimilation of technology. This also needs to be coordinated with the other functions for developing appropriate manning norms and identifying the necessary training needs for handling and absorbing the new technology. Similarly, R&D, marketing and operations need to work very closely to understand the process and ensure constant upgradation.

The experience of other countries, especially South Korea, indicate that understanding the process aspects is much better when R&D professionals are fully involved in the entire transfer process. In fact, in some organizations in South Korea, technology transfer takes place to R&D, which in turn transfers it to operations. The advantage of involving the R&D people right from the beginning is that they understand the process aspects and can consider upgrading the technology on their own wherever required.

For any transfer and assimilation of technology, a systematic documentation of the present status of technology used in different industries is important. In addition, the systematic documentation of the entire process of assimilation and technical details including any upgradation or modification is essential from time to time. Proper documentation of all relevant information enables simpler and quicker information sharing and review of the level of technological development. At the organization level also, continuous documentation of technology is very essential so that the status of technology development and upgradation is available in case of any employee turnover.

## Government Role in Technology

The experience of Singapore suggests that the government can play a significant role in facilitating a technology transfer process as well as its subsequent assimilation and upgradation through various incentives. The government or its agencies can take the initiative in identifying the emerging areas of technology advancement, assessing existing technology levels in the country and offering appropriate incentives to cover the identified technological gaps. If required, the government can also take the initiative in buying the latest technology from outside and disseminating it to the local industries. The government can also identify the priority industries where internal capabilities can be built up and initially concentrate on these areas, both in terms of research and investment. Value-added manufacturing activities can be given priority to ensure faster growth of the economy.

## Pooling of Technological Resources

Small and medium enterprises often do not have adequate resources to continuously upgrade their technology with the result that they are unable to compete with the new enterprises who have the latest technology. Singapore has tried the experiment of pooling technological resources together, especially in the retail outlets such as bakeries, where they provide common manufacturing centres for a number of small and medium enterprises. There is also a continuous effort in upgrading the technology with government support. These experiments are worth emulating by other countries. Even in the USA, many small apparel firms have similarly pooled their resources and thus have continuous access to new technology which has enabled them to stay one step ahead in global markets.

# Human Resource Development

## Planning for Human Resources

A major challenge before us today is how to harness the new technological revolution for the welfare of the maximum number of people. To most of us, the word 'technology' conjures up images of sleek machines and computer-controlled systems. These machines are undoubtedly the products and tools of the technological age but the real engine of technology remains the human mind. The challenge, therefore, is to develop the minds and skills of the workforce so that they can intelligently and fully utilize the machine power.

The training tools and institutions which we have developed over the past century, unfortunately, often have not kept pace with the geometric advances of technology. This is especially true in the case of developing countries. Formal training institutions are, for no fault of their own, under-financed and often reduced to purveying the skills of an outdated technology. In many cases, the teachers themselves are unfamiliar with the latest technology. The organizations which need this skilled manpower for their advancing processes, often have to choose between the available options on the basis of obsolete techniques. This further inhibits the introduction of new technology because of the lack of skilled operators. There could also be instances where the teachers who know how to convey the knowledge and skills and the organization that knows what needs to be taught often have no effective means of communication. Therefore, for any technology change and development, there is need for both short-term and long-term planning of human resources.

For this, technological planning as well as human resource planning must go hand in hand.

The objective of the planning activity is to establish a framework for evaluation and the evaluation process should then feed the next cycle of the planning process. Developing people is the centre of the planning circle. Planning leads to the setting of objectives—specific, measurable, outcome-oriented statements—which can act as the linchpins for the planning, administration and evaluation functions. It is comparatively easy to theoretically develop the planning and evaluation process but extremely difficult to carry it out in a very complex, technologically fast-changing environment, as there are many points at which it can break down.

Before starting the actual planning process, some of the major questions to be answered are:

❑ To what extent is the planning process routinely tied to specific data?

❑ Is there sufficient data for taking programme decisions for human resource development?

❑ Is there a well-designed management information system for the implementation of the programme?

❑ To what extent are the plans evaluated and used in the next planning cycle?

❑ Is the plan reviewed at the end of the plan period or the outcomes reviewed? Is the data from the evaluation of the current plan recycled into the next plan?

The human resource development plan should be specific enough in order to determine where a country or organization can best obtain or train the human resources needed to accomplish the desired objectives. In such cases, the objectives have to be clear and possibly measurable and the plan should be seen as being fairly related to and visibly assisting the country's programmes.

Usually, human resource development is sidelined when technological and developmental planning is done. If such is the case, there is little that professionals involved in human resource development can do. However, there are several things that human resource development planners can take up in the course of technological development:

❑ Developing a human resource plan even if there are no specific country-level developmental objectives

❏ Effectively integrate the development of specific development plans taking into consideration the new technologies

❏ Ask planning questions. For example, how many and of what types of personnel and what skills would the country need in various segments of the economy over the next five to 10 years to achieve its objectives? What new knowledge and skills will the country or the different sectors of economy need to have over the next few years to facilitate technology development and the country's progress?

❏ What major problems do the planners envisage in the near future to meet the objectives. (All these may not be subject to human resource development solutions but some will certainly be.)

Some initial steps that could be taken are given below.

❏ Given the planning requirements, we may need to look at the future, but how far ahead we should look depends on many factors. Many experts feel that 15–20 year plans may become outdated because of the rapid technological changes and difficulties in predicting that far in advance. Therefore, the long-range planning period in many countries is limited to five years

❏ Each segment of the economy must be tied to the overall country's goals. Therefore, each segment, including its human resource development wing, should base its plans on the national plans

❏ Provision for the review and modification of the plan are necessary. There has to be an annual review of the long-range plan to take care of environmental and technological changes

It is important that the human resource development and technological plans are linked with the budgetary allocations. In a sense, the budget is also a plan. Each human resource development segment should have a planning time-table which provides for completing the plan before the budget is 'locked in'. This will ensure that the plan is realistic and that the resources needed to fund the plan are appropriate and available. This requires data-based planning.

## Education and Training

In developing any human resource plan for technology changes, the basic prerequisite is elementary and higher level education of the people. One of the reasons for expansion of higher education in many countries, including India, is the main concern of planners with forecasting and meeting the needs of higher level manpower. However, there is usually a tendency to err on the side of excess. This happens because the demand for higher level professional manpower is determined on the assumption of fixed output-skill ratios. The possibilities of substituting physical capital and skills among different skill categories are ignored, leading to rigidities in the system.

Also, education investments tend to be made without any reference to socio-economic criteria. Educational institutions are established without due regard to the availability of material and human resources, adequacy of catchment areas, optimal size and socio-economic needs of the people. Often there is greater emphasis on expansion rather than on improving the quality and efficiency of the existing resources. Some of the indicators of malfunctioning of educational systems in the Indian subcontinent are:

❑ High rate of unemployment among the educated

❑ Scarcity of certain skills

❑ High level of brain-drain

❑ Under-utilization of employed skills

❑ High rate of failures and dropouts

Though there is wastage of resources at all levels of the educational system, it is maximum at the school level. For example, in India, there is a very high dropout rate—almost 50 per cent—in the first four years of school. This is very high as compared to Japan (1 per cent), Taiwan (8 per cent), South Korea (less than 10 per cent), Afghanistan (15 per cent), and the Philippines (about 20 per cent). Even in engineering colleges, the dropout rate in a country such as India is fairly high and unemployment among engineers is fairly common. It has been estimated that one dropout from an engineering college can take care of at least one primary school for a year.

The Indian subcontinent has a large number of scientists and engineers but in the absence of a systematic approach the linking of theoretical technical training with the socio-economic environment has been slow. In these countries, technology has been imported even for simple industrial processes. This can lead to a failure of educational policies on the criteria of investment, redistribution and creation of socially relevant needs. Consequently, this can lead to inefficiencies in production and utilization of human capital.

Another factor is that the academic training distinctly designed for human resource development is not widespread in universities and colleges. It should be understood that human resource development presumes not merely development of literacy or education but developing people for the required skills with specific laid-down objectives. In other words, educational institutions need to be developed with a distinct human resource development focus. This is not to indicate that investment in school education is irrelevant; it is not because they provide the foundation for higher technical education. If the basic material is poor, then investment in higher technical education may not yield the desired results.

With the objective of modernizing the conventional production system, machinery and technical know-how are initially imported from advanced countries either in exchange or export of primary goods or as external assistance to be repatriated in the future. But these practices cannot go on for ever. Some countries have now started giving emphasis on developing their own technical personnel to operate the complicated technological systems. Therefore, for faster development of educational policies, more investment will be needed at the higher stages of education which can lay emphasis on the development of skills for new technologies.

For appropriate skill development, many countries have started vocational training institutes as well as apprenticeship training schemes. However, there are two senses in which it can be argued that the quality of the training schemes is deficient. One is, at the end of the training, the trainee is unable to carry out a specific job although he is regarded as being capable of doing that job. The other is when the training fails to reach a certain standard. In other words, when training is being judged against criteria accepted as good in themselves. In this case, any relationship between training and the ability to do a specific job is being established and the emphasis is upon the development of the trainee's talents for work in general or for a broad range of jobs. Here, the concept of training merges with the concept of education.

Thus, it is conceivable that the product of a 'bad' training in the second sense, can be a perfectly good worker as far as the employer is concerned. Similarly, good training in that sense can produce, from the employers' point of view, a 'bad' worker. Therefore, there is a strong movement to improve the quality of training. One reason for such demand is the advent of the 'micro chip' revolution. A second reason can also be the reason for increasing youth unemployment in a country such as India. There is a sense of expectation that immediately after leaving school, the young person must get a placement of some form or another. Thus, training for the unemployed is a more emotionally charged issue than training for the employed or about to be employed. In countries such as France or West Germany, 40 to 50 per cent of young people enter full-time vocational education after compulsory schooling; in countries such as India, it is almost less than 10 per cent.

Similarly, the apprenticeship training in industry is normally treated as a cheap substitute for permanent employees. The training given is of a very general nature. The objective of these schemes is normally to increase the competitive edge of the young people and get them as quickly as possible into a job. Hence the programme is constrained by these objectives and the quality is necessarily limited. Many of the jobs available to young people require no skill or training. For a need-based training, the starting point must be that jobs already exist for which the training is required. The need, therefore, is for high quality training for high quality jobs.

It is understood that any investment in human resource development would yield results in the long run. On the one hand, the advantage is that they do not depreciate or lose their value during the period of their utilization. In fact, the more use that is made of investment in the knowledge, skill and experience of a country's population, the more is the capital value and the higher the income-yielding capacity of the investment made in them. There is a close relationship between the spread of scientific and technical education and the pace of technical advancement and scientific inventions and innovations, and between the trained manpower and the utilization of the advanced techniques of production.

## Changes in Occupational Structures

A number of recent studies on the relationship between new technologies and skills have arrived at quite different conclusions. Some feel that there is a definite trend towards deskilling. In the printing sector, for instance, photocomposition and facsimile satellite transmission can render much of the traditional know-how of the professionals obsolete. The same is true in the metal trade. Highly skilled milling, grinding and lathe machines are being replaced by Computer Numerically Controlled (CNC) machine tools. The introduction of robots too will lead to a general decline in qualifications because these machines take over not only the manual but also the intelligent human functions. Others, however, do not agree with these conclusions and argue that the production, setting-up and monitoring of these machines require vast and sophisticated know-how and skills. Yet others foresee a different polarization of skills that, on the one hand, require an elite corps of engineers-technocrats, controllers, repairers and on the other and a huge army of machines-minders.

Such a variety of functions may not be so surprising. In the first place, with the introduction of new technologies, there are vast changes in occupational structures. Moreover, micro-electronics is applied in many different production processes and can, therefore, lead to very different skill patterns. With the changes in technology, occupational activities are less concerned with production processes than with control and support activities. Manual activities and craftsmanship are getting transferred to maintenance and repair tasks which will become more complex as the machines become more sophisticated. A very high degree of occupational skill required will need to be combined with higher level of general and technical education. Therefore, the general level of education will be a very relevant factor so that the worker can understand the 'whys' and 'wherefores' of limited operation for which he is responsible. He will then be able to absorb the successive training and retraining which the technical change is certain to entail—at the level of the factory, of the occupations and of the industry. Another development is that at least in certain occupations, information technology is playing an increasing role in skills from which it was totally absent till only a few years ago. Given these trends, a broad basic education in which a solid general initiation to the methods of science will be a valuable asset for future members of the active population who are called upon to work with the new technologies.

Another trend that is visible is the growing mass of employment in the service sector. For example, in one of the studies conducted in OECD countries, it was found that the share of employment in the service sector rose, on an average, from 43 per cent in 1960 to 63 per cent in 1991. It now accounts for two-thirds of the total employment in the USA and Canada, though it is still far less than 50 per cent in the countries of southern Europe and Ireland. It grew at a faster annual rate during 1973–90 than from 1950–73. The service sector is mainly engaged in trade, restaurants, hotels, transport and communications, public health, insurance, postal services, education and other business services. There is a trend towards introduction of modern technologies in these services which can result in temporary displacement requiring training and retraining of personnel in these sectors. There is need for specialized training programmes designed specifically for the service sector.

In planning for human resource development, it is necessary to analyze and examine the demand-supply relationship on a continuing basis and periodically check the 'rolling forecasts' so that suitable adjustments, if necessary, can be made while determining priorities. The long-term forecasts should go far beyond a statistical analysis given a qualitative as well as quantitative evaluation and appraisal of changing demand-supply relationships. While forecasting future manpower shortage, one should take into account the changes in occupational skills which are likely to take place in the future. For example, a new technology will lead to the development of new skills, making old skills redundant. Introduction of CNC machines is an example. This can sometimes create a dilemma for the economy because, in many cases, the organizations may just go in for recruitment of new persons easing out old ones. This could result in the creation of additional employment while, at the same time, causing unemployment of the existing manpower. Thus, the human resource development strategy should take into account the upgrading of skills of the existing manpower as well as training of new personnel. This has to be linked with providing basic educational requirements and standards, right at the selection stage.

In any case of technology transfer, especially from developed to developing countries, the normal practice is to plan on the basis of manning standards originally given by the developed countries. However, in developing countries such 'speed-feed' technology transfer and manning standards result in problems owing to different norms, cultural values and socio-economic conditions as well as the current basic education and skill level of the employees. As a result, all manning standards become distorted as they were, in the first place, developed by developed countries to meet their own peculiar needs. Therefore, some research may be needed to identify the various factors which influence manning standards in cases of technology upgradation. Case studies of a few organizations can be prepared to see what were the originally specified standards and what actually has happened over a period of time and what the implications are for the organization in terms of productivity and human resource development. The norms could perhaps gradually change in future, but it is important to make such estimates.

## Strategy for Developing Human Resources for Employment

One of the objectives of any country, especially a developing country, is to ensure full production and employment for all who are available and seek work. Therefore, a country's human resource development strategy must be linked to investment and fiscal policies with the objective of developing economically sound production-oriented employment rather than relief-oriented employment. In other words, it should stimulate and not impede the process of economic development. Therefore, a well-designed employment promotion policy should lay down in quantitative terms the employment and training targets for different sectors of the economy and also lay down the measures necessary for the realization of these employment objectives. It is essential that such a policy is carried out within the overall framework of national development plans. Experience shows that only those countries from the Asian region which were able to achieve a compounded rate of GDP of 8 per cent or more, succeeded in securing a progressive decline in the rate of unemployment.

It would be useful to work out a detailed inventory of the technology alternatives available for each industry, and within each industry, for each of the major processes, for the guidance of planners and policy-makers. The general approach of the human resource development strategist should take into account the following factors:

❑ Identification of the areas of economic activity which are seriously handicapped owing to shortages of technical, professional and skilled manpower

❑ Initiation of necessary measures for the development and training of strategic manpower

❑ Initiation of appropriate policies for efficient utilization of the available human resources in the country

The problems of manpower shortages are discussed under separate broad groups.

♦ *Current Availability of Positions*  These are positions for which suitable manpower possessing the required skills and knowledge level is not available. In the present context, for example, there will be shortages of computer programmers, experts in Computer-Aided Design (CAD) and Computer-Aided Management (CAM) positions. There could even be shortage of some types of skilled workers such as machinists. At the supervisory and technical levels, there could be shortage of, say, electronic, electrical and metallurgical engineers and supervisors; while at the professional level, there could be shortages of trained craft teachers and instructors in certain areas. There can be shortages at the top management level as well. There is often a dearth of qualified and experienced technical and managerial personnel in specialized fields. Possible shortages can be identified through enquiries from major establishments who routinely employ skilled workers, as well as by checking registrations of vacancies among employment or placement services.

♦ *Partially Filled Positions*  Partially filled positions constitute a concealed portion of manpower shortages. Where it is difficult to locate the manpower of requisite skills, the employing organizations lower their educational and vocational training requirements or at times upgrade already employed personnel even though they may not have the requisite skills. The problem of identifying partially filled positions is one of judging cases where an increase in skills would lead to significant increase in the production or in an improvement in the quality of services. In these cases, one approach could be to develop certain standards for satisfactory performance of an occupation which may be linked with training. The type of training already given to the employees in such occupations could be examined to identify where the training falls short of the required standard. This can also be done by making an assessment of the proportion of manpower employed in an occupation whose inadequate performance is resulting in low levels of production or poor quality services. This could be done on the basis of the employer's opinion, trade testing or even the trade unions.

*Manpower Requirements Linked with Shortages of Key Inputs*
In many developing countries, especially in Asia, organizations are not able to work to their full capacities owing to certain infrastructural bottlenecks, such as shortage of power, unavailability of raw material, inadequate spare parts, poor transportation, etc. Fuller utilization of the installed capacity can create additional demand for scientific, technical and skilled manpower.

♦ *Replacement of Foreign Technical Experts* Many developing countries at the initial stages of technology development, need the expertise of the developed countries. However, each country must try to train its own personnel to replace such foreign experts who have highly specialized and critical skills.

♦ *Manpower Shortages due to Employment Abroad* The countries of south Asia, such as India, Pakistan, Bangladesh, etc. have been experiencing an exodus of certain skilled categories of employees to other countries, particularly to those in the Middle East since there they get much better compensation. Such a drain is unavoidable and each country needs to prepare adequate manpower at various levels to take care of such eventualities.

## Training Strategies

An attempt has been made in the preceding part to highlight some of the basic considerations which should weigh with planners and policy-makers concerned with technological and human resource development. The different types of human resource developmental programmes are described below.

♦ *Institutional Training* Technical and vocational training can be at the professional level, technician level or at the artisan, craftsmen and skilled-worker level. Professional training can be provided at the graduate level in various fields of specialization. For technicians, institutional training facilities can cover the intermediate group falling between professionals and skilled workers.

♦ *Vocational Training* Special vocational training programmes can be adopted by various countries depending on their requirements at the artisan, craftsmen and skilled-worker levels. The selection of such programmes should be based on the following:

❏ Flexibility Vocational training programmes at the craftsmen and production process workers' level should have flexibility. They must allow inter-occupational changes within the broad groups of occupations since the rapid pace of technological change often renders some occupations either obsolete or less important.

❏ Adaptability Technological upgradation frequently demands considerable adaptability on the part of the skilled workers to adjust themselves to new processes, new types of machines, new raw materials and methods of handling, new forms of control devices and occupational safety measures. The type of vocational training should facilitate the acquisition of new skills and their application to the production processes.

❏ Economy The results obtained from training should be commensurate with the resources spent. This would involve balancing of costs and the benefits that may accrue from training. The training of employed manpower may, therefore, be preferred to fresh entrants because there is a shorter gestation period before they become productive.

❏ Accessibility The location of vocational training facilities should be such that they are easily accessible to large sectors of prospective trainees as well as to industrial centres. This will enable practical training to be imparted to different branches of industries without much difficulty and cost. This will also entail greater collaboration between educational institutions and the industry.

♦ *Apprenticeship Training* Apprenticeship training is a system where an employer undertakes, under contract, to employ a young person and train him for improving his skills systematically for a specified period. The existing apprenticeship training facilities in many countries in the Asian region are not adequate and suffer from some defects and limitations. There is often a shortage of adequately trained instructors in theoretical and technical subjects. There is also considerable confusion regarding the importance of the apprenticeship scheme and the methods by which it should be established and conducted. During one of our studies in India on graduate engineer trainees, we found there was no set syllabus for the apprenticeship training; nor was there a methodical and balanced programme of theoretical and practical instruction. Supervision was often lacking and in most cases, apprentices were used as cheap labour. There is need for organizing and developing a systematic national apprenticeship programme to:

❏ Determine the apprenticeship trades

❏ Fix minimum standards of training

❏ Establish methods of examination

❏ Determine the number of apprentices and skilled workers needed for each trade and occupation

The Government of India had set up an Apprenticeship Board to introduce better standards and uniformity in their apprenticeship scheme. It is desirable that each country enacts an apprenticeship legislation laying down the rights and obligations of employers and apprentices and prescribing rules governing organization and supervision of training.

Apprenticeship training and institutional training should be dovetailed so that students are equipped with a broad-based knowledge of their specialized engineering functions including possible future changes in technology and production methods. At the organizational level, there should be a long-range training plan. Each organization should be encouraged to prepare an annual three to five year plan of plant-based education and training. The basic aim should be to meet the needs of technicians and engineers for knowledge and skill and pave the way for foreseeable changes in occupational and skill structures owing to technological changes. Another aspect linked to training is the task of selecting technicians and engineers who have the aptitude and are capable of upgrading their education or skill levels to the needs of the enterprise. Proper utilization and placement of engineers after training is another important aspect.

♦ *On-the-Job Training* This refers to the paid or unpaid training which a person receives while working on the job. This covers both in-service and pre-service training. Normally, such training combines theoretical as well as practical experience under the guidance of experts and is normally determined by the needs and requirements of each organization.

♦ *Upgrading Training* This kind of training is provided to those who are already employed for improving their knowledge, skills and aptitude. Upgrading assumes significance in many developing countries where a large number of workers have had no previous formal basic training in the trades they are engaged in. Supplementary courses should be available for all workers who wish to improve their general, technical or even commercial knowledge in order to facilitate their growth in the organization. Such training could be within the plant itself or in outside institutions through evening classes. Normally, in the case of smaller establishments, outside institutional, centralized training systems can be more useful. In Japan, for example, there is 'company school system' where certain establishments offer upgrading training courses to their own employees as well as accept employees from other smaller establishments which are not equipped with their own courses.

♦ *Accelerated Training*  There is sometimes need for quick training in certain trades and occupations where there are serious shortages of qualified personnel. This is particularly useful in meeting the urgent needs of developing countries for semi-skilled workers and workers not requiring highly specialized training. Such training is possible when the trainees have the necessary basic educational background and some work experience. The instructors need to be skilled craftsmen with good teaching ability. Close coordination is needed between the industry and centres of accelerated training, which must be equipped with adequate shopfloor facilities, teaching and training materials.

In addition, there is need to provide incentives and facilities to the personnel so that they can update their knowledge. These can be in the form of:

❑ Incentives for those who follow short-term or long-term courses outside the organization but concurrently with their employment

❑ Participation in short, off-the-job training courses;

❑ Wage and promotion policies that provide an incentive to training and motivate the personnel to continue their education

♦ *Training for Traditional and Non-formal Sector*  A large number of artisans, craftsmen and production workers in some Asian countries are traditionally trained, or acquire the skills in the form of 'learning by doing' under the guidance of an experienced artisan/craftsman/skilled worker. Though such trainees do not pass any tests, they do acquire technical competence. However, they are often inadequately trained in modern processes. Present employment trends in some Asian countries suggest that a sizeable proportion of the available semi-skilled labour would continue to be met by traditionally trained artisans and craftsmen. Also, there is an informal sector consisting of self-employed personnel or those working in very small establishments which meets a large segment of the market demand.

Many developing countries believed that economic development would sooner or later lead to the emergence of a modern technology sector large enough to absorb additions to the labour force and in the process bring about full employment. The activities in the informal sector would then disappear and its participants would be absorbed in the formal sector. However, the formal sector may not be capable of generating jobs as fast as it can generate output and many developing countries have begun to realize that these informal activities are no longer transitory. In such a situation, it may become necessary to organize training courses even for the so-called 'wayside' semi-skilled or skilled workers. Very little attention has been paid to this sector so far, except possibly in handicrafts because of their contribution to foreign exchange earnings.

♦ *Training of Instructors*   The quality and efficiency of training, both institutional and in-plant, depend to a large extent on the knowledge, pedagogical skills and qualifications of the instructors. One often hears complaints that new institutions have been established without adequate supply of trained teachers. The solution lies in first upgrading the knowledge and skill of the instructors to keep pace with the changes in technology. There is, therefore, an urgent need to constantly train instructors in appropriate technical skills and teaching abilities.

♦ *Supervisory Training*   The need for supervisory training in developing countries is much greater because they have far more workers who have never undergone any sort of basic training and whose knowledge about new techniques or job relations, job instruction and job methods is very limited. The Training Within Industry (TWI) programmes now in operation in a large number of countries can be further extended in scope and coverage and the quality of training improved upon.

♦ *Management Development* Development of management should form the core of any programme for human resource development. It is the management which plans, coordinates, supervises and controls the processes in industries and it is good management which ultimately ensures effective utilization of all available resources. Hence, high priority needs to be given to management development programmes in any human resource development planning. With rapid changes in technologies, especially with the advent of computers, microchips, etc. managers need to be trained in modern technologies so that they can in turn motivate the workmen to adapt to the new systems.

## Training Methodologies

Till now, training has been largely confined to schools, vocational training institutions and colleges. However, in the future, owing to fast-changing technologies, non-conventional methods of training will have to be adopted. This is more relevant for mass-scale training in all sectors of the economy. There may be need to make use of television, satellite communication, telematics, etc. as methods of training. Already, open universities have come up in many developing countries. For example, in India, there is a National Open University as well as regional open universities. Television and satellite communication systems are extensively used for training and development. These need to be supplemented with programmed learning, development of better quality correspondence courses and even appropriate examination and testing systems.

♦ *Computer Assisted Instruction (CAI)* This is a relatively new technique that is being used in a multitude of educational and training situations. In its simplest form, CAI offers an interactive environment in which the computer implements the final information presentation on the basis of communication from the learner. The interaction takes place through display devices, such as audio, tape or slides, to 'connect' the learner with the information being sought.

The computer lends itself to a variety of instructional modes. Tutorial and 'drill-and-practice' applications emerge most frequently as viable ways of CAI training for the industry and business. When using the tutorial mode of CAI, the bulk of the material to be learned is presented via the display unit of the computer. A one-to-one, individualized relationship between the computer and the trainee provides an environment in which the computer explains the concepts and procedures. It displays the information and asks questions. The computer travels to the next level of difficulty only when the trainee's response indicates his or her readiness to proceed.

The following features of CAI provides several potential advantages:

❑ Individualized Instruction   The trainee learns at his or her own rate of progress. The computer responds to the specific needs of the trainee.

❑ Immediate Feedback from the Computer   The amount of time required to master a lesson is often cut down by up to 50 per cent through CAI.

❑ Novelty and Appeal   The learning process seems more enjoyable than conventional methods as the computer has an element of novelty and appeals to a wide variety of age groups and applications.

❑ Reinforced Decision-making Ability   The trainee's decision-making skills are often strengthened because, the computer presents far more alternatives. The trainee can make a wrong decision without serious consequences and learn how to evaluate choices in the process.

The major drawback of the CAI is the initial cost. However, it appears that in the long run its advantages far outweigh its drawbacks.

♦ *Community-based Training*   Training tools and institutions developed over the past century have not kept pace with the geometric advances of technology, even in the case of developed countries. Many formal vocational training institutions are under-financed and are often reduced to purveying the skills of an outdated technology. In many cases, the teachers themselves are unfamiliar with the latest technology. In such a situation, it is desirable to establish community-based, local technical education colleges. Such colleges should be given the freedom to experiment, establish and develop educational programmes suited to the employment environment of the community in which they are located. The curriculum could be suitably designed to meet the needs of local enterprises, while at the same time involving the employers as well. Teachers and instructors should maintain close contact with the personnel and training officials of local firms, seeking their advice on not only current skill requirements but also on what will be needed five to ten years from now. Such institutions can also develop in-house tailormade programmes for a company or training institution to meet the educational needs of specific local enterprises.

## Management of R&D for Industry-Academy Collaboration

In many countries, though heavy investment is made in technical education, equipment, infrastructure and modern computers, the returns in terms of development of applied research projects by which a country can benefit are barely negligible. In many cases, the staff members of higher technical institutions are inclined to do basic research which helps them in publishing papers and enhancing their academic stature. However, this has not been usefully adopted by business and industry in the area of applied research as they do not use sophisticated methodology. Thus, though there may be highly sophisticated institutions of technical education, their spin-off benefits to the surrounding environment are limited. They remain isolated islands of excellence without much direct interaction with the neighbourhood business and industry. Though these institutions are well-equipped with all the infrastructure facilities, no space is earmarked for creating a research environment where academics can share information with representatives from industrial houses and business enterprises. Since business enterprises often lack the necessary infrastructure and facilities needed for research, some countries and institutions could consider establishing 'research parks' along the following guidelines:

❑ Space in the institutions of excellence should be made available to industrial houses and business enterprises on a lease basis with facilities for research

❑ Such facilities should form the nucleus of research parks with the latest amenities and facilities for research

❑ These research parks should have a good working relationship with academic for sharing of applied research results

❑ Research parks may be controlled by specially constituted committees appointed by the governing councils of various institutions and should have representatives from different industries

The expenses for establishing these research parks should be met from the lease money earned for facilities provided to the industrial houses on a time-bound basis as well as any other available sources. These research parks should be exclusively meant for applied research projects and should have no commercial objectives. The projects should have some relationship with the capabilities and potential of the concerned institution. The projects should utilize directly or otherwise the faculties, libraries, equipment and other infrastructure in the institution. Some balancing arrangement of equipment and instruments for research should be made in the research parks. Industries and enterprises should be given full rights to the end-products of such projects. However, the methodology involved for research may be used by academics for teaching and publication purposes. Methodology and data collection could be shared with other institutions. Such research parks have already been established in the USA in as many as 80 institutions.

## Human Resource Re-adjustment

Governmental policies with regard to trade unions and regulations of employer/employee relations can play a significant role in encouraging foreign investment, transfer of technology and technology assimilation. Any technology change or upgradation can cause dissatisfaction among the workforce. Development of micro-level and macro-level policies to handle labour-related issues, such as redundancies, skill changes, redeployment, etc. are essential. While, at the micro level, each organization has to work out its own re-adjustment policies, at the macro level the government has to ensure a conducive legal framework to protect the larger interests of all the parties. In today's environment, there is limited flexibility to redeploy displaced persons because of resistance from unions and associations. Any alliance can create fear of restructuring resulting in potential loss of jobs or even additional cultural stresses. To a large extent, this affects the assimilation and absorption of technology.

One of the methods of reducing this problem would be to adopt a participatory approach to work out a rehabilitation plan for each employee affected by the technological change. In Germany, for example, the co-determination law stipulates that employees have to be forewarned about any major technological change being envisaged and the management then has to work out a detailed joint rehabilitation plan along with the employees' representatives. Such a procedure has considerably reduced the resistance of employees to technology change.

## Voluntary Retirement Schemes

In India, the problem of overmanning and the resultant surplus owing to technological change poses a serious challenge. Labour laws and unions do not encourage retrenchment. In such a situation the possibility of successfully introducing an informal exit policy is more plausible. Several large public sector organizations have tried to reduce their numbers with the introduction of voluntary retirement schemes. Though informal schemes can work in countries such as Singapore or Malaysia where there is acute shortage of skilled labour, in India these schemes do not work as smoothly. Care needs to be taken while identifying surpluses and the schemes should be drafted to attract such surplus staff to the extent possible.

## Labour Laws

Each country needs to develop labour laws that ensure a fair deal to the employees. For example, in Malaysia, the government has tried to ensure through legislation that the redressal and grievance procedures for employees are reasonable and comparatively faster. Once the employees are able to get protection, other matters relating to promotion, transfer, dismissal, reinstatement, allocation of duties, etc. are excluded from the collective bargaining machinery.

## National Wage Council

To ensure healthy industrial relations, Singapore has set up a tripartite body called the National Wage Council which consists of eminent economists, employers and trade union representatives. This council develops guidelines for wages and other related issues which the industries are expected to follow while negotiating and settling wage agreements. It can also offer advice in case of any disputes. This experiment has so far worked with reasonable success in Singapore. Other countries could also try establishing such councils with necessary modifications to suit local needs.

## Skill Development Fund (SDF)

As we have seen earlier in this book, Singapore and Malaysia have created a skill development fund for continuously upgrading the technical skills of their workforce. Training is subsidized through the fund and the fund money is raised by levying a cess on the industries since they are the ultimate beneficiaries of the fund. Other countries could also follow this example.

Many MNCs who have the resources and technical capabilities can be persuaded to help in the training process not only for their own employees but also for employees from other organizations and students from technical institutes. Organizations such as IBM, FEST and Singapore Airlines have set up training institutes in Singapore which are subsidized through the skill development fund.

## Incentives for Innovation

For any assimilation and absorption of technology, incentives are needed for innovation, assimilation and upgradation of technology both at the macro and micro level. The process has to start right from the school level. In Malaysia, efforts are being made to change the school curriculum in order to encourage creativity among students with greater emphasis on science and technology-oriented subjects.

There is also need for built-in incentives for technicians. However, in some countries such as India, employee growth prospects are higher in administrative jobs, with the result that even capable technical R&D professionals often aspire to do administrative work. In contrast, in South Korea, technicians can rise up to the master craftsmen level by passing certain examinations and meeting specific criteria. According to Korean law, master craftsmen have to be paid a salary equivalent to that of a professor. This has enabled the specialized skills to be retained and improved in the country. This policy has also resulted in a reversal of brain drain and provided built-in incentives for employees to constantly upgrade their skills.

## Increasing Trainability

With rapid changes in technology, the obsolescence rate of human resources is bound to increase unless the employees are constantly trained and retrained in the emerging technologies. Singapore and

Malaysia are making continuous efforts to not only train the workforce in specific skills but also increase their trainability so that the workers can be quickly retrained to use new technology when the need arises. In contrast, in India, the training imparted to workmen is haphazard and weak. More investment needs to be made in skill upgradation as well as in increasing the trainability of employees, especially in sectors where there is fast-changing technology, such as in the field of electronics. Investment in training should not only be targetted to meet the immediate needs but also for future skill development.

## Development of Ancillary Industries

Technology transfer has come to be looked upon as an easier method of accelerating economic development. The Japanese industry completely restructured itself to accommodate the sub-contracting system. The government also provided training and appropriate legislative guidelines. Big business houses began to share the production process, technology and innovation with small and medium industries. Modernization of traditional industries and technology sharing among local companies were encouraged to take advantage of the synergistic impact of innovation, competition and mass production. Larger firms concentrated their investments in core production processes using the latest technology and contracted out to suppliers for parts and components. This model was emulated by Malaysia and South Korea with suitable variations. In India, with the introduction of exit policy and divestment of public sector units, the problem of surplus manpower can be partially solved by promoting ancillary industries set up by the employees themselves.

## Transfer of Managerial Technology

In the process of technology transfer, the MNCs bring along their managerial expertise to the developing countries. It is easier to transfer and assimilate the technological know-how than transfer managerial technology because of cultural variations. For an alliance to work successfully, it is crucial that proper adjustments are made in the managerial technology to suit the environment and culture of the recipient countries. Adjustments are required in human resource related policies, manning norms, production yardsticks, promotion policies, appraisal systems and even salary structures to suit the local environment.

Planning on the basis of manning standards originally given by developed countries can lead to problems. In developing countries, 'wholesale' technology transfer and such manning yardsticks cannot work owing to different norms, cultural values, socio-economic conditions, and different levels of basic education and skills. Also, it must be remembered that in most cases there is no wholesale transfer of technology. There is a blending of technology—partly indigenous and partly imported. Therefore, any wholesale adaptation of manning norms becomes inapplicable.

Each country and organization needs to take into account various factors to evolve more practical and applicable manning standards. Again, owing to different conditions, it would be unwise to lay down standards for productivity levels based on labour productivity per man hour in developed countries which have more or less full employment, higher skill levels and correspondingly much higher wages. On the other hand, in developing countries the social and technical competence as well as wage levels are very low, apart from different values and traditions which affect the employees' attitudes in terms of abseentism, overtime, etc. In such a situation even the norms for measuring productivity may need to be based on investment per person or production per unit of capital employed.

## Implications for Organizations

Previous chapters have dealt at length with the implications of various aspects of macro- and micro-level policies and practices relating to economic restructuring, technology transfer, assimilation, upgradation and meeting the challenges of human resource development in the context of the changing global scenario. The challenges being posed for organizations worldwide and how they should prepare themselves to meet these challenges have also been discussed earlier in this book. Various macro- and government-level policies, socio-economic structures and environmental factors could have major implications for organizations. The changes in economic structures, technology and requirements of skilled human resource entail certain restructuring of organizational policies and practices to prepare themselves for the change. Some of the areas where organizations may have to give special attention are summarized as under:

❑ With economic restructuring and financial reforms, competitiveness will increase. This will necessitate modernization and constant upgradation of technology. Internal resources being limited, organizations at the micro level should develop an investment strategy through raising funds from external sources. This may necessitate also developing strengths to build successful strategic alliances with other organizations who can provide the necessary technology.

❑ To improve quality, the technology has to be transferred. This will also imply developing competencies for appropriate assessment of technology.

❑ An organization's R&D set-up could play a crucial role in appropriate technology assessment and transfer. Therefore involvement of R&D personnel during the assessment processes could be crucial.

❑ To develop successful alliances, it is important for the organization to delineate its core competencies and make R&D investment in those areas so that they are in a stronger position, not only in developing strategic alliances but also in providing certain core strengths to the strategic alliance partners. Keeping this in mind, the organization should develop a long term R&D strategy and a policy of technology assimilation, upgradation and reverse engineering. Such a policy may also include association with scientific and academic institutions for constant upgradation of technology.

❑ Organizations need to develop human resource development strategies by first making proper assessment of current human resources and then predicting future requirements in relation to the new technologies. All these gaps have to be filled by developing appropriate training policies including increasing the trainability of existing employees.

❑ Wherever appropriate, organizations should develop ancillary industries and train redundant employees to become ancillary suppliers.

❑ Medium and small enterprise with limited resources, could come together through their chambers and associations and develop common technology centres to meet competition. This has been done in Singapore and emulated by Malaysia and other countries.

## Conclusions

Any human resource planning process must take into account the level of development of each country. Therefore, there cannot be uniform technology transfer and human resource development strategies applicable in all situations. Even within the country, there could be wide variations in terms of the development of technology in different segments and sectors of the economy. The transition from traditional to modern technology must be managed sensitively. New markets and technologies do require a highly skilled, better educated, more mobile workforce, which is capable of shifting from manual jobs to more white-collar jobs. However, in many countries workers are still struggling in a work environment that has not altered much since the middle of the last century. Many workers are still caught up in the movement towards greater automation performing mindless jobs. It is impractical to assume that there will be a sudden change of technology in all spheres of business activity in all countries. For some time to come, modern technology will have to co-exist with traditional technology in the informal sector. Therefore, each country and each organization needs to develop and train its people with different skills to suit the requirements of traditional and modern technologies.

# BIBLIOGRAPHY

**ABDULLAH, MAISOM**, 'Transfer of Industrial Technology of the Manufacturing Sector: The Case of Malaysia', ISU-TSCP, 1988.

**AGRAWAL, PRADEEP, SUBIR V. GOKARN**, et. al, *Economic Restructuring in East Asia and India: Perspective on Policy Reform*, Macmillan, New Delhi, 1996.

**AJAMI, R.**, 'Co-operating to Compete: Using Technology to Link the Multinational Corporation and the Country', *International Journal of Technology Management*, 5(2), pp. 165–78, 1990.

Alien Business Law of 1972, Government of Thailand, 1972.

**ANSHAR, AZMI M**. 'Making Use of Local Incentives', *New Straits Times*, June 6, 1992.

**ASHFORD, NICHOLAS A**. and **CHRISTINE AYERS**, 'Policy Issues for Consideration in Transferring Technology to Developing Countries', *Ecology Law Quarterly*, Vol. 12, No. 4 pp. 871–905, 1985.

'Asia-Pacific Tech. Monitor', *Technology Atlas*, Asian and Pacific Centre for Transfer of Technology of the UNESCAP, Bangalore, March 1987.

*Asian Development Outlook 1995 and 1996*, Asian Development Bank, Oxford University Press, 1995.

**BALASUBRAMANAYAM, V.**, *International Transfer of Technology to India*, New York, Praeger, 1973.

**BARPAL, I.R.**, 'Business Driven Technology for a Technology Based Firm', *Research Technology Management*, 33(4), pp. 27–30, 1990.

**BARTLETT, CHRISTOPER A**. and **SUMANTRA GHOSHAL**, *Managing Across Borders: The Transnational Solution*, Boston, Harvard Business Schools Press, 1991.

**BHALLA, AJIT S**. and **JAMES, DILMUS D**., 'Technological Blending: Frontier Technology in Traditional Economic Sector', *Journal of Economic Issues*, 20(2), pp. 453–62, June 1986.

**BHANOJI RAO, V.V.**, *India's Economic Reforms: Government, People and Attitudes*, New Delhi, Tata McGraw-Hill, 1994.

**BIDAULT, FRANCIS, BRIAN PAGE, (Tr.)** and **PETER SHERWOOD, (Tr.)**, *Technology Pricing: From Principles to Strategy*, New York, St. Martin's Press, 1989.

**Bin Mohammad, Mahathir**, 'Malaysia: The Way Forward (Vision 2020)', working paper, Malaysian Business Council, 28 February, 1991.

**Blomstrom, M.** and **H. Persson**, 'Foreign Investment and Spillover Efficiency in an Underdeveloped Economy: Evidence from the Mexican Manufacturing Industry', *World Development*, 11(6) pp. 493–501, 1983.

**BOI**, 'Impediments to Backward Linkages and B.U.I.L.D, Thailand National Linkage Programme', paper prepared by the Foreign Investment Advisory Services for the BOI, 1991.

**Brunsell, M.A.**, Struggle to Acquire High-tech Knowledge: The US, Japan and Europe', *Industrial Management*, 33(6), pp. 23–30 1991.

**Burrill, Steven**, 'Managing the Technical', *Management Review*, American Management Association, December 1986.

*Business India*, March 27–April 9, pp. 51–54, 1995.

*Business Times*, Singapore, 'Growing Intra-Regional Trade Cushions Asia-Pacific from World Slowdown', 14 April, 1993.

*Business Today*, 6 January, 1996.

——————————, 7–21 October, 1995.

——————————, 22 October–6 November, 1995.

'CAI: Who's in Control Here?', *Training HRD*, p.54, September 1977.

**Carland, J.A.C.** and **J.W. Carland**, 'Paths to Successful International Technology Transfer', *International Journal of Management*, 9(3), pp. 343–48, 1992.

**Cascio, Wayne F.** and **Elias M. Awad**, *Human Resources Management: An Information System Approach*, Reston Publishing Company, Reston, Virginia, 1981.

**Chen, E.K.Y.** (ed.), *Foreign Direct Investment in Asia*, Asian Productivity Organization, Tokyo, 1990.

————————, *Multinational Corporations, Technology and Employment*, London, Macmillan, 1983.

————————, 'The Newly Industrializing Countries as Exporters of Technology in Asia-Pacific', In Fu-chen and K. Salih, (eds.), *The Challenge of Asia-Pacific Cooperation*, Kuala Lumpur, ADIPA, pp. 122–38, 1987.

**Czinkota, Michael R., Pietra Rivoli and Ilkka A. Ronkainen** (eds.), *International Business*, (2nd ed.), Fort Worth, TX, Drydeb Press, 1992.

**David, A.**, 'CAI: Yesterday, Today and Tomorrow', *Momentum*, p. 9, May 1978.

**Davidson, W.H.** and **McFetridge, D.G.**, 'Key Characteristics in the Choice of International Technology Transfer Mode', *Journal of International Business Studies*, 16, pp.5–21, Summer 1985.

————————, 'International Technology Transactions and the Theory of the Firm', *Journal of Industrial Economics*, 34, pp. 253–64, 1994.

**Davies, Howard**, 'Technology Transfer through Commercial Transactions and the Theory of the Firm', *Journal of Industrial Economics*, 26, pp. 161–75, 1977.

**DAWSON, LESLIE M.**, 'Transferring Industrial Technology to Less Developed Countries', *Industrial Marketing Management*, 16(4), pp. 265–71, 1987.

**DESAI, ASHOK V.**, *Development and Change*, 21(4), pp. 723–49, 1990.

**DHESI. A.S.**, 'Aspects of Human Resource Development in India', *Social Science Research Journal*, 2 (1 & 2), pp. 1–5, 1977

**DAVID, DICHTER, ROBERT HUSBANDS, ANNI ARESON** and **MARK FREY**, *A Guide to Technology Transfer for Small and Medium-Sized Enterprises*, Gower Pub. Co., Hants, UK, 1988.

**DUNNING, J.H.**, *Multinational Enterprises and the Global Economy*, Workingham, Berkshire, Addison-Wesley, 1992.

'Economic and Social Council, United Nations, Experience Gained in Technical Cooperation Activities Involving Privatization and Foreign Investment', Report of the Secretary-General, Commission on Transnational Corporations, April 1993.

*Economic Times, The*, 7 December, 1995.

——————————, 22 February, 1996.

——————————, 2 May, 1995.

**EDWARD, K.** and **Y. CHEN**, 'Intra-Regional Investment and Technology Transfer in the Asia-Pacific Region in Intra-Regional Investment and Technology Transfer in Asia', a symposium report, Asian Productivity Organization, Tokyo, pp. 11–40, 1994.

**EDQUIST, CHARLES, STEFFAN JACOBSSON**, and **JETHANANDANI KISHORE**, 'Automation in Engineering Industries of India and Republic of Korea Against the Background of Experience in Some OECD Countries', *Economic and Political Weekly*, (20)15, 13 April, 1985.

**EKHOLM, E.L.**, 'Transferring Technology to Developing Nations', *Engineering Management International*, 5(1), Netherlands, pp. 45–52, 1988.

**ENOS, J.L.**, 'Transfer of Technology', *Asian-Pacific Economic Literature*, pp. 3–37, 3 March, 1989.

**ERNST, D.** and **D. O'CONNOR**, *Technology and Global Competition: The Challenge for Newly Industrializing Economies*, New Delhi, Oxford & IBH, 1989.

**FOMBRUN, C.J.** and **A. KUMARASWAMY**, 'Strategic Alliances in Corporate Communities', *The Evolution of Telecommunications 1980–88, Japan and the World Economy*, 3(3), pp. 243–60, 1991.

**FORREST, J.E.** and **M.J.C. Martin**, 'Strategic Alliances between Large and Small Research Intensive Organizations: Experiences in the Biotechnology Industry', *R&D Management*, 22(1), pp. 41–54, 1992.

*Fortune*, 11 May, 1987.

**FRY, M.J.**, *Foreign Direct Investment in a Macro-economic Framework: Some Further Findings*, University of Birmingham, International Finance Group, 1993.

GEORGANTZAS, NICHOLAS C. and CHRISTIAN N. MADU, 'Cognitive Processes in Technology Management and Transfer, Technological Forecasting and Social Change', *An International Journal* 38, pp. 81–95, 1: 81–95 EN 1990.

GHOSHAL, S. and others, The Learning Alliance between Business and Business Schools: Executive Education as a Platform for Partnership', *California Management Review*, 35(1), pp. 50–72, 1992.

GRANSEY, E. and S.M. WRIGHT, 'Technical Innovation and Organizational Opportunity', *International Journal of Technology Management*, 5(3), pp. 267–92, 1990.

GUGLER. P., 'Building Transnational Alliances to Create Competitive Advantage', *Long Range Planning*, 25(1), pp. 90–99, 1992.

HABIBIE, B.J., 'Sophisticated Technologies: Taking Root in Developing Countries', *International Journal of Technology Management*, 5(5), pp. 489–98, 1990.

HAGEDOORD, J., 'Organizational Models of Inter-Firm Cooperation and Technology Transfer', *Technovation*, 10(1), pp. 17–30, 1990.

HAGEDOORD, J. and J. SCHAKENRAAD, 'Leading Companies and Networks of Strategic Alliances in Information Technologies', *Research Policy*, 21(2), pp. 163–90, 1992.

HAMEL, G., 'Competition for Competence and Inter-Partner Learning Within International Strategic Alliances', *Strategic Management Journal*, 12, pp. 83–104, Summer 1991.

HARRISON, ANN, 'The Role of Multinationals in Economic Development: The Benefits of FDI', *The Columbia Journal of World Business*, Winter 1994.

HARTMANN, GERT, IAN NICHOLAS and others, 'Computerized Machine Tools, Manpower Consequences and Skill Utilisation', *British Journal of Industrial Relations*, (21)2, July 1983.

HARVERY, JAMES L., 'Effective Planning for Human Resources', *Personnel Administrator*, p. 45, October 1983.

HARVEY, MICHAEL G., 'Application of Technology Life Cycles to Technology Transfers', *The Journal of Business Strategy*, pp. 51–58, Fall 1984.

HEIBA, F.I., 'International Business Negotiations: A Strategic Planning Model', *International Marketing Review*, 1(4), pp. 5–16, 1984.

*India Today*, 31 January, 1996.

_____, 31 March, 1995.

_____, 15 August, 1995.

*International Country Risk Guide*, International Business Commission Ltd, London, 1991.

'Intra-Regional Investment and Technology Transfer in Asia' a symposium report, Asian Productivity Organization, Tokyo, 1994.

*Investment in Thailand*, Paper prepared by the Foreign Investment Advisory Services for the Board of Investment (BOI). September, 1991.

KELLER, ROBERT T. and RAVI R. CHINTA, 'International Technology Transfer: Strategies for Success', *Academy of Management Executive*, 4(2), pp. 33–43, 1990.

KENICHI, OHMAE, *The Borderless World: Power and Strategy in the Interlinked Economy*, Fontana through Harper Collins, 1991.

KIM, YOUN-SUK, 'Managing Technological Transfer with Korea as a Catalyst, *Human Systems Management*, 8, pp. 217–23, 1989.

KOJIMA, K., 'Transfer of Technology to Developing Countries: Japanese Type versus American Type', *Hitotsubashi Journal of Economics*, pp. 1–14, 17 February, 1977.

KONZ, LEO E., 'The International Transfer of Commercial Technology: The Role of the Multinational Corporation', (ed.) S. Bruchery, Salem, NH: Ayer, Arno Press, New York. 1980.

KRISHNAMURTHY, G.V.G., 'Legal Aspects of Technology Transfer: A Conspectus', *Chartered Secretary*, 21(4), pp. 273–76, 1991.

LALL, S., 'Developing Countries as Exporters of Industrial Technology', *Research Policy*, 9(1), pp. 24–52, 1980.

_____, 'Foreign Direct Investment in South Asia', *Asian Development Review*, 11(1), 1993.

LEI, D. and J.W. 'SLOCUM, 'Global Strategy, Competence-Building and Strategic Alliances', *California Management Review*, 35(1), pp. 81–97, 1992.

LIM, L.Y.C. and P.E. FONG, *Foreign Investment and Industrial Restructuring in Malaysia, Singapore, Taiwan and Thailand*, OECD Development Centre, Paris 1991.

LIM, L.Y.C. and N. SIDDAL, 'Foreign Investment, Trade and Technology Linkages in Asian Developing Countries in the 1990s', paper prepared for United National Centre on Transnational Corporations Project on Globalization and Developing Countries, 1991.

MACKLIN, THOMAS, 'Remodeling HRD', *Training and Development Journal*, pp. 46–50, June 1982.

MADU, CHRISTIAN N., 'Perspective Framework for The Transfer of Appropriate Technology', *Futures*, 22(9), pp. 932–48, 1990.

_____, 'Transferring Technology to Developing Countries: Critical Factors for Success', *Long Range Planning*, UK, 22(4), pp. 115–24, 1989.

MALHOTRA, R.N., 'Economic Reforms: Retrospect and Prospect's, Foundation Day Lecture at Administrative Staff College of India (ASCI), December 1992.

MARTON, KATHERIN, *Multinationals, Technology and Industrialization: A Study of the Implications and Impact in Third World Countries (Contemporary Studies in Economic and Financial Analysis*, Greenwich, Jai Press, 1987.

_____, *Multinationals, Technology and Industrialization: Implications and Impact in Third World Countries*, New York: Free Press, 1986.

_____, 'Technology Transfer to Developing Countries via Multinationals', *World Economy*, pp. 409–26, December 1986.

**MEHTA, M.M.**, *Human Resource Development Planning*, New Delhi, Macmillan, pp. 7–59, 1976.

**MUKERJEE, SWATI**, 'The Impact of Liberalizing Imports: India, A Case Study', *The Journal of Developing Areas*, pp. 521–34, 28th July, 1994.

**NAIDU, GOKUL**, The Emphasis on Training in View of the Changing Environment in Malaysia, Paper presented at the conference on workers' training held at Singapore on behalf of National Productivity Board, 1991.

*National Research Council: US-Japan Strategic Alliances in the Semiconductor Industry—Technology Transfer, Competition, and Public Policy*, Washington, National Academy Press, 1992.

*New Technologies and Industrial Transformation in Asia-Pacific Developing Economies*, UNDP, ESCAP, 1992.

**PANG EMG FOND**, 'Emerging Trends in Intra-Regional Investment in Pacific Asia: Implications for Industrial Restructuring and Technology Transfer in Intra-Regional Investment and Technology Transfer in Asia', a symposium report, Asia Productivity Organization, Tokyo, 1994.

**POAPONGSAKORN, NIPON**, et al, 'On-the-Job Training in the Manufacturing and Services Industries', report prepared for the National Social and Economic Development Board, 1992.

**RAO, KALA**, 'Economic Restructuring, Technology Transfer and Human Resource Development', *Personnel Today*, October–December, 1994.

**ROBERTS. E.B.**, 'The Technological Base of the New Enterprise', *Research Policy*, 20(4), pp. 283–98, 1991.

**ROBINSON, L.G.** and **T.A. ROBINSON**, 'CAI in Health Education: A Pilot Study', *International Journal of Instructional Media*, 5(3), 1977–78.

**ROSENBERG, NATHAN** and **CLAUDIO FRISCHTAK**, (ed.), *Trade in Technology by a Slowly Industrializing Country: India, Hall Sanjaya, International Technology Transfer: Concepts, Measures and Comparisons*, Praeger, New York, 1985.

**RUFFIN, R.J.**, 'The Role of Foreign Investment in the Economic Growth of the Asian and Pacific Region', *Asian Development Review*, 11(1), 1993.

**SHAHID, N. ZAHID**, 'Inter-Regional Investment and Technology Transfer: A South Asian Perspective in Intra-Regional Investment and Technology Transfer in Asia', a symposium report, Asian Productivity Organization, Tokyo, pp. 57–75, 1994.

**SINGH, RANA K.D.N.** and **PREMILA NAZARETH**, 'Perspectives on Foreign Investment in India: New Delhi Round Table on FDI and Technology Transfer', *CTC Reporter*, pp. 17–21, 23–24, 33, 1990.

**SIRILLI, GIORGIO**, 'The Technology Balance of Payments as an Indicator of Technology Transfer in OECD Countries: The Case of Italy', *Technovation* 11(1), pp. 3–25, 1991.

SMILOR R.W. and D.V. GIBSON, 'Technology Transfer in Multi-organizational Environments: The Case of R&D Consortia', *IEEE Transactions on Engineering Management*, 38(1), pp. 3–13, 1991.

'Special Issue on Global Competition and The Effective Impact of Innovation', *Technovation*, 12(2), 1992.

STEWART JR., CHARLES T. and YASUMITRA NIHEI, *Technology Transfer and Human Factors*, Free Press, New York , 1987.

'Technology Development, Adaptation and Assimilation Strategies at Corporate Level', survey report, Asian Productivity Organization, Tokyo, 1994.

TEECE, D.J., 'Technology Transfer by Multinational Firms: The Resource Cost of Transferring Technological Know-how', *Economic Journal*, 87, pp. 242–61, June 1977.

'The Economic Administration Reforms Commission: Technology Development and Acquisition', *Journal of Indian School of Political Economy*, 4(3), pp. 542–67, 1992.

TIPTON, BERYL, 'The Quality of Training and the Design of Work', *Industrial Relations Journal*, 13(1), p. 27, Spring 1982.

'Transnational Corporations and Management Division', *World Investment Report 1992:* Transnational Corporations as Engines of Growth, New York, United Nations, ST/CTC/130, 1992.

TRAN, V.T., 'Technology Transfer in the Asian-Pacific Region: Implications of Trends Since the Mid-1980s', in Ito. J. and A.O. Krueger (eds.), *Trade and Protectionism*, Chicago, University of Chicago Press, 1993.

UNGHU, A. AZIZ, *Strategies for Structural Adjustment: The Experience of South East-Asia,* International Monetary Fund, Bank Negara, Malaysia, Washington, 1990.

VAJPEYI, DHIRENDRA and R. NATARAJAN, 'Technology and Development' *Public Policy and Managerial Issues*, Rawal Publishers, Jaipur,1991.

VIRMANI, B.R., 'Automation and Changing Technologies: Issues and Concerns for Manpower Planning and Industrial Relations', *Indian Journal of Industrial Relations*, 25(4), pp. 323–34, 1990.

———, 'Graduate Engineer Trainees', Hyderabad, Administrative Staff College of India and New Delhi Federation of Indian Chambers of Commerce and Industry, 1983.

VIRMANI B.R., KALA RAO, 'Global Economics, Technological Changes and Human Resource Development', in *Human Resource Development Global Changes and Strategies in 2000 AD*, (ed.) Kohli, Uddesh and Dharni P. Sinha (ed.), Allied Publishers, New Delhi, 1994.

———, 'Policy Initiatives Towards Structural Reforms: Malaysia and India', paper presented at the Retreat of the Secretaries to Government of India, Administrative Staff College of India, Hyderabad, 1994.

———, 'Technology Transfer, Assimilation and Human Resource Management', *Personnel Today*, pp. 3–19, July–Sept. 1994.

**Virmani B.R. and Sunil Guptan**, *The Indian Management*, Vision Books, New Delhi, 1992.

————, *Technology Transfer and its Implications for Manpower Planning and Productivity*, Indian Council for Research on International Economic Relations, New Delhi, 1985.

**Westney, E.**, 'Transfer of Organizational Technology', *International Trade Journal*, 4, pp. 69–90, Fall 1989.

*World Competitiveness Report 1995*, World Economic Forum and International Institute of Management, Geneva, 1995.

*World Development Report 1991, The Triad in Foreign Direct Investment*, UNCTC, New York, United Nations, 1991.

*World Labour Report*, 1984, Vol. I, *International Labour Organisation*, Geneva, pp. 48, 188–89, 1984.

**Yamashita, S.**, *The Role of Foreign Direct Investment and Technology Transfer*, Hiroshima, Hiroshima University, 1992.

**Young, K.Y.**, 'Investigating the Selling Process for Technological Products', *International Journal of Technology Management*, 5, 1991.